SAS – Men in the Making

SAS – Men in the Making

An Original's Account of Operations in Sicily and Italy

Peter Davis MC

Edited by Paul Davis

Pen & Sword
MILITARY

First published in Great Britain in 2015 by
Pen & Sword Military
an imprint of
Pen & Sword Books Ltd
47 Church Street
Barnsley
South Yorkshire
S70 2AS

Copyright © Peter Davis MC 2015

ISBN 978 1 47384 560 2

A CIP catalogue record for this book is available from the British
Library

Typeset in Ehrhardt by
Mac Style Ltd, Bridlington, East Yorkshire
Printed and bound in the UK by CPI Group (UK) Ltd,
Croydon, CRO 4YY

Pen & Sword Books Ltd incorporates the imprints of Pen & Sword
Archaeology, Atlas, Aviation, Battleground, Discovery, Family
History, History, Maritime, Military, Naval, Politics, Railways, Select,
Transport, True Crime, and Fiction, Frontline Books, Leo Cooper,
Praetorian Press, Seaforth Publishing and Wharncliffe.

For a complete list of Pen & Sword titles please contact
PEN & SWORD BOOKS LIMITED
47 Church Street, Barnsley, South Yorkshire, S70 2AS, England
E-mail: enquiries@pen-and-sword.co.uk
Website: www.pen-and-sword.co.uk

*Dedicated to the memory of
Private George Valentine Weston.
A different war and a lifelong battle.*

Contents

Foreword and Acknowledgements

This is my father's story. Using the diaries that he kept, he wrote this book immediately after the war. It filled the gap between coming home and taking up his place at Cambridge University.

I knew of the manuscript's existence, but was never asked to read it. Over the years it was forgotten. My father was murdered in 1994. He was shot in the back of the head, whilst reading a book in his home in South Africa, and his death remains an unsolved crime. After his murder I cleared his house and his personal papers were stored until such time as it wasn't too painful to go through them. During 2012, whilst at last going through his papers, I came across his original manuscript, and read this book for the first time. I wasn't surprised that he hadn't written about being awarded the Military Cross as he had told me that the most memorable times for him were those early years in the SAS. At the age of 20 he was experiencing things and taking on responsibilities which I had never known about. I had never realized quite how lucky he was to survive the war. When I read the book now, I wonder why he didn't talk about that time more. Perhaps the past was too painful.

Much of the book's content was entirely unknown to my brother and I. Where necessary the book has been shortened, but the words are entirely my father's. The only thing we have changed is the title. He had called it 'Stand by to Embark'. For me, reading this book is seeing his journey from boyhood to manhood. We have called it *SAS – Men in the Making*.

This book would not have been possible without the help of various people, including Alec Muirhead's daughter, Colette Baigrie. Alec is mentioned throughout the book and he and my father remained friends for the rest of their lives.

Thanks also go to Simon Fletcher – simonfletcher.8theavenue@hotmail. co.uk – for working his magic on my Dad's old black and white photographs. He brought them back to life, and achieved that difficult balance between clarity and atmosphere.

I would also like to thank the SAS Regimental Association for helping me to make sense of the abbreviations used and filling in many of the gaps in my father's military career.

Lastly I would like to thank my wife, Lisa, for her help, encouragement and suggestions.

Paul Davis

Glossary

XIII Corps	Group of Regiments
AA	Anti-aircraft
BESA gun	Italian Machine Gun
Chota	Hindi Term meaning small, younger or junior
CO	Commanding Officer
CSMI	Company Sergeant Major Instructor
Cwt	Hundred Weight – 20cwt in a ton
D-Day	Invasion Day
DSO	Distinguished Service Order
Duce	A leader or dictator, applied especially to Benito Mussolini
ENSA	Entertainment National Service Association
EY Rifle	Lee-Enfield called the EY Rifle after Sir Ernest Youlle who adapted it
GHQ	General Headquarters
HE	High Explosives
HMS	His Majesty's Ship
HQ	Headquarters
JU 88	Junker, a German Stuka Aeroplane
LC	Landing Craft
LCA	Landing Craft Assault, approximately 12m long
LCI	Landing Craft Infantry, approximately 50m long
LMG	Light Machine Gun
LRDG	Long Range Desert Group
MG 15	Machine Gun
MT	Motor Transport
MTO	Motor Transport Officer
METS	Middle East Training School Paratroops
MO	Medical Officer
NCO	Non-Commissioned Officer
NAAFI	Naval Army Air Force Institute
OC	Officer Commanding
OP	Observation Point

OCTU	Officer Cadet Training Unit
Oerlikon	Anti-aircraft gun. Mounted mainly on ships.
PT	Physical Training
PU	Personnel Utility Vehicle
Provost	Regiment or Naval Police
RE	Royal Engineers
RSM	Regimental Sergeant Major
RAF	Royal Air Force
RASC	Royal Army Service Corps
RSM	Regimental Sergeant Major
RTU	Returned to unit
SBS	Special Boat Squadron
SRS	Special Raiding Squadron
SAS	Special Air Service
SRS	Special Raiding Squadron
VE Day	Victory in Europe
Wadi	An Arabic term meaning a valley or dry river bed.

Alec Muirhead

Bill Fraser

Captain Francis ('Franco')

Derrick Harrison

Fraser McCluskey

Harry Poat

John Tonkin

Johnny Wiseman

Paddy Mayne

Pat Reilly

Phil Gunn

Sandy Wilson

Tony Marsh

Introduction

There are few of us who fought in this war, who do not, on occasions, find their thoughts wandering back to the past, reliving those former days and desiring them back with some eager longing. Few of us can forget the glamour of travelling through foreign countries, especially as part of a victorious army, or the pride and self-satisfaction which accompany the risks and dangers of battle once these are things of the past, rather than of the present. But more deeply than any of these things do we regret the loss of the carefree, intimate, regimental life which we once experienced but for which there is no substitute in the narrow, peacetime existence to which we have returned.

My own particular loss in this respect I feel most strongly, for I was in the SAS (Special Air Service), a small unit which fought a strange kind of war. This spirit, which ran through the SAS during their part in the Sicilian and Italian campaigns, is one which should be kept alive and spread throughout the country. Loyalty to one's men, to one's officers and to the regiment was the key note of this spirit, but it was a loyalty the rigidity of which was tempered by a freedom from care, a camaraderie, and an unpredictable roguery which served to instil into the unit an atmosphere of unity and of happiness.

It is my wish to recapture, as far as this is possible, the spirit which characterized the SRS (Special Raiding Service, as the unit was called during the period I intend to describe) rather than a bare account of facts and experiences. It is the humorous and personal side of army life that I wish to stress most, since the memories which this recalls are the strongest and the most cherished.

They were a mixed lot, those men who formed the SRS in those critical and decisive days of 1943, when the battle for the Mediterranean was fought and won, and when our army set foot once more on the mainland of Europe. A mixed lot, it is true, such as is found in any service unit, but yet they seemed to be typified by a quality common to them all and shared by few others. This quality is not easy to define: some would call it independence, some might even go so far as to call it conceit, whilst others might describe it as the common gangster mentality, or merely an irrepressible and irresponsible *joie de vivre*. But however regarded, none who came in contact with this little unit, left these men without feeling convinced that there was something different, something unique, about them. At one moment they could appear as nothing more than a band of cut-throats, a mere undisciplined rabble. And yet, as one came to know them better, one found that they all possessed a strange morality, even a code of honour which made them stick together through any kind of hardship or danger, and follow any officer in whom they had put their trust, wherever he might choose to lead them.

Such men as these could either be the salt of the earth, or with a little encouragement, the unscrupulous enemies of society – it all depended on the one to whom was given the opportunity of guiding and controlling them. The qualities which characterized these men no more than reflected the truly remarkable character of their leader, Major 'Paddy' Mayne DSO, one of the outstanding characters of this war.

Few men have possessed so strong a personality as Paddy Mayne. Officers and men alike worshipped him, respected him, cursed him and loved him, and all feared him. This massive Irishman, shy and self-conscious in public, deadly as an enemy, sincere and loyal as a friend, unpredictable and infuriating as a companion, devoted his whole attention to his unit, imparting to it something of his own amazing character. He moulded it by degrees into the light-hearted and unorthodox, but nevertheless strangely disciplined and highly efficient fighting unit, which was to gain for itself a reputation with friend and foe alike.

It is of these men that I wish to write in an attempt to portray them as they were, individually and collectively, in action and out of it. It will not be an easy task to try and describe so complex, irrational and variegated a subject, and although I shall fall short of my object, the attempt at least will be worthwhile.

Chapter One

Gathered Threads

Although gradual, the change over from peace to war was nonetheless fundamental. Slowly but surely, the life we had known, and which we were fighting to preserve, faded away, never to return. Instead, we were faced with a new, more austere existence, one which called for hardier and worthier qualities than the old, and in which the traditional sovereignty of freedom gave way to that of compulsion, in order to fend off the great calamity which so gravely threatened us.

Most men, when faced with the certain prospect of being conscripted into one or other of the services accepted this fate with resignation, and passively allowed the seemingly smooth flowing stream of conscription to carry them exultantly along its tortuous and uneven course. But some, exuberant in their youth and glowing with an adolescent enthusiasm for something which they could not understand, allowed their ideals and ambitions to dive headlong into the still waters, unaware of the dangers and disappointments which these concealed.

It was to this latter group that I belonged. To me the risks, the sacrifices and the sorrows of war meant nothing. The glamour of uniform and the prospect of glorious opportunities gained for themselves so important a place in my mind, that nothing would content me until I too had voluntarily cast myself into this stream. I took this fateful step in June 1940, and from then until the end of 1942, disillusionment came upon me with one anti-climax following close upon another, with the result that my original ambitions and ideals before long were completely submerged.

For no sooner had I entered the army than I seemed to lose all individuality and personality, and to become no more than an unimportant and even unnecessary part of some mighty machine. With zest and enthusiasm I applied myself to my recruit's training, in the hope of being commissioned all the sooner as a result. But my only reward was to be kept hanging around the camp for two or three months, filling sandbags, and helping the Post Office sort the Christmas mail.

Posted eventually to an OCTU (Officer Cadet Training Unit) I worked with a will once more, spurred on by the thought of rapid promotion and a responsible position. But when, as a young and keen second lieutenant, I found myself in a battalion of a well-known infantry regiment, my spirits were once again dampened and my enthusiasm repressed. It was a bad battalion, hardly typical of those which had given the regiment so high a reputation. Snobbery and ignorance pervaded the relations in the officers' mess, and sapped the spirits of the men. Moreover, the work was monotonous and badly organized, merely consisting of erecting coastal defences and pulling these down again.

Despair and disillusionment had worked so powerful an effect on me at the end of six months that a friend and I decided to leave these spiritless conditions with the utmost haste. Our chance soon came and with no regrets we were able to volunteer on a draft that was shortly being sent overseas.

And so I found myself in the Middle East. The journey out was pleasant and uneventful through the smiling seas and under the tropical sun of the South Atlantic. But once arrived at the Infantry Base Depot at Geneifa, the vast reinforcement centre on the banks of the Suez Canal, my hopes were again frustrated. For it was found that the battalion which we were to join had only a few weeks previously set sail for India, and I was in consequence stranded in Egypt without a unit.

A lecture given to us by a major from GHQ who was seeking officer recruits for a special type of work, raised my spirits once more, and I eagerly handed in my name. The work described appealed to me greatly. Small parties were to roam about behind the enemy lines, harassing and sabotaging their lines of communications. Officers chosen would be their own masters and plan the details of their own operations, so that the scope for initiative and individuality were immense. The attractions of such a life after the repression and monotony I had experienced with the battalion in England, were immeasurable.

But ill-fortune still pursued me. My application was disregarded, and instead I, and eight other subalterns in the same position as myself, found ourselves posted to Syria, where for five dreary months we spent our time supervising the native labour employed on the construction of several fortified areas which were being built there with all possible haste, in case the Germans should break through in the Western Desert or launch a strong drive through Turkey, and thence via Syria and Palestine to the banks of the Suez Canal.

My new work was if anything even more distasteful to me than anything which I had hitherto encountered, but at least I was left to myself and was to a large extent my own master. Five months of this ignominious and degrading employment were as much as I could stand, so that eventually I started agitating for a transfer and wrote personally to this effect to the Staff Officer at Ninth Army Headquarters who seemed likely to be in a position to transfer me to the type of work I most wanted.

And at this point my fortunes changed. For the direct result of the interview following my application was my being posted to a unit which completely fulfilled all my original hopes and ideals – a unit eager and willing to fight the enemy in any way chosen for it, a small body of men under young and intelligent officers who abhorred routine and spit and polish, and who lived together in harmony and mutual respect, aware of their own capabilities, and supremely anxious to put these to the test as speedily as possible. It was the one unit in the British Army which was able to fulfil all the exaggerated ambitions and desires which sprang from my youthful exuberance.

It was a peculiar sort of unit in which I found myself, as a result of my interview at Ninth Army Headquarters. It appeared that some months back, the Middle East Commandos, who were the amalgamation of several commando units, sent out to this theatre from England for specific purposes, had been disbanded. All the men being volunteers and specially picked, it was held by some people of influence that it would be a pity to waste their training and special qualifications by allowing them to split up entirely and return to their parent units. Thus attempts were made to keep them together in some form of loose organization in which they would be available for special service operations.

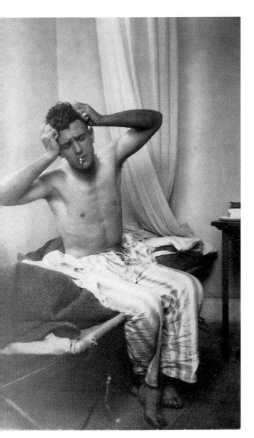

Peter Davis, Syria, April–November 1942.

Many were taken off to form a new unit called the Special Air Service which had been started by two young lieutenants, Stirling and Lewis, who both possessed initiative, drive and originality.

The remaining men had been messed around in frightful fashion, and had drifted vaguely through unit after unit, each formed by someone working on a private and often quite unfeasible idea. But although no profitable work had been done by most of these men for the past six months, they had at least remained together, and at the time I joined them, were embodied in a unit known as 'C' Squadron, the 1st Special Service Regiment.

This was in fact the only squadron of the regiment, the other squadrons having been merged into it only a short time previously. For the last few months they had been employed on preparing the mountainous area on the Syrian–Turkish border, into a defensive zone, especially suited for guerrilla warfare. Caches and sites were prepared for the concealment of arms and store dumps, bridges were reconnoitered and mined, and troops were even sent into Turkey in civilian clothes, to examine the country there. All this, of course, was as a precaution against the possibility of a German drive onto the Suez Canal through Turkey, for it was considered that we had not sufficient troops available for an organized defence, so that guerrilla methods would have to be relied upon.

This work was eventually completed by the end of October 1942. Largely as a result of the efforts of the squadron commander, Richard Lea, and his immense personal magnetism, certain staff officers in Ninth Army headquarters were beginning to take an interest in the squadron, and at the time I joined it, steps were being taken to train and equip the unit for a more active role. It was even hoped that the 1st SAS regiment would consent to incorporate the squadron within its numbers, and allow it to join them in their raids and adventures behind the enemy lines in the desert.

And thus it was that the unit I joined was concentrated at Chekka, (a pretty little village right on the Lebanese coast, about 40 miles north of Beirut) and was about to start on an intensive course of training in driving and vehicle maintenance, demolitions and navigation. It was hoped that this training would prepare the squadron for sabotage and harassment work in the desert, and thus encourage the SAS to take the unit over en bloc.

I settled down to these new conditions quicker than I had ever thought possible. Soon I began to know the men, and to make myself known to them, and from the first I was greatly impressed by their bearing and spirit. No ordinary men were these, such as are found in a normal infantry or subsidiary unit. These men were thinkers, each with a mind of his own, with ambitions, with pride in himself, and above all, with a genuine and heartfelt desire to try his strength against that of the enemy at the earliest possible opportunity. Most of them had seen action before, in Crete, in Syria or in the Western Desert; some had taken part in the Rommel raid where Colonel Keyes had lost his life.

From the first I admired these men and marvelled at the contrast between them and those I had come across in my infantry battalion and elsewhere. The traditional army discipline was not necessary with them. They did not need

Peter Davis, Syria, November–December 1942.

to be trained to follow blindly any officer who was given charge of them, or to obey without thought any order, however foolish it might be, that happened to be passed down to them. With men such as these, co-operation rather than compulsion obtained the best results. If there was a job to be done, however irksome and unpleasant, they would do it voluntarily without having to be ordered to do so, and without an NCO having to stand over them to see that they did it properly.

Naturally with men such as these, a new officer did not at first have an easy time, for being thinkers, they were extremely critical of their officers and would not tolerate fools gladly. Only slowly and even reluctantly, would they grow to trust and rely on their officers and co-operate with them to the full. But once a state of mutual confidence and respect had been reached between officer and men, a bond of such intimacy and friendship was knit between them, that quick to understand each others' every mood and mental disposition, they would work together with the minimum of friction, and consequently with the most successful results.

Such were the men whom I now had to lead, to know and to understand. It was no easy task, especially for an officer as young as I was, but nevertheless it was a most intriguing and fascinating pastime to study all these unusual and always surprising characters, and to attempt to get to know what was going on in their minds. The names of many of these men will be constantly recurring in succeeding pages. They were not mere pawns who followed like sheep anywhere I chose to lead them. They were friends with whom I lived, celebrated, fought and suffered for three long years of war, friends whom I trusted and respected to an extent that can only be reached in a situation where true friendship and co-operation prevail.

As with the men, the contrast between the officers with whom I now mixed, and those with whom I had previously rubbed shoulders struck me most vividly. The officers of this strange little squadron to which I now belonged, were all young, active and eager. An unassuming friendliness and desire to help took the place of the snobbish reliance on rank and status which had been all too prevalent in my infantry battalion. Richard Lea, the major in command, was not more than 27. Desperately keen to make a name for his unit, he spent his time cultivating influential friends in army headquarters, in an attempt to attain recognition and assistance. In these efforts he was undoubtedly successful, for before long the squadron was given an official establishment, equipped throughout with Jeeps for training and operations, and speedily satisfied with all reasonable demands made for stores, transport and weapons. Slowly, under Richard's care, the squadron became bound into something approaching a co-ordinated whole, a unit fully ready for active operations against the enemy.

Richard was friendly, understanding and always courteous, and it seemed to me that these qualities were shared among all the officers in the unit, for I was welcomed into the mess without ceremony, patronage or jealousy. There I met David Barnby, quiet, sensible and considerate for others; John Tonkin, the young and exuberant friend of everyone; and Mick Gurmin and Ted Lepine, more irresponsible than the

Sergeant 'Tugg' Wilson and Private Fred Casey, Syria, November–December 1942.

other two but with a genuine interest for their work and affection for their men. Among such men as these I had no difficulty in settling down and feeling at my ease, and within a week I was truly one of them.

While we were training at Chekka, we were visited one morning by Captain Steve Hastings, who was in the SAS and who, being a personal friend of Richard, had come to give us a talk on how that regiment operated. The general gist of this talk was not very clear or concise, but at the end we were left with the impression of a quite amazing unit, which, fulfilling its motto of 'Who Dares Wins' had committed great deeds of daring and recklessness, far behind the enemy lines. Visions of parachute jumps under almost impossible conditions; of Jeeps, loaded to capacity and equipped with quick-firing twin machine guns, belting into enemy airfields miles behind their lines, and raking the aircraft with incendiary bullets; of small foot-parties stealthily entering these airfields, placing time bombs on the wings and fuselages of the aircraft and then vanishing, leaving flames, destruction and chaos in their wake; visions of actions such as these floated before our eyes, as we sat breathless, listening for the first time to the story of SAS. There was not one of us, who, when the story reached its end, did not hope fervently and wholeheartedly that soon we too, would be members of so glorious a little unit.

'Fishing' at Chekka – Syria. Explosion causing photo to be blurred.

Our hopes were to be realized far sooner than any of us expected. A few days later we all set off in our extraordinary little Jeep convoy for practical training in the Syrian Desert. At an abandoned little petrol station on the oil pipeline, which went by the name of H4, we made our home for the next two weeks and from this base roamed the surrounding area, learning all that the locality offered us in the way of desert driving and navigation.

In the course of this valuable training we were able to explore much of the Syrian Desert, for many were the navigational schemes and night attacks we had to do before it was considered that we had learnt enough. Our work was hard but we nevertheless found our own relaxations – mechanized fox-hunts and long and exciting gazelle hunts at 40 or 50 miles per hour over the smooth, hard surface of the terrain.

We arrived back at Chekka, after two weeks of this practical training, to find the camp buzzing with rumours to the effect that we had been amalgamated into the SAS, and that moreover we would be proceeding to their base at Kabrit in Egypt in a few days' time.

Richard was not long in confirming this news, and 18 December 1942, found our long convoy of Jeeps interspersed with occasional 3-tonne trucks, winding slowly down the coast road, on the long journey to Egypt. Passing through Beirut and Haifa, we motored down the green coastal plain of Palestine, the blue Mediterranean glittering invitingly on our right, and the stony shrub-strewn

Gazelle hunting while training at H4 in Syrian Desert, 1942.

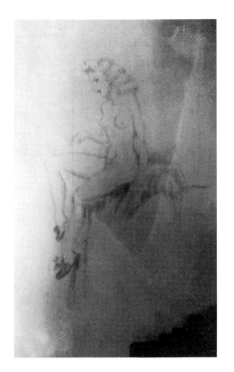
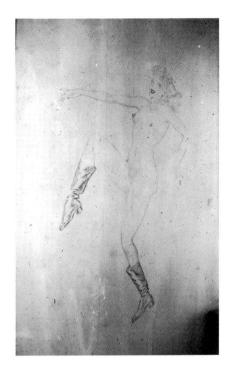

Bar and wall decorations – officers' mess, Chekka, November–December 1942.

hills frowning down on us from our left. A day and a half of driving through the arid, sandy wastes of the Sinai Peninsula found us at Moascar on the banks of the Suez Canal. Familiar territory this, for we were now only 30 miles or so from Geneifa, that vast depot to which I had proceeded on first arriving in Egypt and which bore no very inspiring memories for me.

Kabrit, our final destination, lay a mere 14 miles beyond Geneifa, and at about tea-time on 21 December 1942, our convoy drove through the gates of the camp of the 1st SAS Regiment with a flourish. Carefully the vehicles were lined up in the square, as we clambered stiffly from our seats and rubbed the dust from our eyes in order to look around and absorb the surrounding scenery soon to become so familiar to us. Here we were to meet men who had already done great deeds, men who possessed that same inquisitive pioneering and buccaneering spirit which, in the course of centuries, has served to raise England to her leading place amongst the nations. And it was our honour that we were to be allowed to live with these men, to share in their exploits, to fight alongside them, and maybe to die with them.

It was a proud moment for us all, and one not entirely free from some trepidation, to realize that we now belonged, if only on probation, to a regiment which in so short a space of time had won for itself such fame and honour. Even the thought that we would have to do five parachute jumps before being admitted into the unit, failed to perturb unduly, for our desire to join this regiment far outweighed any scruples parachuting might arouse.

The Motor Transport Officer, 'Franco' as he was called, made us welcome and so organized us that in a matter of an hour or so, all our Jeeps and vehicles were unloaded and handed to the permanent MT staff for overhaul, the squadron was shown to its lines, and officers and men were allotted their sleeping quarters. Richard rushed off on some important business and every one of us was imbued with a peculiar feeling of alertness. We felt that from now on, anything might happen at the shortest of notice. None of us expected to remain long in this camp for it was nothing more than the permanent operational base for the SAS Regiment, where parties were equipped and briefed and then sent out with the least possible delay, to operate in the desert. The place certainly gave the impression that no time was wasted here.

The first impression of mine was not without justification, for after tea Richard called all his officers together and told us that half the squadron was to go on operations in a few days time, and the other half would soon follow it. In the meantime, most of us were to report the following day to No.4 Middle East Training School, where we were to be put through the rigours of a parachute course as the first qualification necessary for our acceptance into the SAS Regiment. So things really seemed to be moving.

But our hopes were not to be fulfilled as quickly or as completely as we had thought, for we found five new officers attached to our squadron who were given priority over us for operational work. There is no doubt that this was a great mistake on somebody's part. Admittedly we were untried in battle but on the other hand so were they and it seemed a very short-sighted policy to separate men from officers who knew them, and to whom they had become accustomed, and to want them to go into action under the immediate command of complete strangers.

But this was done, and Richard added to the original mistake by making another of equal magnitude. He was ordered to pick out half of his squadron for an immediate operation, which, with the exception of one officer, was to be officered entirely by the newcomers. Instead of picking out a typical cross section of the squadron, Richard was so anxious that the squadron should make a good name for itself, that he picked out all the very best men from it and sent them off with this first party! Naturally this left the rest of the squadron in a very depleted condition.

As it happened, the first party left for operations within a week of our arrival at Kabrit, and we were never to see any of them again, for sometime later we learnt that they had fallen into an enemy ambush and had been killed or captured to a man.

Kabrit was a pleasant camp and we soon settled down there. I, and about forty others of the squadron, went on a parachute course the day after we arrived, and the remainder busied themselves with learning their way around and how the regiment worked. The camp was situated right on the shores of the Little Bitter Lake, a few hundred yards south of the 'Point', which was a tongue of land, running out into the lake and which divided the Great Bitter Lake from the Little Bitter Lake. On entering the camp the first thing to catch the eye were the swings, enormous steel tubing structures, nearly 60ft high, which were contraptions erected with the intention of teaching the embryonic parachutist to jump from considerable heights, without so much as a tremor. All around the camp were strewn various odd pieces of parachute training equipment, such as aeroplane fuselages and an assortment of steel scaffolding erections. Prior to the arrival of No.4 Middle East Training School, this camp had been the only place in the Middle East where some sort of synthetic parachute training was carried out. The equipment was not used much now, except for a sort of pre-parachute course under the regiment's own instructor, Company Sergeant Major Instructor Glaze. Right in the middle of camp were two rather remarkable looking buildings. They were remarkable principally for their height, for they were the parachute packing sheds and these had to be built to a considerable height to permit the parachutes to be fully extended when they were hung up to be dried.

The mess was a large double marquee and its main attribute was that it boasted a bar that never closed. In fact Leitch, the barman, stayed up most of the night, and indeed sometimes did not get to bed before dawn when the wilder parties were in progress.

Christmas came along three days after our arrival and it was quite an ambitious event. Colonel Stirling and many of the operational personnel managed to come down for this day. Of these visitors I chiefly remember a captain in full Scots' regalia who was sporting the two most magnificent black eyes I have ever seen. He looked rather sheepish when questioned on their origin, but in spite of his reticence, it soon leaked out that the great Bill Fraser – terror to the Germans in the desert and with a whole string of operations to his credit – had been taken for a ride in a Cairo or Alexandria taxi when he was far from sober and had been ignominiously beaten up and robbed! What a come down! Poor Bill was very ashamed of it!

The most memorable event of that Christmas was when Richard called his officers into the squadron office to tell us that we would all be going on operations within the next week. After months of inactivity, this came to us as very welcome news indeed.

While the men ate their Christmas dinner, Colonel Stirling, who had come down from the desert especially to pay the camp a visit on that day, took the opportunity to speak to all the men. Beyond the usual Christmas clichés he did not say much, but despite this his powerful personality made itself felt, and one could tell by the attitude of those men who knew him, with what respect and even reverence he was held by every man in the unit. And indeed, from all accounts, he was an amazing man. Tall, distinguished-looking and yet surprisingly young for a man of such influence and authority, he gave the impression of knowing exactly his own mind, and moreover of being able to persuade people to do just as he wanted. Although formerly in the Scots Guards, he by no means adhered to the blind discipline of the guards regiments, nor did he give much thought to matters of administration. In fact, it might be said that he was extremely unpractical. But his real character lay in his flair, almost amounting to genius, for planning operations, which for their daring and cheek would not have entered the head of any normal army leader.

He saw openings where others saw none; he planned and carried out operations which had been held by high ranking officers to be impossible, and belonging to the realms of fantasy. But such was his magnetic personality, that having conceived one of these 'hare-brained' schemes, he was able to persuade Very Important People to give them their support. He was known to practically every commander of importance, all of whom had shown themselves willing to fall in with his wishes. He treated his men fairly as human beings, rather than as children, and by thus freeing them from all the irksome and petty military restrictions that were the custom in the army, and by granting them various forms of minor privileges, he gained their undying loyalty and support.

From the start, there came into being through his example, a feeling of comradeship and a spirit of co-operation in the regiment which never died throughout the whole war, and which will still exist in the days of peace. The men knew what was expected of them, even though they were given almost complete freedom in their spare time, and rather than let the colonel and the officers down, they would take it upon themselves to see that they behaved themselves in the proper manner. If by any chance, certain individuals did not abide by this unwritten law, it was too bad for them for all of a sudden they found themselves back with their parent units. This threat of being sent back to their units as being considered unsuitable for the regiment, grew to be regarded by the men as the worst punishment and disgrace that could befall them. This explains the truly remarkable spirit that ran through the unit, and how every single man down to the lowest pen-pusher or sanitary man held their colonel and other operational officers in the greatest esteem and respect.

At this point, I think it would be fitting to add a few words about the origin and work of this most unconventional unit, to which I now belonged. But as I only joined the regiment in December 1942, much of what I am now relating was only gathered by me from hearsay, from casual talk in the mess and in the canteen and from second hand sources, with the result that some of my statements may be inaccurate, for which I hope I shall be forgiven, by those with a greater knowledge of the facts.

As has already been mentioned, the Middle East Commandos were disbanded early in 1941 and many excellent men were left out of a job who were nevertheless anxious to keep together. Two young lieutenants, Stirling and Lewis, had thought out a scheme whereby the enemy lines of supply and rear bases could be harassed, disorganized and damaged by small parties of determined men being parachuted behind their lines. At first this project seemed idealistic and over-ambitious, especially as it had previously been considered to be impractical to use paratroops in the desert, owing to the climate. Even if such a scheme were possible, how were two young lieutenants, unknown to anyone, to make themselves and their ideas felt? But this is where the remarkable character of

Stirling showed itself. By his amazingly powerful personality, he managed to convince the people that matter that maybe there was something behind his idea after all, with the ultimate result that he was given a free hand to form his own unit, and to have a shot at realizing his ideals.

With this in view, Stirling and Lewis gathered together a picked bunch of officers and men from their old commando units and proceeded to set up a camp at Kabrit. Thus was formed the first nucleus of the 1st SAS Regiment. At that time Kabrit was nothing more than a patch of sand, but out of this, Stirling and his men soon managed to build up the camp to the state in which I found it, when joining the regiment. To a certain extent by official means, but mostly by scrounging, stealing and borrowing, they managed to get together the material and stores required. They formed their own parachute training school and made every man go through a course of at least five jumps. This was worked in conjunction with the aerodrome which lay just across the road from the camp. At the same time the unit went through a very rigid course of training for the first operation which depended on a parachute descent. But this, however, turned out to be far from a success, as the men were dropped in a violent gale, and got hopelessly separated and lost on landing. However, this did not deter them, and back they came to Kabrit to try again.

Subsequently, as an alternative method to parachuting to get the men behind the enemy lines, the idea evolved of the unit working in conjunction with the Long Range Desert Group, who had made themselves acquainted with the vast, hitherto unexplored tracts of desert, far to the south of the fighting area. With the aid of this hardy and resourceful little unit, the SAS were enabled to attack the enemy's bare southern flank from secret bases, buried right in the depths of the desert. The Long Range Desert Group were a small group of daring explorers, who had charted and reconnoitred areas of desert never before trodden by white men for all the desert fighting was done in the narrow coastal strip, and because of its treacherous surface neither army made use of the immense expanses of territory lying further

Peter Davis in a Jeep during training, November–December 1942.

inland. Much of this was impenetrable to wheeled or tracked vehicles, as it was composed of soft, shifting sand, known as the 'Great Sand Sea'. It was this area that Stirling now chose for the future lair of his men.

And so a completely new form of training was begun. Instead of aircraft, the unit was now transported by, and mounted on Jeeps, which were found to be more manoeuvrable and to have a better cross-country performance than any vehicle which the enemy possessed. In fact, difficult though this operation proved, they could get through the Sand Sea, which provided them with a sure haven from anything except aircraft. Needless to say for this form of work a very high standard of navigational and driving skill was required. The Jeeps were modified and transformed into something very different from their original design. They were mounted with machine guns of all sizes and calibres, and were converted to carry enough petrol to enable them to travel for 800 miles at a stretch without refuelling.

In liaison with the LRDG, petrol and ammunition dumps were sited in certain points of vantage in the desert and secret operational bases were formed. From these established vantage points, the unit was able to attack the enemy behind his own lines, at any point they chose, and from that time on they made the fullest possible use of this advantage. Small parties of men were thereafter continually sabotaging railways, destroying dumps and attacking airfields, and there is no doubt that they caused the enemy many a headache. Great was the material damage they inflicted but the mental strain which their activities undoubtedly caused must have been infinitely greater. Soon the SAS had formed a reputation for itself that gradually spread through both the British and German armies. Recruits came in rapidly and the regiment was established.

For the most part the SAS concentrated on raiding enemy airfields and had succeeded in destroying an amazing number of aircraft on the ground, even though after the initial surprise, the enemy had taken to posting a sentry on each plane! The methods they used were original also. They would place on the wing of the aircraft a specially constructed bomb fitted with a time pencil mechanism, consisting of gelignite and thermite mixed, and the whole, wrapped up in a ration bag, had both explosive and incendiary qualities.

Unfortunately, Lewis was killed in an early operation, and the regiment lost in him a very able and beloved officer, but by now nothing could stop the regiment's reputation growing. Stirling rose to the rank of lieutenant colonel, and the new unit was officially recognized and respected by GHQ Cairo.

Such then, in very brief outlines, was the type of regiment I had joined and with which I was to remain for the rest of my military career. And this first Christmas among these men helped me greatly towards getting to know them and to adapt myself to their rather unconventional ways. I also learned how we had established ourselves at Kabrit, and this news came as a great blow to our pride for our acceptance at Kabrit was far more the result of a misunderstanding than anything else, and was certainly nothing of which we could be proud.

When at H4, and in that sandstorm, Mac had sent a telegram to Richard, which ran approximately, 'Conditions impossible, heavy sandstorm in progress: please permit immediate return'. This telegram, instead of going to Richard, somehow got down to Kabrit, and was eventually received by the deputy OC of the camp in the absence of the colonel. He of course, was rather taken aback by the message and felt that if conditions in Syria for the squadron were really as intolerable as was made out, then we had better come down to Kabrit. So a signal was sent off summoning us down there. And that is the way in which we were accepted in the SAS!

Christmas ended on a note of disappointment for me, for I learnt from Richard that one officer would have to be left behind at Kabrit to look after the twenty men who were also being left behind. As I was the newest arrival, I was the unfortunate to whom this job was given, and thus I found myself in the unhappy position of seeing all my friends and my men going off without me. Still, I was promised they would call me out just as soon as there was room for me up there, and in the meantime I knew that at least I would be able to finish off my parachute course without fear of interruption.

Chapter Two

Embryonic Parachutist!

The first party left on operations on 31 December and the remainder of the squadron, except for myself and my twenty remnants, left Kabrit about a week later. It was very depressing to be left all alone but fortunately the parachute course took my mind off things.

Parachuting had largely been discarded as a means of getting the regiment to their objective, but nevertheless the colonel insisted that all new recruits should go through the course, and thus be ready to jump into action at any time. The chief reason, I feel, for the course was that it sorted out the recruits; if they could stand up to jumping out of a plane into space, then it showed that they had at least some of the qualities that made up the sort of man who was required.

The course took place about 3 miles from our camp at Kabrit and was very efficiently run. It lasted two weeks on the ground, after which, five jumps from a Hudson had to be completed. The instructors were a mixture from the Army PT School and from the RAF, and a better bunch of men one could not hope to meet. They knew their job very thoroughly and combined such cheerfulness with their efficiency that we all came to enjoy the strenuous physical exercise which the training involved.

No.4 Middle East Training School, must have looked a strange sight when viewed from the Suez–Geneifa Road. Gigantic towers and platforms of steel scaffolding reared themselves up into the sky and aeroplane fuselages lay scattered on the sand in careless confusion.

We first reported to the METS (Middle East Training School Paratroops) on 22 December, the day after the squadron arrived at Kabrit. There followed two weeks of strenuous physical training during which, in addition to reaching a state of physical fitness which most of us had never before achieved, we were made to go through on the ground a synthetic parachuting training which was designed to acquaint us not only with the drill which had to be learned, but also with all the sensations the parachutist experiences when he actually jumps. By the end of those two full and gruelling weeks there was nothing we required to know about the art of parachuting and all preparations were made for our first jump.

But we were not to jump on the day scheduled. That night one of those sudden Egyptian storms arose, bringing along with it a strong gusty wind

Kabrit, Egypt, December 1942 to March 1943

Orderly room, Kabrit, showing swings.

Parachute hanging sheds, Kabrit.

which whipped the sand into every corner of the tents and messes, and created conditions which were quite out of the question for parachuting, let alone for flying! So none of us was surprised to be told on the next morning's parade, that the jumping was postponed until the following morning. This procedure went on for four days, whilst the storm continued to rage in unabated strength, so that the fear of the pending ordeal gradually diminished and the stark reality of the whole thing grew less. As I went to bed each night, and heard the wind battering at my tent, I was able to heave a sigh of relief, and say, 'It's not tomorrow, at any rate!'

And then one morning after going off to sleep with just that thought in my head I woke to the awful realization that the storm was over. All was still outside, and conditions were ideal for jumping. Quickly dressing in all the various knickknacks that went along with jumping, I reported to the packing sheds where we were told that jumping would take place that morning. So this was it!

There was a funny dry feeling in my throat and a heavy feeling in my stomach, as I drew my chute, and I wished I had not had so much breakfast. And then began the waiting. Very few people seemed completely at their ease. Some were quieter than usual, but on the whole there was an atmosphere of forced merriment, all being unnaturally hearty.

There were seven in my stick and we had to jump in pairs. As I was the officer, I was made to jump in the last pair and I was thus the first into the plane. At first everything was exactly the same as the ground training: the inspection of our harness by the dispatcher, entering the plane, crowding into the nose as we took off, and then assuming our proper positions. The dispatcher came round to hook each of our static lines onto the strongpoint, and to ensure, personally, that the safety pin to prevent the claws of the clip from accidentally opening was inserted. All the time we kept up a running flow of hearty, cheery conversation and anecdotes, to try to take our minds off the present. He made us all promise to say cheerio to him as we went out, in the hope that we would worry more about this little detail than what we were actually about to do. I must confess that I was not feeling at all happy, and from the look on their faces, I imagine none of my companions were either. I felt very cold all of a sudden, as though I were even then exposed to the violence of the slip-stream that I could feel rushing passed the plane. At least three times I examined my static line to make sure that I was properly hooked up, and once I was satisfied to that effect, I could not keep my eyes

Parachute training course, No 4 Middle East Training School, Near Kabrit, January 1943.

from the door. This seemed to exercise a malignant attraction for me. Half of me wanted to go as far away from it as possible, while the other half felt a peculiar desire to hurl itself out.

Such were my feelings then, as we sped towards the dropping ground. I most certainly had not the slightest desire to jump, and yet I was possessed by an even greater fear than of passing through that door – the fear of appearing afraid and maybe of refusing. And then, as I gazed out of the window, I saw below me on the dark sand, a little patch of white, arranged in the form of a T. Something jumped up in the region of my stomach and was still. We were there. The T was laid to show us as we descended in which direction the wind was blowing, and of course, to show the pilot where to release us.

'*Running in!*' the dispatcher's shout seemed to awaken us from a bad dream. I saw the first pair leave their seats, and the number one take up his position in the gaping doorway. I felt myself gripping tightly the edge of my seat, for fear that, by some lurch of the plane, he should prematurely be sent hurtling into space. At that moment I felt that I would never be able to bring myself to stand in the doorway like that!

'*Action stations!*' The atmosphere inside was electric. The number one was straining in the door half inside and half out of the plane. So keyed up were his nerves that it would have only been necessary for someone to speak for him to have gone out. But he did not have long to wait. The red light above the door could not have been on for more than a couple of seconds, before the frenzied shout of the dispatcher '*Go!*' informed us that it had turned to green. Numbers three and four prevented me from seeing these first exits, and all that told me they were out, was the sharp crack of the static line extending and the bump as the empty parachute bag hit the tailplane. There were now only five of us left in the plane, excluding the dispatcher. He, in contrast to our decidedly mixed feelings seemed to be enjoying himself hugely. He peered out of the door, and with great glee told us that the first two were on their way down successfully. How I wished I could have changed places with one of them!

A few minutes later, the same procedure was carried out and numbers three and four went out successfully, leaving only three of us to jump on the following circuit. I began to feel rather sick and colder than ever. I had noticed with horror the speed with which they seemed to be whipped around the corner as soon as they had got one foot outside. It appeared to be such very violent treatment.

As we made the final circuit the three of us who remained were made to move right up beside the doorway and soon the by now familiar order, '*Running in*' was applied to us. Slowly we got to our feet and lined up, the one behind the other. Phillips, the number one, took up his position in the door and from

Parachute training course, No 4 Middle East Training School, near Kabrit, January 1943.

where I stood I could see his face clearly, as, with one hand on each side of the doorway, he balanced himself on the threshold with nothing but a few inches separating him from space. The sweat stood in beads on his brow, as we ran in, and his jaw was moving rhythmically and mechanically, as he chewed his gum. The shout of '*Action Stations!*' woke me from my study of Phillips's face, and I realized that I only had a few seconds to go before I would be hurtling through space. My stomach felt as though it weighed a ton and every nerve in my body was so tense that I would have jumped had a pin been dropped. Fascinated I watched Phillips, trying to forget my own fear in the contemplation of his. What was wrong with that red light? Surely it should have turned to green ages ago! Just as these thoughts were flashing through my mind, the dispatcher bawled '*Go!*' in my ear, and muttering a prayer I prepared for the very worst, never having felt so afraid in all my life. An expression of determination, mixed with repulsion crossed Phillips's face, and he made a half-hearted attempt to push himself out with his hands, in the manner taught. But his chute got caught in the top of the doorway and the slip-stream must have been a good deal stronger than he imagined, for when I looked again expecting to see Elwys, the number two, disappearing, Phillips was still in his 'action stations' position and the plane had passed over the dropping ground, so that we had to make another circuit.

Something was bumping violently inside me. Oh why can't we get it over with, I found myself muttering, while I was cursing at having to undergo that awful circuit once more. The instructor was muttering reassuring words of advice in Phillips's ear and I watched his strained and anxious look and the mechanical movement of his jaw, while I wondered if he would make it the next time round. I was not sure how I myself would feel when I stood in that doorway and saw the ground rushing past beneath me. The red light went on again and the tense feeling increased. I noticed in an objective sort of way that I was sweating hard, though I was strangely cold.

'*Go!*' shouted the dispatcher and Phillips went. Before I could realize that my last hope had

Peter Davis before first jump.

Before first jump: Frame, Little, Unknown, Tunstall, Phillips, Elwys.

now gone, Elwys had disappeared and I found myself in the gaping doorway. I don't remember jumping: the next thing I remember was being gripped by an almighty wind which pulled me horizontal and filled me with sheer terror. As if in a dream I noticed the side of the aircraft flash past me, and forgetting all the lessons we had learnt on the ground, I clutched madly in the direction of the tail plane, anything to save myself from this awful sensation of powerlessness. And then before I even felt myself to be falling, came the welcome tug and I looked up to see the lovely white canopy billowing out above my head.

In spite of my shocking exit, for I realized that I had gone out in one mad flurry of arms and legs, everything was completely in order. I was sweating harder than ever and felt boiling hot; after I had settled myself comfortably in my harness and grasped the lift-webs above my head, I took the opportunity of looking around me. The silence with which I was now surrounded was a wonderful contrast to the noise and the vibration of the plane. Everything seemed so peaceful, with the sun shining in the cloudless sky and the yellow sand below, that I found my terror of a few seconds before rather difficult to understand and one of my first impressions was, 'You old fool, what on earth did you make all that fuss about.'

I could see Phillips' and Elwys's chutes slightly below and to the left of me. It was good to know that they had got out safely. I felt on top of the world as I drifted peacefully downwards. Save for the quite considerable swing from one side to the other, there was absolutely no motion at all until I was only a short distance from earth. By this time, the instructor on the ground had started making some rather pointed remarks through a megaphone on the subject of keeping one's legs together, and just in time I remembered the landing training that we had gone through earlier on in the course. I managed to do a three-quarter turn, which put my right side to the wind, as the ground came rushing up at me. I hit it hard, but in accordance with my training, I crumpled up, rolling sideways onto my right shoulder and with a strange feeling of elation, picked myself up unhurt and ran round my chute.

After I had folded this up in the approved manner, I went back to the truck where the rest of the stick were waiting, in spirits very different from those of only a few minutes earlier. Everyone was talking and describing their experiences, and the general impression was that the whole business was not nearly so bad as our imaginations had caused us to believe it would be. But the next time we went up, the tension, and the strain, and the silence in the plane, were as apparent as they had been before, and for my part at any rate, the sensation of sheer panic as I went through that door never diminished. The high spirits that were displayed on the ground after the jump was over, were certainly no criterion by which the pleasures of parachuting could be judged, as they reflected nothing more than the welcome release from the considerable nervous tension, to which we had all just been subjected.

I accomplished my remaining four jumps successfully in the following three days, after which I was able to celebrate the completion of my course by spending a weekend's leave in the magic city of Cairo!

I shall never forget that first trip to Cairo and the sight again of large hotels and civilized surroundings. I started my leave by joining in the drinking that went on round the bar under the auspices of the very efficient barman, Corporal Leitch, who was up half the night attending to our wants and having a quiet laugh at the officers in the shelter of the bar. I had often heard the expression 'a dour Scotsman' but its meaning was never really clear until I met Corporal Leitch, who fitted the description admirably. He never said two words where one would have sufficed and always gave the impression of having a rather jaundiced view on life, especially when there was no whisky to be had!

At the bar I met John Bell, an officer the same age as me, and who had arrived at about the same time. Johnny was a frank, sincere and conscientious chap,

Parachute training near Kabrit, January 1943.

whom one could not help liking and we immediately struck up a friendship. As we drank and chatted, a stranger came up to the bar beside us. There was nothing spectacular about this visitor; on the contrary, in fact, he was a mild, kindly-looking old gentleman, whose youth was already well behind him. He seemed perfectly at home in the mess, and as soon as he had reached the bar, began to sink pink gins at a prodigious rate. He soon started up a conversation with Johnny and me and revealed that he was far from being the mild old gentleman that he appeared. He was the revolver-shooting specialist, Major Grant-Taylor, and must have been the best shot with the revolver in the whole of the Middle East. He had started a course in the pistol and close combat methods which many of the unit had already attended, and at which I was lucky enough to be present a few months later. Apparently this meek looking little man was able to give one of the most blood-curdling and morale-boosting lectures on the offensive spirit that has ever been delivered. But I did not know all this about him then, and we chatted until well into the following morning while one pink gin after the other slid down his throat.

There is nothing impressive about the trip to Cairo from Kabrit. I cadged a lift in a Jeep the following morning which brought me safely to the city by lunch time. Although the distance is about 90 miles the road is so flat and straight that the trip can be comfortably completed inside two hours. No town or village lies on the route and, as far as the eye can see, the road runs for the whole distance through a stretch of flat, sandy desert, sprinkled here and there with patches of brown camel grass and scrub. Rocky hills rose up in the distance for the first part of the run, but soon even these were left behind and nothing except the kilometre stones that lined the roadside gave indication of how much of the distance was yet to be covered. Almost exactly half way was the Half-Way House, which catered for the weary traveller and where, at regular Spinneys prices one could obtain a meal or a cup of coffee and a dry bun.

One or two army camps were dotted about here and there along the roadside, but the very bleakness and monotony of the landscape always made it seem something like a miracle when, after topping a long gentle rise, the great city of Cairo came into view. It seemed unnatural and out of place somehow. Before you realized it, you were in the city with its teeming pavements and hooting taxis, rattling gharries and clanging tramcars, with its fine modern buildings, its primitive native houses and its spacious and beautifully kept parks. Only 2 miles outside Cairo you might still have been in the middle of a vast desert, thousands of miles from any civilization. I could not quite believe it and all of a sudden felt rather lost in the middle of this noisy, active and hurrying throng.

Cairo was a wonderful city if one went there just to have a good time, with the intention of spending an unlimited amount of money in a limited space of time. It can truly be said that anything could be bought in Cairo at that time, for a price. But food was reasonably cheap and plentiful, and so the best part of a weekend's leave was spent in eating and drinking. Hotel accommodation was desperately short, for officers at any rate. A room to yourself was an unheard of luxury, for the Cairo hotels used to squeeze as many beds as possible into all their rooms, so that we got the impression of sleeping in a dormitory. But nevertheless, the price of a room was demanded from each of the occupants, so the war must have certainly been welcomed by the Cairo population.

I met up with Douglas Stobie and Ken Lamonby, two officers who had just joined the regiment, and we spent the rest of my leave together. We soon learned that one had to have one's eyes wide open in Cairo, if one did not want to be fleeced right and left by the civilians. It seemed a point of honour with the Egyptians to make as much money as possible out of the unsuspecting British soldiery who went there to spend their leave and have a good time. In this, the Egyptians did not bear the whole guilt for Cairo is such a cosmopolitan place that one comes across all nationalities there, especially Greeks, Turks and French. But no matter what the nationality, their intention was the same, to make use of the war to their greatest possible advantage, by making the celebrating and pleasure-seeking Eighth Army leave-troops pay through the nose for everything.

So that was Cairo – a city where anything could be bought at a price, where for a short leave, a wonderful time was to be had, but where the characteristic Arab graft and love of money was rampant.

Back at Kabrit I busied myself with getting to know my twenty-odd men, keeping them well occupied and preparing them for operations to the best of my ability. Soon all of them had successfully gone through the parachute course, except for one who refused and another who fractured his spine on landing, and who consequently never returned to the unit from hospital. Training hours were not long and we enjoyed plenty of free time. The day started with reveille being blown on the bugle and half an hour later, at half past six, we had to double out into the chilly misty morning, onto the square by the boxing ring. There Company Sergeant Major Instructor Glaze, our jovial PT instructor, put us through our paces with a rigid set of exercises, followed by assault course training on the parachuting apparatus. Twenty minutes later it was a weary body of men who returned to their tents to dress for breakfast. But irksome though this training might have been, it certainly made us fit, which was to serve us in such good stead later on. Training hours were from half past eight to half past four and mercifully I was given a completely free hand in how I arranged it.

The original adjutant of the camp when I first arrived, had been so 'guards' that he seemed to be surrounded by a veritable halo of spit and polish, and was only remarkable for his extreme lack of intelligence, but he was succeeded by John Verney who, despite being unacquainted with the job, could not have done better at it and was a joy to work under. All he wanted from me was a weekly training programme, and in return I could always rely on him for help in arranging exercises etc. To begin with, we concentrated entirely on driving and navigation, demolitions and firing foreign weapons, and it did not take long before I had all my men fairly adept at these subjects. We were only passing the time away as profitably as possible, for we were under the impression that on 25 January, we would be going up to join the squadron and thus were very determined to learn as much as possible.

But in this expectation our hopes were once again dashed, for on 22 January, Tripoli fell to the advancing Eighth Army, and we were told that there was no scope for us and that the squadrons would shortly be returning. I was very disappointed, for it seems strange to spend eighteen months in the Middle East, without once having taken part in any of the desert operations, and it is something that I shall always regret. But we had no alternative but to remain at Kabrit making the best use of our time as possible.

Peter Davis at Kantara Station, Palestine, March–June 1943.

Excellent instruction was given us in demolitions by Bill Cumper's engineer section. A wonderful character was Bill. He possessed the most cheerful disposition and quickest wit of anyone I have known. He had risen through the ranks, and was now a permanent fixture in the regiment. If anyone felt depressed they only had to talk to Bill for a few minutes and I defy them to have kept a straight face for long. Since I am rather small in size, Bill always called me 'Chota', and I do not believe to this day that he knows my real name. In the mess he was always remarkable for the fact that he never drank anything stronger than a lemonade although, on occasions he was known to add a dash of lime, to keep his spirits up. But it was surprising what an effect these drinks could have on him, for he could hold his own even in the most hilarious of parties, and it is only further proof of the spontaneous cheerfulness of his nature that he never felt tempted to stimulate it by artificial means. Bill was a ranker and proud of it; he would often come into the mess, chose an empty seat next to a newly arrived young officer, asking permission to sit next to the 'officer', and then in a loud voice would inform the mess waiter that he was ready for lunch, by telling him that he could bring in the 'swill'.

It was a great event when 'Jumper' Cumper was going through his parachute course, and on the occasion when he had done two out of his five jumps, he came strolling quite unconcernedly into the mess, with two fifths of the parachute wings sewn onto his sleeve, which he proudly displayed to as many people as he could.

Bill was extremely violent in his declamations against the 'spit and polish' brigade, and he kept his independent character, no matter who he had to meet. The story goes that when the Duke of Gloucester inspected the camp, Bill absolutely refused to wear a 'Sam Browne' in his honour, and he is reported to have greeted the royal visitor with the words, *'Hello, Duke, meet the lads!'*

This same individuality and lack of embarrassment which he displayed towards his superior officers, was revealed to the full when Bill was in action. Nothing scared him or caused him to lose his light-hearted, carefree attitude. When the regiment was raiding Benghazi, they found their way barred by a gate. Bill, who was in one of the leading Jeeps, jumped down and with a flourish and many exaggerated gestures, threw it open, in a loud voice proclaiming as he did so, *'Let battle commence!'* No sooner had he done this than the enemy who were in prepared positions nearby, opened up with all they had got and battle certainly commenced with a vengeance.

No one could help liking Bill and he remained always one of the most popular figures in the regiment, a first class technical engineering officer, as well as a sincere friend and a most amusing companion.

Peter Davis, Cairo, January 1943.

Outside the camp there was not much in the way of amusement in the immediate vicinity, except for the local cinema, and it is proof enough of how the men found time hanging heavily on their hands, that this was so remarkably well patronized. The Egyptian cinemas were indescribably awful and it was always a source of wonder to me how the authorities allowed such conditions to exist. Apparently they had accepted the offer of a local contractor to provide entertainment for the troops in the canal area, and paid him vast sums of money for this purpose. But he must have made his fortune out of the contract, for everything was skimped and shoddy. The buildings themselves were foul and many of them actually waved about in the wind. The seats were hard, uncomfortable and sordid and the sound system was so distorted that it was impossible to hear. The films were so old that they were always breaking and the operators were so amateur at their job that often they would show separate parts of the film in the wrong order! The troops took all this in very good humour, I thought, and usually just went to have a good laugh at their primitive surroundings. However, I cannot blame them in the least for the few occasions when they felt they had had enough of a good thing, and had set fire to the whole wretched contraption.

And now I think it opportune to say a few words about various people I met and with whom I had to work at Kabrit. As I have already mentioned, very few of the operatives were at the camp, as both 'A' and 'B' Squadrons were chasing up the German retreat at the time I arrived in the regiment and were now somewhere in the vicinity of Tripoli. The camp was left in charge of an elderly non-operative major, whose job it was to look after the administrative and disciplinary side of things in the absence of the colonel. He was a typical regular soldier, of the type who had worked his way up from being a 'boy' in the regimental band, and as a result he was not too easy to work under. As far as I could see he had only two thoughts in his head: one was whether anyone had dropped a piece of paper in the camp area recently, and the other was how many officers and men were dodging doing their day's work.

He paid far more attention to the cleanliness of the camp than to the welfare of the men and to their training, and he had not been in charge long before the roads in the camp were all lined with stones. Woe betide the man who accidentally tripped over a stone and dislodged it in his sight – he could be sure of extra fatigues for that! The stones had not been there long before Pat Reilly, the regimental sergeant major, was summoned to the orderly-room, and instructed to find a fatigue party to paint these stones white without delay. Pat was rather taken aback at this strange request, but after a second's hesitation, came out with the reply, *'Oh yes sir; and shall I get them painted on the underside as well?'*

These two did not get on well together as may be imagined, for whereas the major stood for pettiness and unnecessary, trivial discipline, the RSM ruled the camp and the sergeant's mess with an iron hand. So long as everything was going all right he would have nothing to say and gave the impression of being a jovial, friendly person, but as soon as the slightest thing went wrong he was there on the spot and ready to tear a strip off anybody. His one concern was to keep the camp running efficiently and anyone who did not help him towards this goal soon paid for it.

Pat was a massive Irishman, standing about 6ft 3ins, and weighing close on 15 stone. He shared with the leading figures of the regiment, such as Paddy Mayne, the quality of possessing extremely high powers of observation. He would walk about the camp, giving the impression that he was easy-going and carefree and yet all the time, there was not a thing that escaped his notice. And once he noticed anything, he was certainly not slow to act. Pat was the best

RSM I ever met in the army. He was not only respected, but admired by the men, from whom he kept exactly the distance that his rank demanded. In his treatment of them he was completely fair, whilst his ability to judge character, which never led him wrong, was something in the nature of a gift. And added to these qualities he was, purely as a man, one of the best types on this earth. Sincere, a good listener, and always willing to have a laugh at his own expense, he was one of the best natured people I have ever met.

It was natural that a man such as Pat Reilly had qualities which were wasted as an RSM, and thus it was not long before he received his commission, and returned to the regiment in that capacity.

I had been at Kabrit about a month when a startling rumour began to spread around, and shortly afterwards it was confirmed that Colonel Stirling had been captured. It was learnt later that he was almost certainly betrayed by the Arabs, for his party woke up one morning to find themselves surrounded by a crowd of fierce-looking Germans and all they could do was give themselves up. Two of the party lay low and managed to get away, and after a harrowing time, succeeded in making their way to the First Army lines. The news of the colonel's capture was received with dismay at Kabrit and, down to the newest arrival, everyone regretted the loss of so inspired and distinguished a leader. The future of the regiment was now very much in the air, more especially since the wonderful advances of the Eighth Army had made the presence of the regiment in the enemy's rear almost unnecessary. Shortly after the news of the colonel's capture, 'A' Squadron under Paddy Mayne returned from operations, and after a few days reorganizing at the camp, and then some leave in Cairo, they went off to Syria to do the course at the ski-school in the Lebanon mountains.

'A' Squadron arrived back just on the day when General Alexander was inspecting the camp, and everything had been prepared to give him as good an impression as possible, when these bearded, dirty men began to come in. Poor Pat Reilly was tearing his hair trying to hide them all and his patience was put to the highest test, when Johnny Wiseman, a very small and amusing officer, chose to enter the gates sporting a magnificent beard, at the very moment when the general was inspecting the men. Not unnaturally, Pat failed to recognize Johnny and told him to clear off in no uncertain terms.

During their brief stay I hardly got to know any of 'A' Squadron, though I came to know them all very well later. However, I shall never forget my first meeting with Paddy Mayne, the squadron commander, under whom I was to serve for the next three years and who, in my opinion, was one of the most outstanding characters that this war has brought to light. I wanted to speak to

Bill Cumper about some point to do with demolitions and was told that I could find him in Paddy's tent. I walked in and was introduced by Bill.

My first impression of Paddy was amazement at the massiveness of him. His form seemed to fill the whole tent. Standing well over 6ft every part of his body was built on a proportionately generous scale: his wrists were twice the size of those of a normal man, while his fists seemed to be as large as a polo ball. Although he must have weighed close on 17 stone, there was not an ounce of surplus flesh on his body, and I was to learn later that his powers of endurance were unlimited. He seldom worried about keeping physically fit, and yet he could accomplish twice as much as the average man. He was made to look even more imposing, on the occasion of our first meeting, as his face was covered with an enormous reddish beard which he was just in the act of removing. But this could not hide his extraordinary profile, for he was one of those people with a dead straight forehead, so that from the top of his head to the tip of his nose was a straight line. Under great jutting eyebrows, his piercing blue eyes looked discomfitingly at me, betraying his remarkable talent of being able to sum a person up within a minute of meeting him. He received me most civilly and I was struck by the incongruity of his voice and of his shy manner, contrasting with the powerfulness of his frame, for his voice was low and halting, with a musical sing-song quality and the faintest tinge of an Irish brogue. I was soon to learn that when he was excited or intoxicated, this remarkable voice would become so Irish as to be hardly intelligible, and when he was angry it would reach such heights as to be almost a falsetto!

But on this occasion Paddy was courteous and charming, as he always was with strangers. He asked me a few questions about myself and the men left in my care, and then offered me the opportunity of going up to Syria with his squadron to go through the ski-course. I was very tempted to accept, but had to decline the offer, explaining that I was still hoping that Richard Lea had not forgotten me and that he would keep his promise and call me up to the desert shortly. It later turned out that this hope came to nothing and it would have been far better for me to have accepted Paddy's offer.

A few days later Paddy came into my tent and asked if he could take one of my men with him. Naturally there was no reason for me to refuse this request, and moreover, I was hardly in a position to, but what struck me at the time, was that he should have the decency to come to me rather than summon me to him and tell me of his intentions. From the very first moment one set eyes on him, Paddy Mayne gave the impression of being a great man. Not indeed, because he was always showing it or talking about it, but simply from the terrific force and vitality that radiated from him. He was a man of very few words and was amazingly shy when he had to talk in public to the men, and I think his greatest pleasure in those days was to sit quietly in the mess, with a drink in his hand, watching in silence with those sharp, penetrating eyes of his, everything that was going on around him and making a mental picture for future reference of the private, individual character of everyone he observed.

There was nothing stuck-up about him; he would talk for hours to anyone, whether a man, NCO or officer, on terms of absolute equality. But it was a dangerous thing to imagine that by taking you into his confidence in this way, Paddy was showing you a sign of his special favour, for as likely as not he would not so much as look at you on the following day, and by just a look or a gesture, he was able to put himself at the correct distance from you. If there was one thing that he hated, that was a person trying to win favour with him, and it was a rare thing for anyone who practised any self-seeking motives with him to be allowed to get away with it for long.

There were many other officers I met during this stay at Kabrit with whom I was shortly to become much more closely acquainted. There was George Jellicoe who, although a shrewd and a capable leader, was the complete antithesis in character to Paddy Mayne. Possessing a strong personal charm and magnetism, he did not seem to conceive the seriousness and danger of the job that he was training his men to do, and used to lark about the mess on occasions like any high-spirited schoolboy. He seemed too light-hearted to take his job seriously, but people who knew him soon realized that this was only a pose. He was in charge of 'D' Squadron, a newly formed unit which was occupied with a rather different sort of training than that which had previously been practised by the regiment.

'D' Squadron concentrated on training in small seaborne raids, and shortly afterwards they split off from the rest of the regiment to undergo a most extensive training. It should be mentioned that by the end of 1943 they were known and feared by the enemy in Crete, Sardinia, Corsica, Sicily, Italy, Greece, Yugoslavia and all the islands of the Aegean and Adriatic. Many a volume could be written of the dangerous and daring ventures which they undertook.

Another prominent figure in the mess, was Captain Francis, the MTO, 'Franco' as we called him, who was a born staff officer. He had just the right walk, just the right suggestions of a comfortable paunch and that air of knowing all there was to know about every subject, without deigning to reveal his knowledge to anyone. As he walked over to the mess from the MT office, in his customary slow and dignified fashion, carrying the little black brief case under his arm which gave him such an air of importance, he seemed a great man indeed. But Franco was not such a bad sort at all. He never made himself out to be anything other than what he was and could join in the laughter at himself with the best of them. Once you took Franco for what he was, rather than for what he ought to be if you judged him for his stately exterior, he proved to be very good company.

'B' Squadron had meanwhile returned to Kabrit, and from all accounts they had had a pretty bad time of things and casualties had been extremely heavy. They were given leave and then remained hanging around the camp, pending the reorganization that we all knew was inevitable, as a result of the colonel's capture.

By the beginning of March, I had given up all hope of getting out to the scene of operations. The Eighth Army was sitting in front of the Mareth Line, and there was absolutely no scope left for the regiment in this theatre. My squadron was the only one up now, and rumour had it that they were having a pretty good time in Tripoli and would shortly be returning. So we at camp just filled in our time as best we could.

My squadron returned about the middle of March. It was grand to see them all again, and to be able to chat with John and Ted and Mick and learn all their news. Apparently they had not done very much, for by the time they had got out there, there was hardly any useful work which they could do. In fact, beyond reconnoitering some of the enemy positions at the southern end of the Mareth Line, and taking some useful photographs of ready-prepared enemy defences which at that time were not yet manned, their time had been completely wasted. In fact they envied me having completed my parachute course, and having been able to spend the period more or less profitably.

A few days after the arrival of 'C' Squadron, as my squadron was called, Paddy Mayne's 'A' Squadron returned from the ski-school in Syria, rather more quickly than they intended, as a result of the mysterious disappearance of a large amount of chocolate from some place or other where they had been. The whole regiment was now back in camp, and it was clear that now at last the long expected reorganization of the unit was to take place.

After the usual rumours it was learnt from fairly sound sources that the regiment was to split into two groups, one under Paddy Mayne, of about 250 strong, and the other under George Jellicoe of about 150 strong. Paddy's squadron was to be called the Special Raiding Squadron, and Jellicoe's was named the Special Boat Squadron. These high sounding names were meant to indicate to some extent the different roles that the two squadrons were destined to play, for the SRS was to be trained in parachuting and land operations, while the SBS was to concentrate entirely on sea operations. As it happened, when both units went into action some months later, it was the SBS who landed in small parties by parachute, while the SRS were landed in assault craft, but no one was to know that then.

Both squadrons were to be under a central headquarters known as HQ Middle East Raiding Forces. Heaven knows who invented these names, but modesty certainly does not seem to be one of his predominant virtues!

The question naturally arose, how was everyone to be fitted into this new organization, and it soon became clear that many people would have to go, especially among the officers. We were kept in suspense for a few days until one morning Richard called me into the office tent and told me that I was to be given a section of twenty men in the new organization. It can be imagined with what relief I heard these words, and I was even more pleased to learn that I could take with me the twenty or so men who had been left with me during all the time the squadron had been away on operations, and whom I had come to know and like, very well indeed. I was also told that the new squadron was to be divided into three troops, each troop being approximately equivalent to the three squadrons, as they then existed. But as each troop was to consist of only three sections and my present squadron could raise four, I would be the odd section, and would thus take my twenty men into a strange troop, and away from the squadron I knew. I did not like this news at the time, but had no reason to regret the change, for I found that I was in a rattling good troop, which I felt was considerably better than the one I was leaving.

And so it was that the old 'A' Squadron, formed No.1 Troop of the new organization. The old 'C' Squadron formed No.3 Troop, and the second troop was formed by a section from each of the three squadrons, for the old 'B' Squadron had suffered such heavy casualties in the desert that it could not raise much more than one section.

A day or so later, I was introduced to my new troop commander Captain Poat. Harry Poat was a typical Englishman of the old school with all the qualities and none of the defects. To look at, he was of medium height, very broad and tanned. He seemed to radiate health and energy. Two shrewd blue eyes surmounted a fair moustache, and no matter where he was he was always perfectly dressed! To speak to he was not striking. He gave the impression of never quite knowing what to say, and although whatever he said was sound common sense, and often even brilliant, the process of thinking it out seemed rather a strain, as though his brain was rusty and not accustomed to the effort of thinking. When he read it was at half normal speed and he would follow each word as he read it with the end of his forefinger, so that by the time we, looking over his shoulder had finished the page, he would only have read two or three lines. Harry possessed very fine common sense, which resulted in his being one of the finest officers the regiment produced, added to which he was as brave as a lion.

My fellow section commanders in No.2 Troop were Tony Marsh, captain and second-in-command of the troop, young, bouncing, blonde, and extremely good looking. He was always up to some trick or the other, would never seem to care about a thing except about having a good time, and yet in actual fact no one could be more conscientious and he knew everything there was to be known on the subject of training and of handling men. Unlike Harry, Tony preferred the unconventional in matters of dress, and unless he was wearing something slightly different from everyone else, he was not content.

The third section commander was Derrick Harrison, who had joined the regiment about a month after me, whereas Tony and Harry had come to it over two months before. He was one of those thin, nervous types, who can never do anything slowly. When he walked he would give the impression that were it not be for propriety he would far rather be running. He paid the strictest attention to detail and would dwell on small points which we thought not worthy of attention until he had got right to the bottom of them. He was intensely keen and interested in the training, almost to excess. But like Tony he was extremely human and sincere and we made good friends right from the start.

Our troop staff sergeant was Bob Lilley, a veteran of the regiment since its foundation. Bob is difficult to describe for I have never met another man like him and it is impossible to include him in any particular set type. He had had the worst possible education and yet had worked on his own and raised his standard, not only on the narrower issues, but on the wider ones also, and many is the argument he would have on economic, political and social subjects, in which he showed his sceptical views to be as unshakeable as a rock. As a sergeant in charge, he was excellent. There was rather a harmful tendency in the regiment for the NCOs to be scared of using their authority, for fear of being unpopular with the men, so that they would rather side with the men and not with the officers. Over-familiarity was a danger of which we always had to be careful, but if everyone had been like Bob Lilley, we need have had no worry on this score. The men disliked him, principally because he would stand for no nonsense from them. He was a fine example of loyalty to his officers and controlled the sergeants under him with an iron hand. Nor would he be content just to sit back and take shelter behind his rank. One of the men, who had more conceit than good sense, chose to accuse him of this on one occasion. Bob Lilley promptly took him outside and, in spite of the fact that Bob was getting along in years, being on the wrong side of forty, he gave him the good hiding he so richly deserved. Bob Lilley was just such a staff-sergeant that a good troop needed, and on whom his officers could rely completely.

About 20 March, the regiment took up its new formation. Paddy, in his shy, halting, barely audible speech, gave us a short talk, in which he informed us that we were about to start off on a period of very intensive training. What it was for no one knew, but we were told sufficient to show us that it was for some important job. Paddy also told us that we would be leaving Kabrit within the week for a new training area in Palestine which provided a more suitable terrain.

A few days later we were given a talk by our new colonel. His speech did not impress the veterans very much, but it hardly mattered, as we hardly saw anything of him. To all intents and purposes Paddy was the boss and took no orders from anyone. The new colonel was purely administrative, and much as he would have liked to, was given no opportunity of meddling with our training. In fact, we hardly ever saw him.

On the last night of Kabrit we had a wild party in the mess, which left the place looking as though a hurricane had passed through it. Our old naval friends of HMS *Saunders*, the camp next door, gave us a right good send off, and seemed genuinely sorry to see us go. The following night, we scrambled ourselves and our belongings onto the waiting transport, and amid waves, cheers and farewells drove off into the darkness to the station. In typical Egyptian fashion, our train had run out of coal on the way, with the result that it turned up eight hours late, so that we had to spend an uncomfortable night in the open. But nothing lasts and just after dawn the train actually condescended to arrive; wearily we slung our belongings in, and settled ourselves down to the long and tiring journey, which we knew was ahead of us, and which I had already covered once before. So it was goodbye to Egypt, and a new phase had started in our varied existence.

Chapter Three

Invasion Training

We left Egypt about the beginning of April and arrived at Azzib (Palestine) after a typically slow, monotonous journey lasting over forty hours. As is usually the case with such journeys, our arrival was so timed that we reached our destination at about two in the morning, and in consequence, all the rush and bustle of de-training had to take place in pitch darkness. There was no station and we found ourselves up on the grass verge of the track, a very disconsolate group. But gradually some sort of order began to make itself felt, for the unit transport which had been taken up with the advance party arrived shortly afterwards, and was soon busy ferrying the men to the camp. Eventually I found myself a tent where I lost no time in getting stretched out on my bed.

I woke fairly late the next morning, and quickly got up to have a look around. Looking towards the sea about half a mile away, the main coast road could be seen skirting the hill on which the camp was situated, and this was fringed with orange groves of a refreshing greenness after the arid wastes of Egypt. Looking inland one could see the coastal range of hills which runs the length of Palestine, rising up beyond the intervening two-mile wide strip of cultivated land.

The camp itself was centred around the top of the hill, on which were situated the various messes and cookhouses, and the slopes of which were freckled with the tents of the men's lines, neatly arranged by troops.

It did not take us long to find out where we were. The camp lay on the coast road about 20 miles north of Haifa, and 3 miles south of the Syrian border. A mile or two to the north of it lay the small arid village of Azzib, and the same distance to the south was the small Jewish holiday resort of Nahariya.

Around midday, of that first morning Paddy summoned a meeting of all the officers, in order to lay down the procedure of training that was to be adopted. We were still not told what we were training for, or how long a period of training we were likely to have.

In view of the fact that the regiment was recruited from all arms and from all different types of unit, the necessity was recognized of starting off the training completely from scratch on the assumption that no one knew anything. Only in this way was it thought that we could build up a unit of a high and constant standard of individual efficiency. So for the first month, every man in the unit had to go through a second recruit's training, and pass a test in all elementary subjects, before going on with the more advanced training.

Paddy then discussed in detail the new organization and the function of each sub-unit in it. Each of the three sections which made up a troop was further divided into two equal sub-sections, each under the command of a corporal, or lance sergeant. These sub-sections were again divided into three parties of specialists: the light machine gun (LMG) party, the rifle party, and the rifle bomber party, each of which comprised three men, armed with the appropriate weapons. It can be seen therefore, that each sub-section was, on paper, a highly efficient little fighting unit, capable of providing its own support in many of the usual situations that are met with in battle.

All the training was carried out on the shore, just short of the beach. Here, was a thin line of sand dunes and scrubby country which separated the cultivated land from the beach itself. Through this rough land ran the coast railway. It proved to be ideal training country, for it afforded ample cover, and the sand-dunes formed natural butts for firing practice. Also it was only five minutes march from the camp.

We were kept busy for the first month at Azzib, getting ourselves fit and hardened up for whatever was before us, and making sure that everyone had the most complete basic training that was possible, before we turned to the more specialized forms of training. Many demonstrations were arranged, experiments were tried with equipment and loads to be carried, and also with lightweight nourishing rations. Gradually there evolved a complete scale of arms, ammunition, rations and equipment to be carried by each sub-unit, in such a manner that every individual man was given a specific load to carry.

Raiding Forces Headquarters, was officially, the headquarters which controlled the Special Raiding Squadron and the Special Boat Section, both administratively and as far as the training was concerned, but it soon turned out in actual fact that we were pretty well independent of this rather superfluous organization. Paddy had made this a necessary condition for his taking command of the squadron. As far as Raiding Forces HQ were concerned, they might not have existed, for all the effect they had on our training or our life. All decisions rested solely with Paddy and it was he alone who controlled us.

During our first month at Azzib, Bill Fraser joined us again and also Sergeant Johnny Cooper who had been with Stirling's party when he was captured, but who had made good his escape. Bill had been up with the Eighth Army at the time when they sent the New Zealand column to turn the southern flank of the Mareth Line. Johnny Cooper had had a very exciting time. After escaping from Stirling's party he and Mike Sadler, another sergeant, walked to the First Army lines. They were completely unarmed, and according to them, their most frightening experience was when they were attacked and stoned by some marauding Arabs who had the intention of killing them and robbing them. They either ran or bluffed their way out of this uncomfortable situation, and it was with some surprise and considerable distrust that the American outposts of the First Army saw these two dishevelled and ragged creatures approaching their lines. It was only with difficulty that they believed their story, and then they were flown back to the Eighth Army and thoroughly questioned. Mike Sadler was an expert navigator and it eventually transpired that the route he had taken in order to reach the First Army lines, was the route chosen for Freyberg's mobile column, which so successfully turned the flank of the Mareth Line, and joined up with the First Army.

During this initial elementary training I was given ample opportunity to get to know my section and supervise their training. In this I was ably assisted by my three senior NCOs. Sergeant Andy Storey my section sergeant, ex-Scots Guards and very much the solider, was a hard-headed Yorkshire man, slow but infinitely sound – nothing could perturb him.

Corporal Bill McNinch, my leading sub-section commander, was the direct opposite. Worshipped by the men, he was the humourist of the section. He had a violent character of his own but none could get more out of the men than he, when he so wished.

My second sub-section commander Corporal Bill Mitchell was an NCO who had been under me when I first joined the unit in Syria. A shrewd leader and excellent soldier, Bill Mitchell proved to be one of my most loyal NCOs, and he remained with me right until the end of the war. All three of these NCOs had been proved in action and indeed were veterans of several operations, a fact which was of invaluable assistance to me in my own green and untried state.

After about a month of abnormally hard work it was considered that a satisfactory standard in the elementary training had been reached by every man in the unit, and we now turned to better things which were to have a more direct bearing on the task we were ultimately to be called upon to do. Side by side with the elementary training, steps had been taken to ensure that the men became as fit as was possible and capable of feats of endurance more exacting than any which the normal soldier was called upon to do. So the first item on the programme of the advanced training was to test the fitness of the men by making them march under conditions approximating to those of war, from the shores of Lake Tiberias, which was 600ft below sea level, over the coastal hills

Alec Muirhead and Peter Davis, Azzib, May 1943.

Sandy Wilson, Jerusalem, March–June 1943.

and back to our camp, which was situated on the coast. The distance was about 45 miles and we were to do the march in as short a time as possible.

This rather violent and unpleasant form of training was entered upon in a competitive spirit, for each of the three troops did it independently. No.3 Troop was the first to do it and, judging from their results, it seemed a formidable endurance test indeed. Out of a troop of about sixty, only eight men succeeded in completing the course. Apparently they had decided to march in the heat of the day with the result that they were fainting and passing out like flies under the glare of that summer sun. No.1 Troop fared little better, even though the majority of the troop completed the march, for they managed to take the wrong turning, and march for miles off their course before they realized their mistake. As a result they took nearly forty-eight hours to get back to camp.

And then it was our turn, and very apprehensive we were after examining the mediocre results of the other two troops. We had the advantage of course, of learning by their mistakes, and we certainly did not go out with any false ideas about what we were going to have to do. We left camp by truck early one morning and arrived at the starting point close on midday. The weather was typical of the Palestine summer, blazing hot, without a cloud in the sky, and throwing up a brilliant glare from the chalky white road. But while we were in the trucks, we were tolerably comfortable, for the breeze of our motion served to keep us cool.

Not until we got down from the trucks at Tiberias, did we fully realize how hot it was going to be. Our starting point was 600ft below sea level, and of course not a breath of wind was able to reach down into the depression in which we were. It was a stifling, sticky heat that left us feeling limp and clammy and made our heavy packs seem double their weight. And so we set off, hoping to cover as much ground as possible, before people started to tire or feel the effects of the sun.

Little need be said about the first part of that march, as it was so hot that it was as much as we could do to keep the sweat out of our eyes, to shift from time to time the heavy pack which, every few minutes, became stuck to the shoulders, and to fix our eyes firmly on the centre of the back of the man in front, or on the ground a bare yard in front of our feet. Tony's section took the lead and we followed by sections in single file. We kept climbing all the way, along a narrow path which ran through thick corn fields. As soon as we reached one crest another one spread itself before us. Amid muttered curses we plodded on mechanically, sullen in the realization that our ordeal was only just beginning.

Eventually we came to a crest and to our joy found that the ground ahead actually started to drop. We descended steeply until we reached a small stream whose valley we followed as it wound up a hill. What a relief to our eyes was the high vegetation and the clear cool water, but the temptation which this offered soon added to our torments. We would have given anything to have been able to plunge right into it and drink our fill. But it was useless thinking along those lines, for strict orders had been given beforehand that no water was to be drunk until the word was given by the troop commander. The sight of this water so near and yet so unobtainable, only served to aggravate our thirst, but we were at least able to derive some comfort from it, by dipping our handkerchiefs into it, and tying them round our heads. But this, needless to say, only afforded relief for a few minutes.

Meanwhile the sun had been steadily rising and was now directly overhead, from where it beat down mercilessly upon us cruelly and inescapably. By now

The 'Tiberias' march, Palestine, April–May 1943. Training for the invasion of Sicily.

everyone had some sort of protection for his neck in the shape of a handkerchief or the canvas neck shield with which we had been issued. By about one o'clock the column was subjected to various short halts through some man passing out from the heat, and we all had to wait until arrangements had been made for his disposal. These halts became more and more frequent until about nine had succumbed. When three went down together, Harry very wisely decided that it was no good continuing further under these conditions and gave orders that we should rest until evening.

This order did not need to be repeated to be obeyed, and everyone scrambled for a bush or shelf in the rocks which would give some sort of shelter from the sun. We were allowed a short drink and then made ourselves comfortable and, despite the flies which proved to be an absolute menace, dozed and rested until the shadows lengthened and the noises of the day grew quiet.

About six we set off again, having only covered about 8 miles in six hours. But now the marching was far more comfortable and everyone felt far more cheerful after the very necessary rest. We covered a further 6 miles without anything of interest occurring and then we noticed signs of habitation. The country became more enclosed, and we began to pass one or two Arabs, shuffling along in the direction we were going. In the distance could be heard the occasional bark of a dog and the shouts of a child. Soon we came to a village through which we passed. The track widened and then became a stony lane. At this point we were halted and fell out to prepare our evening meal.

For the march, we were experimenting in rations which would give the maximum amount of sustenance and yet were to be extremely light and compact to carry. So Bob Merlot, our intelligence officer, had prepared for us a ration scale of his own devising which fitted into a cartridge bandolier and weighed next to nothing. The mainstay of these rations was oatmeal and we had been shown how to make out of this, porridge, cakes or biscuits, or how, when the occasion demanded, a handful of it could be eaten raw with good effect. In addition we had dried lentils, bacon (which we could eat raw), and of course the invariable and very essential tea, dried milk and sugar.

We had our meal in a romantic setting. The cooking was done in parties of three, for the rations were so designed that three could cook together with the mess tins and water at their disposal. Quickly numerous little fires sprang up, and as the darkness deepened nothing could be seen but these orange glows with eerie shadows bending over them. The stream at whose edge we sat, reflected the scene: numerous Arabs passed with their donkeys, sheep or cattle and a brisk trade started in which eggs and bread were exchanged for cigarettes.

We were not hurried over our meal and, after we had eaten, were allowed to lie in the cool of the night, smoking and resting for a further half hour before we set off again. After about half a mile, the track we were following came out onto a metalled road, down which we turned. To make us more compact, we formed up from single file into threes, and with our boots ringing out clearly on the road, we swung along merrily enough.

We passed through another village, through the gardens of which we took a short cut, thereby probably waking up every living thing in the neighbourhood, judging by the noise which greeted us. From every garden a wretched cur would bark and howl, women and children scream and men shout. A short pause while Tony checked up on our route and then off again, through a small gate, down a narrow track, until we came onto another road at the foot of an enormous hill the top of which we could hardly see in the darkness. If at first we had fondly imagined that this road would lead us along the foot of the mountain, we were soon disillusioned, for on rounding a bend we found ourselves faced with a steep and seemingly interminable climb.

We climbed for over two hours up that cursed mountain, with the road winding ahead of us like a silver ribbon, zig-zagging its way in a series of sharp hairpin bends into the moon-softened darkness. After about an hour of this, the climb began to tell on us; the light-hearted chaff quietened, footsteps began to drag and the pace became noticeably slower. But these dangerous symptoms were not permitted to last for long, for McNinch, one of my corporals and always the man in an emergency, quickly started up a song. The rest of the section were not long in joining in, and from then until dawn the men were singing without a single break. It really was a magnificent performance. The other sections, not to be outdone by McNinch's choir, started up in rivalry and for the rest of that night we were swinging along that road, eating up the miles in a very creditable fashion.

We covered over 20 miles that night, all of which were along the road. After we had reached the top of the first crest, the road was seldom level, and we had to spend the rest of that night's march ascending and descending the slopes of this coastal range of hills. Eventually it grew lighter in the east, and we were halted close by a large Palestine police barracks, where we were able to wash the dust and grime from our bodies, and tend our blistered and lacerated feet. We had completed 32 miles in eighteen hours. Surprisingly few had dropped out, either through heat or foot trouble, and we were now only five or six short of our original strength. But although we had only about 15 more miles to do, it was clear that this last part of the journey was going to be the most difficult, for by this time, most of the men's feet were in a very sorry condition, and there were few of us still able to walk normally. Also we had to put in an attack on an old ruined castle which lay on our route, and which was to be defended by some of the permanent camp staff who were to be transported there, in readiness for us.

We were allowed to breakfast in comfort. We had previously washed and cleaned ourselves up and changed our socks, and felt considerably refreshed. Oatmeal porridge, followed by boiled bacon and lentils, proved to be a very nourishing meal. We moved off again after a halt lasting an hour and a half. This time, it was the turn of my section to take the lead, and it was not long before we sighted the 'enemy' fortress nestling among the shrubs at the head of a deep gorge.

The attack was, of course, a complete farce. We made very little effort to take cover, as by that time, we were past caring about what the defenders or umpires would think of our assault. All that we could think about was our tiredness and our aching and smarting feet, and in consequence felt in no mood to play soldiers with members of the camp staff who had spent a comfortable night in bed and who had been taken to their position by transport.

But we need not have worried ourselves, or even tried to make the slightest show of the attack, for we soon found the place to be deserted and we were able to enter the castle without seeing a soul. We stopped there for about fifteen minutes for a rest and a smoke, and then pushed off on the final stage of the march, after scribbling a few rude notes on the walls of the castle for the benefit of the defenders, in case they should condescend to turn up later. We found out when we got to camp that the defenders had indeed been sent out but they never dreamed that we would reach the castle so soon. So we arrived at the objective several hours before the defenders, which saved both us and them a lot of trouble.

The first seven of the remaining 10 miles was along the side of a small fast flowing stream which in the course of centuries had worn a deep gorge for itself, and which wound below grim and rugged cliffs of black rock, rising up vertically on either side. At first there was a sort of path along the side of the stream but presently this disappeared and it was found that the easiest route to follow was along the river bed itself, which was not more than a few inches deep. What a wonderful relief it was at first to be able to cool our burning feet in the ice-cold water. The men's spirits revived; they started splashing and larking about. Often someone would unwittingly step into a hole in the water, the depth suddenly increasing from about 12ins to around 5ft, much to the confusion of the involuntary swimmer! And then someone would slip and lose his balance and fall headlong into the water, amid the laughter of his fellows.

Thus although we were by now extremely tired, this was the most pleasant part of the whole march. The gorge was so steep that we were able to walk in the shade almost the whole way, while the cool water rushing past our feet was most refreshing. When we came to a spot where the river formed a natural

Peter Davis, Azzib, May 1943.

Derrick Harrison (left) and Alec Muirhead, Palestine, March–June 1943.

deep pool, we were halted and those who wished to were given the chance of a swim, whilst the remainder rested on the bank and looked on, barracking and hurling cheerful insults at the bathers. Many of us welcomed this opportunity to examine our feet and change our socks, for it had not taken us long to discover that walking in the water as we had been doing for the last 4 or 5 miles, was the worst thing we could have done. The water had made the feet go completely soft to such an extent that it felt as though the very arches had dropped. In the limited time at our disposal, we patched up our feet as best we could, wishing fervently that the whole wretched exercise were over.

Those last 3 miles were infinitely the worst. When we eventually emerged from the gorge, it was to see before us the broad, flat plain which separated the range of hills over which we had just passed from the coast; and there, shimmering in the heat haze, a cluster of red buildings could clearly be seen. The end of our march was in sight for those buildings, which looked as though they were only a few hundred yards away, but which were in reality the best part of 3 miles from us, were our camp.

But now it was really hot and the majority of us had 'had it'. Out in that open plain, we were at the mercy of the pitiless sun. Our feet had been so softened by their immersion in the stream, that every stone, every small unevenness in the ground over which we passed, made itself felt in all too painful a fashion. We followed a very narrow path through the standing corn, which was high enough to prevent us from seeing where we were treading. We were thus unable to avoid the numerous pebbles and larger stones, with which our way was strewn, and which served to aggravate all the more the very tender condition of our feet. The gay chatter of earlier in the morning had by this time died away and we plodded on in sullen, tortured silence, scarcely able to keep tears of exhaustion from our eyes, so great was our fatigue.

But all things come to an end, even unpleasant ones, and at 1.30, we found ourselves, to our intense relief, ascending the small slope on the top of which our camp was situated. We were, at this point, very spread out and nearly all were limping badly. But Harry decided to show the rest of the regiment that we thought nothing of the little march we had just completed, and passed the word back calling for a final supreme effort. The order to slope arms was given and we formed up into threes. As soon as we reached the tarmac road of the camp, at which point our steps could be heard plainly ringing out on the hard surface, everyone fell into step and we swung into camp as though we had only been a few miles. In some remarkable fashion everyone's limp had disappeared and the troop must have been an impressive sight. We had reason to feel pleased with ourselves, for we had covered a distance of 48 miles over very rough and difficult country, and in the middle of the Palestine summer, in just over twenty-six hours.

The Tiberias march was a foretaste of the seriousness of our training and the strenuous days that were to follow. But I had the good fortune to be granted a little holiday from all this exertion. Bob Merlot, Sandy Wilson and I, together with a dozen men, were sent to Jerusalem to attend the Grant-Taylor revolver course. Bob Merlot, the unit intelligence officer, was one of the most perfect gentlemen I have ever met. A model of patience and tolerance, he was friendly to everyone, and the way he looked after our small party during that course at Jerusalem was typical of his kindly, easy-going but shrewd nature. The men worshipped him and would make every effort to abide by his wishes and not let him down. Bob was considerably older than us all – in fact, he had been a pilot in the last war – but to look at him you would never notice his age. In fact he was more capable of enduring hardship and pain than most of us and was more than able to do anything the regiment did.

Sandy Wilson was the quiet dreamy type with many hidden depths, but when you came to know him, you realized that there was a lot hidden beneath that gauche, shy and clumsy exterior. Poor old Sandy's clumsiness was the watchword of the officers' mess. He was extremely tall and possessed the largest pair of feet that I have ever seen. It may have been because of their very size, but at any rate, Sandy seemed to have no control over his feet whatever, and if he could put them into anything, he would. The result of all this was that whenever he entered the mess, people would make a rush for their glasses to bring them to a place of safety, before Sandy got near, and often the quiet of the evening was interrupted rudely by angry shouts of, '*Oh Sandy!*' which was just an indication that Sandy had done it again. This was a most unfortunate characteristic for he had a heart of gold and was never ruffled even by the frequent and general expressions of disgust at his clumsiness. He would just give his quiet smile, a polite apology, and then promptly walk on and knock over someone else's glass, or step on someone else's toe.

We often found our way into the cabaret bar known as the 'Queen's', which was situated in the main street. Bob, who was Belgian by birth, was attracted to this place because it had a girl crooner who was also Belgian, and the first night he came in, she took one look at him, and then came straight up and asked if he were Belgian! Thereafter, we found ourselves there practically every night.

The men from our regiment, who were also attending the course, were often at this place too drinking up their credits just as fast as they could in the limited time at their disposal.

One evening, only extreme good fortune prevented rather an ugly and unfortunate incident from taking place. Sturmey, one of the men, had had far too much to drink and was in a decidedly aggressive mood. In looking around for a suitable opponent, he picked on a young major who was looking very smart indeed, in a beautifully tailored cavalry uniform. He had a string of medals up, including the MC. But the bone of contention was apparently, a parachute wings on the major's arm, which admittedly were of a design that none of us had seen before. Sturmey marched straight up to this officer's table and accused him of being an imposter. Of course, then, the fat was in the fire with a vengeance. The major had the MPs called up and handed the very aggressive Sturmey into their tender charge. Still persisting in his accusation, Sturmey was marched off to spend the night in the guardroom, while Bob, Sandy and I vainly flapped around trying to soothe the irate major.

The next morning we were all amazed to see Sturmey turn up for parade, for we had thought he would certainly be up for court-martial. And so he would have been without the slightest doubt, were it not for the stroke of luck that despite the fact that his accusations were made solely through a surfeit of alcohol, the military police chose to look into them and have a private check on the major's identity. By some extraordinary coincidence, which was fortunate for Sturmey, they discovered that he was in fact an imposter, being some lieutenant in a base job who wanted to look big. He had no right to wear either parachute wings or the MC and other ribbons. We left shortly after that narrow escape without any more of the men getting into trouble although this was due more to the leniency of the Military and Palestine Police whom we had come to know pretty well while attending the course at their barracks, than to any particular restraint on the part of the men themselves.

We found the camp to be humming with activity on our arrival. The main cause for excitement lay in the fact that during our absence the regiment had been visited, inspected and addressed by General Dempsey of whom we knew nothing beyond the fact that he was in command of some corps or other somewhere. General Dempsey had watched our training with the greatest of interest, then called the regiment together and for the first time since we started this training had given us some sort of indication of what we were training for. Apparently our regiment was to be under his personal command in some operation to take place at an undivulged, but not far distant date. Our role was to land in the first wave of the assault by landing craft, and to storm and capture a vital and probably very strongly defended coastal gun battery. The general made no bones about the importance of our task and even told us that the whole

Cliff climbing training, Palestine, April–May 1943.

success or failure of the operation under his command might depend entirely on our own individual success.

Training was speeded up from then on, and the form it now took gave us several indications of what the job we were going to do would be like. For instance every night from then on, almost without exception, was spent in practising cliff climbing in total darkness, and perfecting the drill of this to such a degree that the whole operation could be carried out from start to finish, without a word being spoken.

Each troop would then be given a certain area in which to practise while Paddy would be roaming about up on top ready to come down in fury on any section which was doing it wrong. Many amusing incidents used to occur during these exercises, one of which I remember all too clearly. As part of our equipment each section was provided with two lengths of rope fitted with a toggle attachment so that they could be joined together or looped around a rock. The officer and his batman were the first to climb the cliff, each carrying his rope, and when they had reached the top they would lower their ropes and the rest of the section would climb up one by one, and then take up a defensive position immediately they arrived at the top. It can be understood therefore, that for the first part of the operation, until sufficient men had been brought to the top to provide satisfactory protection, the whole strain of holding the ropes firm rested with the officer and his batman. Percival my batman/runner was not much heavier than me, but in addition he was a stock joke with the section because he would get into a violent flap at any situation.

One night we climbed a cliff as usual and took up our positions to take the strain of the next to climb the rope. Unfortunately in the particular spot where we were, no suitable projections in the surface of the rock were to be found, round which we could hook our ropes, and so we had to take the whole weight of the climber without assistance. We just managed for the first one or two and then we naturally began to feel rather tired.

All of a sudden, Percival found himself slipping. An almighty shriek of '*SIR! Save me! Save me! Help! Help!*' rent the air, with scarcely any attempt at a whisper, so great was Percival's panic. I looked round to see him slowly slipping down the cliffside and of course could not do anything to help him, as I had my own rope to deal with, up which someone was in the process of clambering. But I and most of the others nearby could not fail to see the humour of the situation wherein such a melodramatic cry should be raised in a serious exercise in which no word was meant to be spoken. I found myself so doubled up with laughter that I could scarcely hold my own rope and almost suffered the same fate as Percival. McNinch, who had just come up, quickly rushed to give Percival a hand and to restore the situation, but it was a long time before our amusement died out, and before we were able to regard the exercise with any degree of seriousness.

Harry Poat (left) and Phil Gunn, Palestine, April–May 1943.

Great amusement, principally among the officers, was caused by the horses and mules which we had with us for training. In theory it was decided that we might, on the coming operation, find ourselves without transport and therefore, if we could capture any enemy horses or mules, all the better. So we obtained from the RASC two horses and four mules, ostensibly to teach the men which end of the animal was which, and to learn how to manage them to some small degree. For obvious reasons the mules did not arouse nearly so much interest as the horses. But John Tonkin showed a marked attraction to these animals based, I believe on some experience of them in Syria, and he and Ted Lepine and Mick Gurmin appointed themselves their keepers. They even formed such an attachment for them that they moved out of their tent and went to live in part of the stables which had been boarded off into a kind of hut. Richard Lea was the horse-riding enthusiast and I think it was at his instigation, that Franco (very ex-cavalry and all that) was prevailed upon to give certain of the officers riding lessons each morning before breakfast. (Not that it takes much prevailing upon to give an ex-cavalry officer something to do with horses again!). So any interested spectator could see certain officers dodging PT by riding sedately round in a circle obeying Franco's very cavalry words of command to t-r-r-o-o-o-t, or c-a-n-t-e-r.

Richard Lea, who by that time was training officer, could not keep away from these horses and used to take them out on every possible occasion on the very plausible excuse that he wished to organize some training exercise, until the day when No.2 Troop did their Tiberias march. He thought this would be a good chance to take out a horse, to observe how the troops were bearing up under their ordeal, and so set out to find us. But we were so much ahead of schedule that he completely failed to contact us, and moreover, to his dismay, he found that the going was so rough that he had to dismount. And so after spending the best part of the day trudging about the mountains, dragging an unwilling horse behind him, he had to return to camp almost as tired as we were and pretty fed up with horses in general. From that day on, Richard's interest in horses showed a marked decline!

By the middle of May there was a definite 'operational' feeling in the air, a feeling of suspense and tension. One day all three troops were independently given their first briefing. A sketch map of our actual objective was drawn for us and it was intended that we should learn every detail of this by heart. In addition, we had to learn the exact route we and the other troops would take. The initial plan was roughly as follows. No.1 and No.2 troops were to land on the south coast of a promontory about 200 to 300 yards west of our objective, a gun battery of three, or possibly four, heavy guns. No.1 Troop was to make straight for the camp buildings, and systematically clear them out while No.2 Troop was to make a detour around the western side of the target and come onto the guns from the north, from where they would put in their assault. Meanwhile No.3 Troop had been landed about half a mile further still to the west and was to cut the only road leading to the battery and occupy two farms which held strategic positions in that region.

These were the first orders we received about the coming operation. From then on, we practised our respective roles, day in and day out. Whenever we went out on a night exercise, climbing cliffs, or some similar occupation, to attack a prescribed imaginary target, No.1 Troop would always go straight in while we would make the detour and assault under cover from No.1 Troop's fire-power. This procedure was so ingrained into us that it became second nature, and we learned only to make an assault when covered by a very healthy amount of fire-power from another sub-unit. This principle was even applied right down to section, sub-section and party training and a kind of battle drill was evolved, which we were to practise day after day, so that in the end every man would be trained automatically to carry out a certain reaction at any given situation.

Along with this battle drill, great attention was paid to our marksmanship, and towards the end we spent nearly the whole time firing with live ammunition, and in combining this with the battle drill we had just learned. Much time was spent on range practices at first, but this rather artificial form of training was soon substituted by one which proved to be far more useful. Mere accuracy, it was considered, was not good enough by itself but had to be combined with speed to be really effective, and so the system was adopted of competitive shooting by parties at tin plates. A party would vie with another in knocking down its six plates before the other. This not only encouraged the desired combination of speed with accuracy, but also made each man give some thought to the most effective distribution of his fire. It was a most enjoyable and profitable form of training, causing any amount of cheerful rivalry.

The next stage in our practical training was combining our battle drill with using live ammunition. One night, right towards the end, the whole squadron went out practising this movement with live ammunition and using tracer to direct their fire. The effect was striking. Fire seemed to be pouring onto the target from all directions until the whole sand hill seemed to be aflame. The tracer bullets would ricochet off the hilltop and go shooting straight up into the air like miniature rockets. Were it not for the seriousness underlying the whole procedure, one might compare the effect to Blackpool Illuminations. At the height of this exhibition one of our fighter aircraft chose to fly around just above, curious at what was going on, until all of a sudden the ricochets rising straight into the air must have given it a fright for it replied with a burst of cannon fire into the sea and made off smartly. Later that evening the squadron was officially reprimanded for firing at friendly aircraft!

To Alec Muirhead was given the task of training an efficient 3-inch mortar section. Alec had never seen a mortar before, but this ignorance on his part was put to good effect, for he trained his section entirely along his own lines and in complete defiance of the training manual. As a result of his conscientious experimenting, he was able to mount the mortar and get off his first round with considerable accuracy within eighteen seconds. Of course his lack of acquaintance with the subject did not always stand him in good stead especially on the occasion when, through some miscalculating, he inadvertently directed his crew to fire five bombs rapid, straight down onto his OP position which was about 500 yards in front of the actual mortar. As soon as he heard the first bomb in the air he knew he had done something wrong and immediately realized what it was. The awful suspense of knowing that there were four bombs still to come, any one of which might be a direct hit on him, can well be imagined. He was very lucky indeed to get away with only a cut on the back of the head from a piece of shrapnel.

The manner in which Alec's mortar crew had been recruited was rather amusing. As soon as it had been decided to use 3-inch mortars, a message had been sent off to the Infantry Base Depot at Geneifa, asking for forty trained mortar men, as we thought there would not be time enough to train a crew from scratch. The men arrived all right, but it did not take long for Alec to find out that very few of them had ever seen a mortar in their lives before. It seems that in typical fashion the message had got muddled at some point during the course of its journey, so that the IBD thought that the men were wanted to go on a mortar course. So these poor lads all arrived thinking they were going on a nice cushy mortar course, and were instead launched straight away into a programme of intensive operational training. It says something for them that nearly every one of them turned out well, and were only too keen to be embodied in the regiment once they had come to know us and the work we were to do.

With long night schemes on a full-scale model of the target area, our training at Azzib ended. What had been a motley and relatively untrained force only two months previously had now reached such a peak of trained efficiency that there were, I am sure, very few fighting units in the British or German army to beat them. They had mastered a thorough knowledge of their own and of the enemy's weapons. Their average marksmanship was extremely high, and combined with this accuracy, a very creditable speed. They had learnt to work as a smoothly running machine from the whole squadron, down to the smallest sub-unit, and each man knew how to react to any given eventuality. In addition, they had grown accustomed to working under fire.

Everything down to the slightest detail of the load each man was to carry had been worked out and tested and the regiment was drilled into a state of perfection. Above all, they were as physically fit as any human beings could possibly be. Their offensive spirit, or 'morale' as it is commonly called, was excellent. Not out of patriotic fervour, but solely out of the lust for excitement and the supreme confidence they had in their own capabilities, did these men long for the time when they could show that all the trouble they had been taking during this gruelling training had been worthwhile, and the knowledge that they were completely equipped and trained for the fight made them all the more keen to meet it. As a fighting body they were perfect.

We left Azzib for an unknown destination at dawn on the morning of 6 June 1943. On the principal of 'let us eat, drink and be merry for tomorrow we may die' there was a mad party that night in which both officers and men attempted to consume every drop of liquor to be found both in the camp itself and in its immediate surroundings. Many were the Jeeps 'misappropriated' and taken out for a final binge in Haifa, many alas, were the Jeeps found deep in roadside ditches at the break of dawn, and many were the recumbent bodies that were littering the mess shortly before we were due to parade about 3.30am. It still amazes me how, when the train steamed out of the station no one had been left behind.

It was still dark when the transport took us all to the station. Dawn was just lighting the horizon when we climbed into our allotted and very crowded cattle trucks which were to take us slowly and painfully along the first stage of our journey to Haifa. None of us had the slightest idea where we were going. Many of us, in the condition in which we were at the time, were too merry to care. All we knew was that sometime soon, within a matter of weeks, if not days, we would be given the chance to match our strength against that of the enemy. And of the ultimate result, none of us had the slightest doubts.

Chapter Four

Final Preparations

Right until we found ourselves at Suez at dawn the following day, none of us had the slightest idea of where we were bound, and even then we had to hang around on the platform for a considerable period, still guessing wildly about our immediate future.

Our certainty that we were going to be employed operationally very soon was even increased when we learned that we were all to be transferred onto a ship. It seemed certain that we would be sailing for our unknown objective within the next few days.

Tenders ferried us out to the ship, a smart, fast looking little steamer of about 3,000 tons. She was a two-funneller named the *Ulster Monarch*. As her name suggests, in peacetime she had been a steamer transporting passengers across the Irish Sea between England and Northern Ireland. But the war had given her a new job for she had been taken over by the navy to be used as a Landing Ship for Infantry and had been modified to take six assault landing craft. These could be lowered fully loaded straight into the water, when the time came for them to leave the 'mother ship'. Nothing about her suggested a dirty little crossing steamer. The white ensign flew proudly at her masthead and in true navy style she was clean and orderly, giving out an air of quiet efficiency.

Little did we know then, that the *Ulster Monarch* was to be our home for the next five weeks and a very happy home it was. She was manned by a really grand crowd of men, both officers and ratings, and it says something for inter-service co-operation when it is considered that our men and the navy boys immediately began to feel a sincere respect and admiration for each other, and 'mucked in' to the fullest possible degree. The troops did not get in the way of the crew nor the crew in the way of us. Friendships were formed both individually and collectively and the outstanding spirit that made its appearance on the *Ulster Monarch* was that of co-operation and concord.

We were housed very comfortably without the overcrowding to which we had become accustomed on troopships previously. Each officer had a little cabin to himself, while the men were established on spacious mess-decks. A week or so after we came aboard conditions were further improved, as regards space by the transfer of No.3 Troop to another ship, *The Dunera* from which they would operate.

The navigator and some of the officers of the *Ulster Monarch*, Egypt, June 1943.

General Montgomery making his 'invasion' speech aboard *Ulster Monarch*, Egypt, June 1943.

For the first few days we anchored at Suez, and remained on board the whole time. We were given ample opportunity to study aerial photographs and last minute details concerning our objective. In the mornings we carried on with our PT but beyond cleaning and inspection of arms, the time was our own to discuss among ourselves and with the section any new details about the operation.

The afternoons were devoted to the special training for which it had been considered necessary to transfer us to the ship so long before the actual D- Day. As I have already mentioned, the *Ulster Monarch* carried slung on her davits, six LCAs (Landing Craft Assault), which were to take us onto the beaches. They would be partly lowered until they came to a height just opposite the doors from where we would climb into them. When we were all in position, they would be let down gently (at least that was the idea) into the water and cast loose by the naval crew aboard them. The LCAs were manned by sailors from the training ship HMS *Saunders* which had been situated on the 'Point', just next to our old camp at Kabrit, and so a mutual bond of recognition was established between us from the first. These *Saunders* men were a keen and capable crowd, well disciplined and excellently officered. They made it a point of personal pride that they were going to land us at the right place and take us safely to shore however strong the opposition might prove to be. And thus, the most important result of this combined training was to inspire in us a complete confidence and trust in the men of the other service in whose hands we would be immediately prior to the operation.

Entering the boats could be a tricky business, especially on a dirty night when the operation had to be carried out in complete darkness and when there might be considerable movement of the ship. For in rough seas, if the boat was not lowered completely level, it was liable to be swamped, and if the crew were not extremely quick in casting loose as soon as it was in the water, there was a great danger of the small craft being dashed against the sides of the mother ship. The navy personnel who had to do this tricky job had been carefully trained, and it was thus up to us in our own interests to acquaint ourselves with the drill required, to such an extent that there was no chance of anything going wrong in the embarkation operation as a result of our own inexperience or inefficiency.

From the above account it might be assumed by those unacquainted with the characteristics of the LCA that it was a small and flimsy craft. This is however not exactly true, although in a rough sea and badly handled it was not exactly foolproof. But, being 3 tons in weight and driven by powerful twin engines, it was certainly no cockleshell. In addition to its crew of two or three, it was built to carry from 20–30 fully loaded troops, and was protected from small arms fire by armour all round. At slow speeds the engines were completely inaudible and hardly any betraying whitewash in the wake of the craft was visible. Thus in every respect it was an ideal craft for the landing of troops on hostile shores under conditions of the greatest surprise and secrecy, and especially since its draught was not more than 2ft. Once we knew where to assemble, which boat to occupy, the order in which we disembarked, and our respective positions in the boat, we had nothing further to learn from the point of view of embarkation.

The final thing still left for us to learn was disembarkation and beach drill, and we certainly had a bellyfull of this in the weeks that followed. Every afternoon we were taken out in the LCAs, in order to practise the landing drill time after time until perfection had been reached. Our positions in the boat had been worked out, not only so that we could take them up without confusion during the process of embarking, but also, and even more importantly, so that as soon as we hit the shore the section could leave the craft as a fully prepared combat unit. It was therefore arranged that each of the two sub-sections would be seated respectively on either side of the craft, with section headquarters in the centre. As soon as the doors were opened, headquarters, led by the officer, would disembark and without waiting, move straight up the beach until a suitable vantage point was found, where the whole section could be assembled in a good defensive position.

To reach the required stage of efficiency it is natural that we had to practise the landing again and again, and this we did several times each afternoon for the first few days after we came aboard the *Ulster Monarch*, until Paddy was finally satisfied that we had reached the desired standard.

When we had spent a few days on the *Ulster Monarch* in the manner described, we learned that we were going to carry out a full-scale rehearsal of the operation for which we were being trained at Aqaba, an isolated and rugged spot at the head of the Gulf of Aqaba, at the point where Sinai, Palestine and Transjordan met. In every respect the whole rehearsal was treated like the real thing. Before we sailed from Suez, maps and aerial photographs of the Aqaba area were issued and full operational plans made so that we all knew exactly what to do. These maps and photographs were studied thoroughly with reference to the objective and the route we would take to reach it, until the layout of the ground was absolutely clear to us. We set sail one morning under conditions of active service.

Aqaba was an unprepossessing looking spot. The natural harbour formed by the head of the gulf was a vivid blue offering a striking contrast to the glaring sandy mountains which rose up sheer on either side. At the water's edge were a few palm trees beneath which were scattered one or two native huts, and that was all. Obviously the area was extremely poor. The local inhabitants were dirty, servile and shabby, and it could be clearly seen that they led a hand-to-mouth sort of existence.

The rehearsal took place that evening and about 11pm we were due to embark in the landing craft. The earlier part of the evening was spent in going over details of the attack – our objective was an imaginary gun battery situated on the top of a mountain whose sides were almost sheer. It was to be defended by Indian troops and every advantage of the terrain lay with them. In addition we would obtain no help from the value of surprise as our attack would obviously be expected and awaited.

At last we were in the craft, chugging slowly towards the shore which appeared as a blacker outline against the blackness of the night. The boats touched down in line, about 50 yards apart, and without a word we formed up and moved off. It was all so easy; we had been drilled in this procedure so thoroughly that every step of it was so much child's play, coming to us as second sense. Just as we were moving off, I noticed a small group of men standing within 20 yards of where we landed, who were watching us intently. Little did we know it at the time, but this group included Jumbo Wilson and his staff. From all accounts, he was

Landing craft training at Suez and Aqaba from the *Ulster Monarch*, June 1943.

impressed with our landing and especially with the fact that he never heard a word spoken the whole time we were in earshot.

The rest of the attack was chiefly a combination of blood and tears! Not only did we have to climb that very steep slope, but also we had to do it silently, which was no easy task. Stones would persist in being dislodged and go clattering down the mountainside and it was impossible to prevent oneself from slipping at many points. But the objective remained out of sight all the while as the slope was convex, which proved to our advantage as it meant that the 'enemy' could not see us either. Although they obviously heard us, they were kept in suspense as to when we would actually appear. We had succeeded in reaching a point which, as far as we could gather, was no more than 75 yards from the hilltop, and were just on the point of dispersing ourselves for the assault, when an irate, high-pitched voice emerging from the shadows of a neighbouring wadi came bellowing over towards us, proclaiming that Paddy was on the war path, an eventuality which indeed we had feared when we saw him drinking so much on the ship. Apparently we were moving too slowly for him, but lashed by his fury, we soon remedied this, and reached the top in double quick time. With the knowledge that this was only an exercise, we had a far more healthy respect for the 'enemy' behind us than for that in front. So we cast away all our laborious attempts at gaining surprise and went straight in, rather like bulls in china shops. The Indian defenders must have been quite surprised by these tactics, for they had become so used to listening to our slow and painful approach for the last hour, that we were on top of them almost before they realized it. The assault was the usual mixture of blanks, Very lights, bangs and confusion, until we had passed right through the lot to our consolidating position, when we promptly collapsed and obtained as much rest as we could. We contacted Bill's troop on the top, and shortly afterwards began the even more difficult march down the slope. Eventually we reached the shore just on dawn and a signal was sent to the landing craft to fetch us back to the ship.

Back at Suez, we hung around, doing nothing in particular for over three weeks. General Montgomery came aboard to inspect us one morning, and only half way through his inspection did he connect us with the unit who had operated behind the enemy lines in the desert. Of course this knowledge gave him just the opportunity he wanted to impress us in the usual speech which he was accustomed to make to each unit he inspected. He told us how pleased he was to meet us all again, and promised us that we would soon be given the chance of 'chasing the Hun still further', and then he went on to utter a remark which was so unexpected that I do not believe it rang true to anyone who was listening. He said that were it not for the work of our unit behind the lines in the desert, his army would never have been able even to reach Tripoli. I can't help thinking that it is lucky this speech did not get into the press, as it would have offended to a marked degree the majority of those units who played a spectacular and important part in the victorious advance of the Eighth Army from Alamein, in addition to undermining the enormous publicity that had been given to the Eighth Army. It was in fact, just one of those remarks which Monty was very fond of giving out to whatever unit he inspected, with a view to increasing the factor of pride in one's unit which is so important to morale.

It had been decided beforehand that we would not give Monty the cheer to which he was accustomed, and which he was undoubtedly expecting, until he had entered the launch which was to take him to the next ship. This delayed applause rather took the general aback and he took his leave in some confusion. He did not know why we did not cheer and whether he should leave until we did. So he slowly backed up the companion way, muttering almost under his breath, '*Wonderful discipline, wonderful discipline! Very smart! I like their hats*'. However, as the launch took him away he was made happy again by hearing our cheers coming drifting over the water towards him.

On the afternoon the Derby was run, for which of course we had the usual sweepstake, we were sent out on a marching cum intercommunication exercise. Section headquarters went out by troops, about 100 yards apart, in order to practise communications over the little No.38 transmitting and receiving sets the section runner carried. This was a very effective little instrument and much reduced the problems of control. But in order to obtain the maximum effect from it, it was essential that every operator should learn the general procedure for its use and this was the purpose of the present exercise.

Percival, my runner, was a real character. He certainly was not an ideal wireless operator for he would become so agitated when he had to speak into the set that any procedure that he had learned was scattered to the winds, and he came out with something completely unintelligible. Already, back in the training at Azzib, he had caused us many a laugh. Often when we were doing a mock attack in pitch blackness, walking with the utmost care to avoid dislodging a stone, and cursing under our breath if a rifle should knock against somebody's equipment, or if someone's pack was rattling, the silence would suddenly be sharply interrupted by a shriek from Percival, who, with the earphones over his head, was shouting at the top of his voice, although he imagined he was scarcely whispering. '*SIR!*' he would shriek, '*a message for you.*' I would try to calm him and at the same time persuade him to speak just a little more softly, but to no avail. The whole contents of the message would be carried away triumphantly by the wind, and in our tense imaginations, we could hear it echoing round the neighbouring hills and valleys for many minutes to come.

In addition, Percival could never get his procedure right. When asked to report signals, instead of giving the correct answer *'and receiving you loud and clear'*, he would always forget at the crucial moment just what it was he had to say, so that the final result was usually something like, *'can hear you normal and loud'*, or *'Everything loud and satisfactory'*! It did not take the section long to see the funny side to this and they would wait with rapt attention to hear exactly what Percival would say the next time.

And then on one occasion while we were taking part in a long night scheme, Percival was pursued by a shrieking soprano – not quite literally of course – but this wretched female kept on cropping up just when he was trying to make out a signal, and she would drown out everything. At first Percival was really worried by this phenomenon, and his job was not made any easier for him by the barely supressed laughter of the rest of the section who could clearly hear the shrill, shrieking notes emerging from his headphones. Eventually Percival saw the funny side of it also and started to laugh. Not only did he laugh, but because of the deafening effect of his head phones, he laughed extremely loudly, and the rest of the exercise was spent in trying to restrain our very giggly and vociferous wireless operator. We all saw that he had been drinking that night which accusation he vigorously denied. We still do not know what to believe!

To get back to the communications scheme at Suez, by this time Percival had more or less mastered the intricacies of the No.38 set, and when he remembered himself, was tolerably efficient at operating it, he even managed to pass onto the section the results of the Derby which had been run that afternoon, and which had been relayed out to us from the ship; and what is more, the results he gave coincided with the official results when we got back to the ship. Although I was never too inclined to trust the messages I received over the wireless via the stuttering lips of Percival, I need not have worried as he worked the set extremely well during the operation which ensued.

It was decided to make us do yet another endurance march whilst we were waiting at Suez. We started marching as soon as it began to get dark, and except for the usual ten minutes halt every hour, we kept on marching until dawn. Luckily we were not heavily loaded, but it can well be imagined how boring and monotonous the conditions of the march soon became. Everything we saw was sufficiently uninspiring to prevent us giving our tired bodies the additional mental boost which makes so much difference. Once we were feeling tired, the fact that we disliked what we were doing so much made it decidedly more difficult to carry on. This was undoubtedly Paddy's intention. He wanted to test not only our physical, but also our mental, endurance.

Paddy was terrific that night. When we were splitting ourselves trying to keep up with the immensely fast pace that was set from the front, we would see Paddy striding along on his own, catching us up and overtaking us without the slightest apparent effort. His enormous stride just ate up the ground, and despite the fact that he never ran he could leave the best of us standing. In this way he was able to form from the various reactions of sub-units to this most unattractive, energetic and apparently unnecessary form of training, an accurate idea of which of them were most likely to be operationally efficient.

Paddy tried an experiment on us, which I imagine he had been wanting to try out for some time. The MO had obtained a stock of Benzadrine tablets, which Paddy now dished out to various chosen sections to watch their reactions, and to discover if this artificial stimulant would improve their physical endurance capabilities. These tablets were a mild drug, especially used by aircrews to keep themselves awake and alert when they were on a long and fatiguing night raid. Paddy hoped that by stimulating our minds in this way, our bodies would be correspondingly stimulated with the result that we would not feel fatigue, and that we would be refreshed for further efforts. I can give no accurate description of the effects of this treatment, as No.2 Troop, probably on account of their Tiberias march achievement, were not doctored and were kept unpleasantly normal as a sort of yardstick by which the added vitality of the other two troops could be measured. So all I know about it is that on the way back we had to keep up a splitting pace, but whether this was a result of the predominance of Benzadrine addicts in the regiment, or because of Paddy's slave driving tactics, I shall never know. The latter was certainly very evident – Paddy seemed to be everywhere, and like the Red Queen in *Alice in Wonderland*, kept on shouting '*Faster! Faster!*' when we felt that we were already putting up as fast a pace as we possibly could.

Our troop was leading on the way back and under Paddy's rather violent 'persuasion' we found ourselves marching the last 2 miles in almost forced march time. The cursing, which had at first been under our breath, began to get audible. The leading file of my section, sponsored by McNinch, formed a trade union among themselves and decided that they would not keep up this outrageous pace. So they decided upon a go-slow policy, and from this the rest of the section were not slow to benefit. So on looking round, I found Sergeant Storey and I about 10 yards ahead of the section, with the interval rapidly increasing in the meantime. Paddy could be seen approaching like a whirlwind, from the rear, and the matter had to be quickly remedied. Eventually the men realized that there was some reason behind this apparently senseless driving because for the rest of that march Paddy fastened himself pretty firmly onto our rear, and even the most rebellious of my section realized that it was just not worthwhile arguing with him, as he exhorted us to go even faster still. So, despite aching limbs and blistering feet, we sufficiently proved the superiority of mind over matter by licking up those last few miles in record time, and although we had not been drugged we succeeded in holding our own with the other troops.

Paddy did say afterwards that the effect of the Benzadrine was quite striking: it was first administered to No.3 Troop who were the first to show signs of tiring, and who were beginning to shamble along with dragging steps and heads held low. The transformation was remarkable. The next time Paddy saw them they were swinging along together in grand style, singing and cracking jokes.

While waiting at Suez we did one more training exercise in addition to our normal activities. This was in fact, another rehearsal for our coming operation. There was a big AA Battery on the coast about 2 miles from where the *Monarch* was anchored, and it was arranged that on a certain night we should attack them, and see just how efficient their defence plan was. The attack took the usual form. No.3 Troop cut the road while we made a detour right along the beach under cover of the supporting fire and sundry diversions provided by No.1 Troop. The attack was an outstanding success in every way. I do not think it any exaggeration to say that those gunners were completely at a loss. Bill Frazer's troop made an immense commotion, firing Very lights, 2-inch mortar flares and blanks, while our troop was in the meantime slinking along the coast, in dead ground. Then at the given word Bill stopped his fire and we swept through the gun positions in extended line, while the defenders stood completely taken by surprise. They had been so occupied with the diversion provided by Bill that they never dreamed of the possibilities of a flank attack. They said afterwards that we appeared as if from nowhere and they had no idea where we came from. And so, in every respect, this exercise was a great success from our part and gave us much encouragement.

So much for the training we carried out during those five long and monotonous weeks while we lay anchored at Suez, awaiting the D-Day for the invasion of our unknown objective. Owing to the small size of the ship we were cooped up tight on one another and thus not much happened which was not generally known almost immediately afterwards. For instance, for the first time I came to learn by personal experience, of Paddy's extremely disturbing habit, of 'persuading' all of his officers, whether willing, or unwilling, to join him in his drinking bouts.

Paddy was a very typical Irishman in many of his characteristics, which fact explains his unlimited capacity for consuming liquor and the unlimited length of time for which he would go on drinking. As a result, if he started drinking slowly at about 8pm, just for the sake of having a quiet drink on his own, by about midnight, he would have collected a few stalwarts around him, and the drink would begin to flow more freely, but by 3am, he would be really aroused and decide that he would like to make a party of it. So one of his henchmen would be dispatched to wake up all the officers and summon them, under pain of the CO's extreme displeasure, to report forthwith to his cabin. And then, when everyone was assembled, clad in pyjamas, and stifling their yawns, the real party would start. The drink would begin to flow, stacks of food would appear from nowhere, and we knew that we were all set for the night! Woe betide any of us who were so foolish as to revolt. If we locked our cabin door, it would be broken down, and the first thing we would know about it would be to be borne triumphantly by a gang of toughs into Paddy's cabin, certainly clad too insufficiently to cover up our offended dignity.

It was on just one such of these occasions that we received our first operational orders from Paddy. The CO's command for us to assemble in his cabin was transmitted to our unwilling ears about 3am or some similar impossible hour. With eyes half closed and dragging step we found our way into Paddy's cabin and were just sufficiently awake to notice the terrific disorder there and to accept with resignation our proffered drink. We would then sit down by the table, more or less resigned to take what was coming to us, and since we would undoubtedly be there until breakfast time, to make the best of things. Suddenly Paddy took it into his head to unpack the relief model of the objective which lay in a corner, heavily crated and sealed. So we all got to work and soon drew the model from its numerous protective coverings. It was a really beautiful job. Every rock, every building, and every military position was marked on it in relief, and completely to scale. So simple did it make our task of getting to know the area that Paddy straight away decided to run through the plan of the operation. In normal times, Paddy is a very shy speaker, and his delivery is hardly audible being hesitating and disjointed. But on this occasion he gave the best operational orders he had ever given. Clearly, with a firm and audible voice, he proceeded to run through the whole plan of the operation in perfect textbook style, with no single unimportant detail omitted and with everything brought in, in its logical sequence. Although it had certainly been far from his original intention Paddy succeeded in making this drinking party a very instructive and beneficial one for all of us.

And yet it is only fair to mention that while training was in progress and an operation imminent, Paddy would completely divorce himself from all alcoholic desire and temptations. His chief concern was the efficiency of the little unit under his command, and he was far too wise to risk any evil effect which might arise from him being the worse for alcohol at a critical time, when clear and split-second decisions were expected from him.

The request programmes which were broadcast over the loudspeaker systems were also a source of amusement to us during these monotonous days, and gave the wits of the regiment a welcome chance of practising their talents. Song titles were connected with names and characters in such a way that a certain person would seem to have requested a song title that reflected his own personal wishes. For instance, some person unfortunate enough not to have had the chance of going through his parachute course before we left Palestine, and who was in consequence not entitled to wear his parachute wings, was announced over the loud speaker as requesting the song, 'If I only had Wings'. Later, when the ship was receiving undue attention from enemy aircraft, it was planned to broadcast a request in the name of the skipper for 'Whose Rocking my Steamboat?', but for obvious reasons the jokers checked themselves from going this far.

As each day passed the dark cloud of impending action seemed to come nearer, and the strain of waiting for something unpleasant was beginning to be hard to bear. We knew that it was coming soon, but no one knew exactly when, and planning for the immediate future was always affected by this consideration. But all things come to an end and one day we found ourselves standing on the deck watching the big ships slowly reshuffling their positions. One by one they disappeared up the entrance to the Suez Canal and we knew that at last this was it. Our turn came with the rest of them, and early that morning we found ourselves slowly steaming towards the tall white pillar that marked the entrance to the canal.

We knew that this was not just another training scheme. In a matter of days now, we would be taking part, and an important part, in an invasion that might well prove to be one of the decisive turning points of the war. Our feelings were mixed, as we steamed up the canal, but it is no exaggeration to say that our predominant one was that of relief.

Chapter Five

'SRS Embark' – Murro Di Porco

It was with a feeling of intense and scarcely supressed excitement that we watched the banks of the Suez Canal slowly drifting past us. We had the opportunity of seeing in the distance our old camp at Kabrit to which we waved goodbye, as we steamed through the Great Bitter Lake; and as we rounded the 'Point' all the HMS *Saunders* men in the vicinity gave us a hearty wave, exchanging back chat with the *Saunders'* personnel who were manning the landing craft aboard us. Many were the good wishes they shouted at us as we passed, though they must have had even less idea of where we were going than we had ourselves.

The time passed very quickly and that afternoon we arrived at Port Said, to see a great fleet of liners, cargo ships, and escort vessels assembled there, all doubtless bound for the same destination as we. Only now did we begin to realize something of the scale of the operation that was to take place shortly and in which we were to take part. All around were great ships, loaded to capacity with troops and fully equipped with landing craft and similar equipment to enable these troops to be taken ashore. The navy, too, were conspicuous, and busy little corvettes, destroyers, and landing craft were fussing around continually. Port Said is a much smaller harbour than Suez, with the result that the ships were packed much closer together, and all this helped us realize more markedly something of the size of the invasion fleet which was here being assembled.

The next day we learned that the whole invasion force was going to be allowed ashore rather than be cooped up the whole day on board their ships. For security reasons, this had naturally to be done on an organized basis, but I still do not think that the results achieved were justified by the immense amount of trouble that had to be taken to get us ashore. Firstly, all badges, decorations and regimental signs had to be removed. This seemed a rather silly precaution in itself, as I imagine that the Germans would have been far more interested in learning that there was an invasion force assembled at Port Said, and its approximate strength, than in what individual units went to make it up. But by marching through the streets of Port Said we seemed to be doing no more than to advertise our presence there, to whoever was interested, and moreover to give a very good indication of our approximate strength! We looked on the whole thing rather sceptically, and the best interpretation we could put upon it all was that Monty was so supremely confident about the ultimate success of the venture, that he really did not mind if the enemy did know we were coming.

It was quite an impressive sight. The seemingly endless column, made up of every type of unit from many nations, marched straight and erect through the broad, palm-flanked main streets of Port Said, while an awed crowd gathered to watch them as they passed. I wonder what thoughts were passing through their heads as they watched, and whether any secret radio to Germany was kept extra busy that day, as a result of this parade through Port Said.

After a lot of muddle and waiting around for a ferry to take us back to the *Monarch*, we eventually arrived aboard, and from then on the atmosphere was tense and expectant. We knew that we had not long to wait now, and it came as no real surprise to us when we found ourselves slipping out of the harbour about 11am the following morning and heading straight out into the blue Mediterranean. But we were far from being alone. Both ahead and astern we could see ship after ship slowly manoeuvring into position. Soon we were formed up into proper convoy formation, and hugging the coast of Egypt, we at last really started to move towards our still unknown objective.

But there was no point in keeping us in the dark any longer for security reasons about where we were going to land, for we were now out to sea and completely out of touch with any chance friend or acquaintance whom we would be likely to bump into ashore.

So it hardly came as a surprise to us to receive a little blue book telling us all that the soldier or tourist might like to know about an important island in the middle of the Mediterranean – Sicily, the stepping-stone to Europe. Many of us had thought that it might be Sicily that we were bound for, and as soon as we had received this little book which contained a large scale map of the island, all the pieces of the jigsaw puzzle immediately fell into place.

From a close study of the map, we found that the little foot-shaped promontory on which we were to land, was situated on the south-east shore of the island, about 5 miles or so south of Syracuse, the capture of which port was undoubtedly one of the immediate objectives of the operation.

Officers were summoned again for final briefing and last minute aerial photographs were issued. From then on the ship was a hive of activity as we realized that we had no time to lose. The photographs were studied, discussed and interpreted both individually and collectively, and a large-scale relief model of the objective area went the round of all sections in the regiment. Right back in the days when we were at Azzib the general plan of the attack had been defined and rehearsed. This had been passed down in further detail from

troop to sections, and we were now busy passing it down from sections to sub-
sections and parties, and the individual men themselves. Large scale plans of
the objective area were drawn and studied, until each man knew where he had
to be, what was expected of him, and which flank to cover, at any given moment.
The plan was so completely instilled in us that the whole operation, from the
moment we touched the coast to the time we assaulted the gun positions, could
be carried out in all its detailed intricacies without the need for a single order
being given.

The photographic interpretation which we did was extremely thorough –
too thorough in fact, for many far fetched and conflicting conclusions were
drawn. For instance, there was one mark on the photograph which caused a lot
of trouble and no one could quite decide what it was. Then it was noticed that
there was a figure of a man close beside it, and this man was studied carefully
to see if he could give us any indication as to the nature of the position. It was
decided that if the man were running away from the position, it would most
likely be an ammunition or bomb dump, while if he were running towards it, it
would probably be an air raid shelter, as the arrival of the reconnaisance plane
would almost certainly have caused an air raid alarm to have been sounded. The
only trouble was that there was considerable difference of opinion as to which
direction the figure was running, and right up to the last no definite conclusion
about this point had been reached. It turned out later that we need not have
troubled ourselves about this, and many other similar details, for the object in
question was found on arrival to be no more than an innocent haystack!

On the practical side as well as the theoretical, we were also very busy. Our
equipment had to be sorted and the weight of it carefully distributed over our
bodies. Weapons had to be cleaned and loaded, grenades primed and protective
coverings made for arms and ammunition to prevent them from coming to harm
as the result of immersion in seawater. For this last purpose many dodges were
devised. Oiled silk was issued which we sewed into little waterproof bags for
our valuables and ammunition, while certain rubber articles designed for a very
different purpose were placed over the muzzles of our weapons and our watches.
With a final check up and fitting of our equipment, a final glance at the maps
and photographs with which we had been issued, we were at last completely
ready for any eventuality. We were even provided with inflatable 'Mae West'
life belts, just in case we should have to swim for it – an uncomfortable thought
considering that most of us were carrying the best part of 80lbs weight on our
backs!

Once all these final preparations had been completed there was nothing
left for us to do but wait and talk over the coming operation among ourselves

and with our respective sections. The scene was an unbelievably peaceful one. Out of a cloudless sky the sun shone happily down on the unruffled surface of the blue-green Mediterranean. On the port horizon could be seen the dim outline of the Libyan coast, while the great ships in convoy formation moved lazily, effortlessly and imperturbably towards the enemy shores which we hoped would remain unaware of our impending arrival.

We all realized how much easier our job would be if we could make a surprise landing, but we considered this to be extremely unlikely and too much to hope for in view of the immense scale of the operation. It only needed one enemy aircraft to sight this vast mass of ships for our secret to be out and for the greater part of the surprise element to be lost. And so we kept our fingers tightly crossed during the five-day voyage, and many were the anxious glances cast into the air from time to time in the fervent hope that enemy aircraft would stay away. The tension became especially marked when we drew level with the enemy-held island of Crete, for we realized that the danger would first come from there. But by the grace of God we apparently got by completely unobserved and were unmolested during all the time we were at sea. At the height of the danger period it was reported that a four-engine reconnaissance plane, thought to be a Focke-Wulf had flown over the convoy at great height, but I never saw it myself, and the fact that we received no unwelcome attentions from enemy aircraft during the whole of the trip rather belied the report. In all probability it was one of our own bombers which caused the scare.

We learned later that the squadron that had separated from us when we left Kabrit, and which formed the SBS (Special Boat Squadron), had been given as one of its primary tasks, the job of raiding Crete with a view to keeping the planes there on the ground. It is very likely that we owed the apparent total inactivity of enemy aircraft during the whole time we were at sea to the success with which they carried out this operation.

Our feelings while we were sailing towards Sicily are hard to describe, but it is no exaggeration to say that we were extremely uncomfortable! When I became more experienced in action I grew to realize that far worse than the actual fighting itself is the period immediately preceding the engagement. During that time the waiting, the inactivity and the considerable nervous tension would completely occupy our minds, and the temptation to spend our time brooding and thinking morbid thoughts was hard to resist. It was at times like these that fear of the unknown would take the strongest hold of us. It was too easy to look at the group of faces we had come to know so well and to let the thought possess us that almost certainly there would be many we would not see again after a few days time. We knew that there was a great chance too, that we ourselves might be among the unlucky ones who would not return – we would look at all our intimate personal possessions, our photographs and letters from home – as we packed them away and wonder if we would ever see them again, and what would happen to them if we did not come back. The uncertainties and dangers of the coming D-Day filled our whole horizon, and caused us more mental torture than any hardships of battle.

These were our feelings during those tense and care-laden days before we were due to swarm up the Sicilian cliffs. We had been told that Sicily was the best-fortified island in the whole Mediterranean – a veritable fortress, with which inspecting enemy generals and commanders had expressed themselves well satisfied. And when we came to think that the task which had been allotted to us was to breach this steel wall at one of its strongest points, our natural forebodings become easy to understand. We never dreamt that we would be able to capture the battery without intense fighting, and deep down inside us was the firm belief that many of us would be expended in the effort, and would never come back.

But to counteract these very natural fears was the supreme confidence we had in our own ability, resulting from our previous thorough training. We knew that we were trained to such a degree of efficiency that we would be able to take on enemy forces greatly superior to us in number, and still win the day. All we hoped and prayed for was a speedy end to this deadly waiting and uncertainty, and a normal amount of luck and favourable conditions, to allow us to *show these "Itie" bastards exactly where they could get off!*

We left Port Said on the morning of 5 July and during the next three days nothing occurred to make us think that we were not on just another exercise safe in home waters. But on the afternoon of 9 July one small announcement over the ship's broadcasting system brought us all back to reality with a jump. No longer were we going through a restless and disturbing dream, this was the real thing! The calm voice of the navigator announced, '*If you care to look out to the starboard bow, you will just be able to make out the summit of Mount Etna, Sicily's highest mountain.*'

This simple announcement caused a stampede to the decks and there we saw clearly on the horizon a beautiful sight of the top half of this regular cone-shaped volcano apparently floating on the clouds. Its lower half was completely invisible.

At the sight of this our fears and nervousness came back with a vengeance. I remember thinking to myself, 'My God what fools! Here we are, having successfully avoided being noticed by enemy aircraft, parading our might just a few miles from the Sicilian shore in broad daylight, as if to show the enemy what is coming to them tonight.' I don't think I was the only one to entertain thoughts such as these at first sight of Etna.

It was then about 4pm, and I noticed with alarm how choppy and unsettled the sea was becoming. Early that morning the sun had been beating down upon us and nothing, save the white lines of foam in the wake of the fleet, disturbed the smooth unruffled beauty of the blue water. But around mid-day an almost imperceptible motion had made itself felt as we had our lunch and this was now increasing to a marked and most unpleasant extent. 'Heavens don't say we are going to have a roaring gale just to make everything more difficult?' but this is what it looked like. The old tight feeling round my head revealed that I was shortly going to feel ill – Derek had succumbed and Sergeant Storey came to see me looking as pale as a sheet. And all the time the gale was increasing in violence and showed no sign of abating. Getting us into the landing craft and onto the shore was going to be a tricky business indeed. Needless to say this added discomfort and danger only served to increase our fears.

It began to grow darker, and with the coming of night the general tension increased. Only a matter of hours now before we would be right in the thick of it. The wind and the seas had by now risen to gale force, and the *Monarch* was bucking about like an unbroken colt. We spent most of the remaining hours lying down quietly trying to fight away the overpowering nausea and lassitude that sea sickness brings in its train. All preparations had been made and all we waited for now was the time to arrive for us to embark. About 1am the ship suddenly slowed and we transferred from normal to invasion lighting. All bright lights were dimmed and for the remainder of the time before we embarked, we walked around in a pale and eerie glow. We staggered up to the mess, where most of the officers had already assembled, and proceeded to force bacon and eggs down our unwilling throats. This and the hot coffee provided, did us good and served to mitigate the damp clammy feeling of sickness which was threatening to take hold of us.

We hung around in the mess for about an hour and then about 2am went down to our respective cabins to get ready.

'*SRS, Prepare to embark!*' Over the loudspeakers came those dread words to which we had become so accustomed and which we had so long awaited. I hurried into my equipment, gave everything a final check over and then sat down on my bunk, waiting.

'*SRS, Stand by to embark!*' As though it were just another of those embarkation exercises which we had practised so thoroughly, we slowly made our way to our boat stations and took up our embarkation positions. The men were all present and in good spirits. Now that we were actually doing something, we did not feel nearly as bad as we had felt a few hours before. The doors were open and through them we saw the dark blue patch that betrayed the blackness of that stormy night. The ship was still rolling and tossing and the sailors seemed to be having some trouble in getting the boats lowered to our level. We seemed to wait there for an appreciable time.

'SRS, Embark!' The calm voice of the naval officer giving the command brought our confidence back with a rush. Even if this was the 'real thing' we had after all practised it so thoroughly that we stood every chance of coming through it safely. I no longer felt any apprehensions for I seemed to be living in a dream. We had been imagining this moment so many times during the previous few months that now that it had actually come, it somehow seemed unreal. I expected any minute to wake up and find that we had merely been taking part in just another exercise!

The files of men moved slowly forward, helping each other cross over to the landing craft. So weighted down by our equipment were we, and so rough were the seas, that it was an extremely difficult operation to get into the boats, and only the welcome presence of a sailor, who was clinging to the door ready to give us a hand, prevented several nasty accidents. Staggering under the weight of my kit, and still feeling weak from sea sickness, I fell into the bottom of the landing craft and after picking myself up, made my way to my appointed seat. I had hardly sat down, when I heard a splash followed by a shout of '*Man Overboard!*' God! Had one of the chaps fallen in? It soon became very obvious indeed that someone had, and frantic efforts were made to pull him out.

'*Never mind about him! Get cracking and get those boats away,*' came the harsh voice of the ship's first officer – this callousness on his part caused many exclamations of indignation from our men in the boat, but I think we all realized that we were now under operational conditions and could not risk a whole boat load for the sake of one man. The longer we were there, the greater the danger we were in. However, the boats were loaded without further incident, and Josling, one of Tony's section was successfully fished out of the water, none the worse for his adventure, save that he was soaked and shivering and had lost his rifle. He was passed into my boat looking very sorry for himself and probably very thankful at his lucky escape.

Then followed the difficult operation of lowering us into the water, a procedure especially tricky owing to the violence of the seas. But thanks to the skills of the LCA crew, no sooner did our craft touch the top of the water, then the cables were cast loose in a moment, the motors roared into life and we glided away from the dangerous vicinity of the ship's side. If there had been any delay in casting off, our heavy craft would have been knocked to pieces against the *Monarch*'s side like matchwood.

We cruised around near the ship until all the landing craft were safely launched, and then formed up into formation and started off on the 3-mile trip to the shore, which could just be seen as a low black line in the distance ahead. It was still uncomfortably rough, and as the little boat dipped and wallowed in the waves we were inundated and drenched to the skin by great sheets of water and spray which came flying over us. Shivering, ill, and making full use of the cardboard buckets provided, we sat huddled in the sides of the boat praying that, no matter whatever lay before us, we would soon be allowed to escape from this hell.

We had not been out for more than thirty minutes when the motion of the boat grew considerably less, and we began to feel slightly more comfortable and were able to take some interest in what was happening around us. The strength of the gale had suddenly abated, and as we approached the shelter afforded by the shore, our motion became more settled. I staggered to my feet and went to join Harry who was standing in the stern. In this position I was able to watch the events on the shore more or less as an impartial observer and so interested in this did I become, that I almost forgot the implications of the position in which we were. Our great worry was caused by a searchlight which was sweeping the seas, and as we drew closer, we could not imagine how we were going to avoid being lit up in its dazzling rays, which would mean goodbye to our precious surprise, and probably the end for many of us.

A roar of engines overhead and the crump of heavy bombs falling told us that our bombers were successfully attracting the enemy's attention, and to our intense relief we saw the horizontal beam of the searchlight become vertical as it groped around through the blackness of the skies in a vain search for the intruding aircraft. We breathed again, assured once more. We were then able to watch unmolested quite a display. A stick of bombs seemed to straddle our objective most effectively, while the flack which the enemy was able to send up seemed most ineffective. But irregular and weak though it was, it was not completely useless, for a flash of flame in the sky which dived to extinction into the sea betrayed to us the sad fact that one of our planes had been hit.

At last came the time for which we had all been waiting with nerves keyed up and a prayer in our hearts. Even the most bloodthirsty found themselves praying in moments of danger or uncertainty, so long as they felt convinced of the justice of their coming actions. The engines of our boat went down to dead slow, and all was silent save the whistling of the wind and the tossing of the waves. Inch by inch we crept towards the land which we could now see clearly, everyone almost holding his breath lest the slightest unnecessary noise might betray our presence to the presumably waiting and expectant defenders on the shore.

Suddenly as we were creeping in the silence of the night was rudely shattered. Although we were still about 200 yards from the land, the noise seemed to come from right beside us, and sure enough there, about 20 yards away, we were able to discern a low black shape, from the top of which torches were flashing and men were shouting. For one awful moment we thought we had been discovered by an enemy E-boat, and firmly believed that our last moment had come, in the defenceless state we were in. But to our relief we soon realized that the voices were shouting in English and very violent and unmistakeable English it was. We heaved to, to investigate, and found that it was one of our gliders which had come down in the sea. One of our boats picked up the few (all too few) remaining survivors, and after this delay we continued our slow and silent journey towards the land. We could not understand how all the noise the glider boys had kicked up had not aroused any answering comment from the shore, and we congratulated ourselves on our continued good fortune.

We hit the shore with a slight bump and from then on it was only a matter of carrying out once again the very thorough landing training we had gone through so often. After assembling on the beach we made towards the cliffs which rose up just ahead. Not that there were really any cliffs, as such, for except for a sharp climb out of the boats of about 5ft, the shore rose gradually ahead of us in a series of rocky steps and boulders, so the ropes were found to be unnecessary and we were able to reach the top without any undue exertion. At the top we waited as we had been trained to do, and I quickly made contact with Harry and troop headquarters. He ordered me to remain where I was with his headquarters while he contacted the rest. So we lay there for some time hoping to receive the order to move on.

An ominous whistle over our heads followed by the sharp crump of a bursting mortar bomb quickly livened us up, especially since I heard a sharp exclamation of pain from behind me. Word was passed up that Saunders had been wounded. Aghast at this early casualty I went back to talk to Saunders and found that a bomb splinter had just cut his hand. There was no need to evacuate him, and indeed he was most indignant at any suggestion of our doing so. Mortar bombs were falling fast now, and we were most relieved to realize that they were our own. Alec, with his mortar section, undelayed by picking up glider survivors, must have arrived some minutes before us, and had lost no time in getting into action. His second bomb was right on the target, and set ammunition and grass in the area on fire, so that the whole objective was clearly and very conveniently lit up in every detail. As a result of this unexpected light being shed on the scene, I was able to work out very quickly, from studying various landmarks which we had carefully memorized from the aerial photographs, that we were not, by nearly half a mile, in the position where we should have landed. There straight in front and slightly to the left of me, clearly silhouetted against the growing brilliance of the flames, I could see a tall steel pylon, which I knew should be on the south-west corner of the camp enclosure. If we had landed in the right place, this pylon would have been almost out of sight, and away over to our right. So we must have touched down half a mile further to the east than planned, with the result that we must now be immediately below the battery.

It was this sudden realization that made me remember that we were meeting with a complete absence of opposition, even though we had inadvertently landed on the spot which we unanimously agreed from our study of the photos, would be most likely the centre of the danger area.

Somewhere to our left the comfortable, slow, tat-tat-tat of a Bren gun rang out. Then there was silence once more, save for the intermittent swish and crump of Alec's mortar bombs, which came lobbing over into the target area at regular intervals. Still no sign of the enemy. And then from close at hand, ringing out clearly over the fresh morning air, we heard a pitiful wailing – a sound akin to a small child crying for his mother. It was some member of the Italian garrison who had been struck by the horrible realization that there were enemy within a hundred yards of him, and that the noises of the night were not due to an abortive gliderborne attack or to an aerial bombardment, but were the advance elements of a mighty and overwhelming invasion force. The sound of this voice crying in the wilderness cheered us up immensely. It was so obviously panic stricken that we felt sure that we had achieved complete surprise in our landing, and the enemy defenders were utterly unprepared.

We lay where we were for close on ten minutes listening to the gathering sounds of battle, but still no signs of Harry. Where the devil had he got to? I felt sure that he could not be far and would be coming back soon, as his entire headquarters were lying just ahead of my section. Eventually I decided I could wait no longer, and Bob Lilly and I had a rapid scout round to try and find him. But it was in vain – Harry and the remaining two sections of the troop had disappeared into the night.

Feeling very indignant at being left behind like this I decided that the only thing that I could do was to act on my own. Because we had been landed so far from our intended position, I doubted very much whether Harry had stuck to his original plan and made a detour around to the west of the objective, so as to attack it from the north. So in view of the most reassuring lack of opposition,

I decided to take my section straight in across the stretch of open ground that separated us from the gun battery, which we could now clearly see, lit up by the flames caused by Alec's extremely accurate mortar fire.

Topping a slight rise, we came upon a long low fence of tangled barbed wire. Just ahead of us were some troops, which by their silhouettes we clearly recognized as being our own. I went up to them and discovered they were Johnny Wiseman's section belonging to No.1 Troop. Heavens what a muddle! We should never have met up with them. I got over the wire as quickly as I could, with visions of the whole length of it being covered by hidden machine-gun posts and strewn with booby traps. So anxious was I to get across that I left the entire seat of my trousers behind on the wire, which fact was announced to me by an ominous tearing sound, and a resultant draughty sensation around my nether regions.

By the time that my whole section was across the wire, Johnny Wiseman's crowd had disappeared once more into the night.

Meanwhile, as we plodded on in extended line across this uncomfortably bare stretch of ground, the fireworks started to begin. Streams of red tracer glided slowly and surely into the heart of the target area, in ever increasing volume and intensity. The answering green tracer which we knew would belong to enemy guns, was rare and almost non-existent.

'Sir! I don't think we had better go any further just yet, unless you want us all killed in cold blood!' The calm voice at my side belonged to Corporal Mitchell, my leading section commander, who, a veteran of several campaigns was all too skilled at recognizing the implications of a vicious *psshht* passing over our heads. I had heard the sound too, but being green, did not want to let a little thing like that put me off doing my duty. But Corporal Mitchell pointed out to me that if we were not being actually fired upon, a stack of bullets was passing dangerously close. At this moment we came to another and far more formidable wire obstacle which it would have been suicidal to cross in face of the bullets which were now whipping past us in ever increasing, and ever more threatening fashion. So we made use of a piece of good natural cover in the shape of a low bank which we were lucky enough to find on the spot, and taking up an all-round defensive position, prepared to stay where we were, with a view to giving our assistance wherever it was needed, and in any case to seal off this south side of the battery in case any of the enemy should try to make good their escape in this direction.

Meanwhile the mortar fire had ceased and a veritable hail of bullets proceeded to whip over our heads. How thankful I was that I had followed Corporal Mitchell's suggestion as otherwise casualties among my section would certainly have been numerous.

We had not the slightest doubt but that the fire which we could hear so closely belonged to our own men, and we were confirmed in this belief by hearing the occasional burst of a No.36 Mills grenade and a faint shouting of English voices. Slowly the hubbub died down and now we could see figures walking among the enemy positions firing an occasional burst from Tommy guns, or throwing the odd grenade into the darker corners. I recognized the voice of Chalky White, one of No.1 Troop's sergeants and shouted the password at him.

'*Desert Rats?*' – '*Kill the Italians*', came the prompt reply, and we got up and climbed the wire into the gun position, to mingle with our own men from No.1 Troop.

A rapid review of the situation showed that Bill Fraser, commander of No.1 Troop, had kept to his threat made jokingly to Harry on several occasions, that his troop was not going to be content to capture the camp buildings, and then sit back and leave the guns to No.2 Troop. Oh no! No.1 Troop would go straight in immediately it had cleared its own particular objective and trespass on No.2 Troop's preserves. This is precisely what happened in actual fact, though the

One of the captured guns. Cape Murro di Porco near Syracuse, Sicily, 9 July 1943.

Harry Poat and Bob Lilley on Second Gun Battery, Cape Murro di Porco, near Syracuse, Sicily, 9 July 1943.

change in plans had come through Paddy himself, who realizing the weakness of the opposition had decided to go straight in and take the objective without loss of time and in consequence to abandon completely our original plan.

When we arrived on the scene we found No.1 Troop busy mopping the place up. The pale light of dawn began to clarify the scene and soon we could distinguish little groups of Italians standing shivering by their nonchalant guards. Some of our lads were busy round the entrance to a deep air raid shelter, from which certain noises had made themselves heard, and after repeated threats and exhortations, accompanied by some pretty forceful persuasion through the use of small arms fire and grenades, they succeeded in extracting the occupants. They were a sorry sight. The men came out grinning sheepishly and obviously glad that they had been left alive. Many were considerably shaken and some wounded. But what took us really by surprise was the fact that down in that dug-out were also women and children. They were a poor lot, dirty, shabby and ill equipped, ingratiating and fawning, they formed a startling contrast to the mental picture we had formed of the tough, experienced, and fanatically patriotic defenders we had expected to come up against.

In the centre of all this activity stood Paddy, looking amazingly calm and very pleased with himself; and rightly so too, for we had captured this important position without the loss of a single man. He asked me where Harry was and the rest of my troop and it was unpleasant having to answer that I did not know. But he did not seem to mind and decided to call them in by sending up the local success signal of three green Very lights. They turned up about ten minutes after our arrival, having stuck to the original plan of making a wide detour in order to assault from the north. I sat my section in the well of one of the big gun pits and contentedly we eased the weight of our kit off our shoulders and puffed at our cigarettes.

It was now light enough to see fairly clearly what was happening around us. Everyone seemed most unconcerned about the prospect of a counter-attack, and all were busy discussing with each other their share in this astoundingly simple operation. Johnny Wiseman's section had had a scare when, as they were advancing towards the battery, they saw in the gloom what appeared to be the figure of a man as though in a firing position. The leading man stopped dead in his tracks and the rest of his section did likewise. Had they been observed by this unexpected sentry, or had they stopped in time? Breathlessly they kept still, waiting for the silent and motionless figure before them to make the next move. But all remained still and taking advantage of their presumed concealment, the section carefully brought up the Bren gun, and for lack of any other alternative, threw surprise to the winds, and opened up on the enemy figure. What a laugh they had when they found that what had caused them such worry was no more than the statue of some 'Itie' big- wig.

It was now almost daylight and Paddy decided that we could not stay much longer crowded around the guns. Much had yet to be done before complete daylight, and so the order was given for us to disperse and to organize the prisoners and march them away, so that the guns could be blown up and the success signal sent up to the waiting fleet. The prisoners were the first to be collected and marched off. Already, scarcely 45 mins after we had touched the Sicilian shore, we had collected over 200 of them. One could not help laughing at these childish, dirty little men, such cowards when they were outnumbered and outfought, and such bullies when they had the upper hand. These fawning, friendly, smiling little creatures, who now came up asking for a match, had nevertheless the reputation of treating prisoners in a most disgusting fashion. Of this we had ample proof as the day drew on. Many of the glider troops who had been captured by them had received disgraceful treatment; wounded men had been stripped of their clothes and coverings and left to die from exposure, while other prisoners had been beaten up and robbed of all their personal possessions. We had no cause to love the 'Itie', and when it was we who were in the position of captors his ingratiating advances carried no weight with us.

We formed up into troops and marched a few hundred yards down the only track that led from the battery position, and then sat down among the rocks to await further developments. Meanwhile our engineers were busy preparing the charges with which the guns were to be put out of action, and soon shattering explosions and falling shrapnel announced that this task had been successfully accomplished. All that was left for us to do now was to send up the prearranged success signal to the waiting ships in order to inform them that all was now clear and that they could come close in to shore to discharge their loads. Tony was given the task of sending off these green rockets, but it was only with considerable difficulty that he managed to get them into the air at all. The first two simply fell over on their sides, scattering green sparks in all directions, the third managed to spiral about 10ft into the air, while the fourth and last, performed a remarkable series of acrobatics, in the course of which it succeeded in reaching a height of perhaps 20ft. We wondered if our signals had been sufficient to tell the ships that they could come in, but they must have been watching the coast pretty closely, for it was only a matter of minutes from the sending up of our first rocket that the great fleet, which was just visible on the horizon, began to steam slowly towards the shore. How proud we felt as we watched them, for we realized that it was only by our achievements that they were now able to come within so close to the land.

I think we had every reason to feel pleased with ourselves, and as we heard later, General Dempsey was extremely satisfied with the quick and decisive results of our operation and from then on he began to take a special interest

A glider crashed into a stone wall, Cape Murro di Porco, near Syracuse, Sicily, 9 July 1943.

A crashed glider, Cape Murro di Porco, near Syracuse, Sicily, 9 July 1943.

in our unit and to hold us in high regard. People in the ships told us later that our portion of the coast had given the only sign that the troops had landed and the activity which had been apparent there had been an intense relief to them in their suspense. Then when they saw our success signal so soon after we must have landed, they felt that their worries were over, as they knew from the short space of time that the fighting had lasted, that opposition in that sector at least must have been very slight.

It was by now daylight, and the rising sun helped to give us a more complete picture of the events of the preceding night than we could ever have hoped to have by mere reminiscing. First to attract our attention were about a dozen small black patches floating on the surface of the sea. As it grew lighter we realized with dismay that those dark objects were our gliders which had been cast off too early and which in consequence had been compelled to come down in the water. The crew we picked up as we approached the shore was not therefore an isolated case, but just one of several, and there was no knowing how many men and machines had been swallowed up by the water, now so peaceful and calm, during those few fateful hours before dawn. We counted thirteen gliders still afloat, which meant that in all probability at least twenty had come down in the water, some of which had since sunk. Twenty gliders each holding about fifteen troops meant that this operation had cost us at least 300 men who had not even had the chance to make a fight of it. Our cheerfulness died away on the spot, and it occurred to us with a sudden numbing shock that this war business was not just a game. One just did not refer to an operation as 'having fun' – it was a grim and ghastly business, a matter of pitting one's wits and one's strength, not only against the enemy but also against tricks of fate. It was certainly something in which the word 'fun' did not enter.

And then we let our glances wander inland, noticing a bare, rocky, flattish countryside, studded with small shrubs and stunted olive trees. It bore a parched and dusty aspect: the grass was tall and brown and, except for fields covered with small dusty tomatoes, there was no relief from the all-pervading drabness of the ground and the dark green of the trees. So much we were able to notice, before we saw, about 200 yards away, another glider lying across one of the stone walls with which the countryside seemed to abound. It had obviously struck this with the full force of its landing. Beyond it lay another, with its back broken. Heavens they were all over the place! What a massacre! The thought of the punishment which those glider boys must have received sent a cold feeling down our spines and made us all the more thankful for our own good fortune.

One of our sections had meanwhile been clearing the caves which lay along the coast and our column of prisoners was swelling all the time. Several red berets began to appear among us and soon we had twenty or so survivors from the gliders, including their brigadier who had been found shivering in a cave. He seemed most relieved at being picked up by us and spent a long time chatting to Paddy. He was most impressed by the way our troop commanders did not fail to salute Paddy whenever they went to report to him (this was mostly done for the brigadier's benefit, needless to say). Considerably cheered after his most unpleasant ordeal of the previous night he marched off with the words, *'Well, I suppose I had better look for my bloody brigade'*. He returned some time later and attached himself to Paddy's HQ for the rest of that particular operation.

A roar of engines and an ominous dark shadow passed low overhead, in just sufficient time for us to notice the black crosses painted on the wings, so that we went scuttling for cover in the shadows of a stone wall. It was a German Fokke-Wolf 190 probably on its normal routine dawn patrol, and it passed like the wind without troubling us. We picked ourselves up and fell to discussing the probable reactions of the pilot to the strange sight dawn must have brought to his eyes. How amazed he must have been, how overwhelmed, to see that mass of shipping standing off the coast, and what a report he must have handed in on his return to base, if indeed he ever reached there.

We amused ourselves with such thoughts, as we lay in the scant cover afforded by the rocks and walls that flanked that coastal track leading to the battery. We knew that according to the original plan, Paddy would either signal back to the ship that we were returning aboard her, or else he would state that we would press on until we joined up with our main forces. Up to that moment we did not know on which alternative Paddy had decided, but rumours were strong to the effect that we would be returning to the ship. However, if that had been Paddy's intention, his mind was soon changed for him by events which immediately followed.

A sudden explosion from inland made us sit up with a jerk. What was that? Everything had seemed so peaceful that our reveries were interrupted in the rudest fashion. The noise was easily recognizable as coming from the muzzle end of some big gun, and with tensed expressions we sat by our wall waiting for the trouble that was in all probability coming our way. But there was no tell-tale whine of a shell and the gun fired several rounds without our being able to find out where the shells were landing. Probably it was some activity engendered by the presence of our main forces behind us, or so we thought. And then far out to sea, just short of the steaming fleet and some distance to the left of it, we saw a fountain of water shoot up into the air. So that was the trouble. Another coastal battery about a mile or two inland was firing at our shipping. The fire was very inaccurate and in all probability the guns were trained to the extreme extent of their traverse, for they were firing into an area that should normally have been covered by the battery which we had just put out of action.

But this first sign of organized enemy activity quickly decided Paddy, and word was passed round that we would join up with our main forces, but that we would knock out that battery first. This proved to be easier than we ever imagined, for by a stroke of luck Paddy chose as his headquarters a tall farm building which could be seen across the fields about half a mile away. Our squadron, with its attendant column of prisoners slowly moved towards it, and as we reached it, the fire from the enemy battery ceased. The building which we had just reached was the observation point for the enemy guns. Most of the occupying troops had fled and the remainder were speedily dealt with. We waited among the bushes and shrubs that surrounded this building, while Paddy and troop commanders studied the area. A very few minutes later I was summoned by a runner to Harry's presence. I found him peering over a wall scanning the fields that lay ahead.

'*Oh there you are Peter,*' he said. '*I suppose you realize that that noise we heard recently was fire from a battery further inland. The battery concerned must obviously be that one*', and he pointed out a position on a map, where we knew a gun battery was situated. '*That is where the devils are – no not there, further to the left,*' and following his finger I was able to discern a cluster of men grouped around something that rather resembled an enormous 'T' that was raised from the ground.

'*That is obviously their rangefinder,*' Harry pointed out, '*and we are now going to show them a thing or two. Derrick's section will lead and you Peter will follow. We will make a left flank detour and get into that battery as quickly as possible*'.

With those words I was dismissed to explain the situation to my section as briefly as possible, and then we were off. Slowly we moved for about 200 yards down a narrow stony track in the wake of the leading section. A burst of firing in front and then we stopped. What was up? Had we bumped into opposition already? Apparently we had, for I saw Company Sergeant Major Glaze, our PT instructor, and whom we just could not leave behind on the ship, dash forward with his 2-inch mortar with which he started lobbing a rain of bombs onto a farmhouse about 200 yards away in front of us. We were torn away from the enthralling sight of Glaze in action by being called forward. I took my section up the track while occasional bullets whined overhead, until I found Harry crouching by a wall. He was as cool as ever.

'*There seems to be some opposition coming from that building*', he said, '*but it is not enough to worry about, and as the gun battery is our main objective, we are going to bypass it. So will you take your section on and make your way to the battery on the left of Derrick's section. Just be careful as you go past this house, as there is a certain amount of sniping.*'

With those words Harry left me to take my section past this trouble point, and we were able to enter the comparative cover of a deep shrub-strewn gully, while the noises of battle continued behind us. I learned later, that a minute or two after we had passed, the occupants of the farmhouse surrendered, and it can be imagined how surprised each party was, to learn that our 'prisoners' were a bunch of the glider boys, who had decided to make a stand for it in that house, against all comers. But our 'heavy stuff', which is how they referred to Glaze's rather inaccurate mortar fire, was enough to make them put discretion before valour and they decided to surrender to us. They were firmly convinced that we were 'Ities'. At that time, we were the only troops who wore khaki berets, and these, with the sun shields over our necks, and our blue Indian shirts, did give us a rather foreign appearance. They must have been considerably relieved, even if they were rather ashamed about it all, to find that they had surrendered to their own troops. The officer in charge came running out to Harry and started apologizing most profusely for having killed one of our men, or so he thought. His fears were quickly dispelled however, when the dead man was identified as a very dead Italian, and so the whole contretemps was ended without damage being done to either side.

Meanwhile, our fleet, which must have been rather worried by the intermittent shellfire directed at them, decided to retaliate and one of our destroyers, noticing movement on the building which had formerly served as observation point for the battery, started lobbing shells at it. This gave Paddy and his headquarters, who were by now the real occupants of the building, an unpleasant few minutes, but fortunately he had with him a forward observation officer, who was in direct wireless contact with the fleet, with the result that the disconcerting shellfire was quickly stopped.

The attack on the gun battery now took on a very light-hearted appearance, and far removed from any military training we had ever received. The sections all advanced along the routes they had chosen for themselves, only just troubling about keeping each other in sight, and moving forward steadily despite the erratic and spasmodic opposition they were meeting. It was soon realized that the enemy fire was far from accurate, and whether by accident or design, the first shots were always about 15ft above our heads. The lads soon realized the situation and after a while would deliberately expose themselves in order to tempt the Italians, who by now must have been considerably shaken, to take a pot shot at them and thereby reveal their position. Nonchalantly chewing pieces of grass, or sucking at the small orange tomatoes which were to be found growing everywhere in abundance, and with which everyone's pockets were stuffed, our sections just pressed forward ignoring completely the mild and spasmodic opposition with which they were occasionally faced. As soon as fire or activity was observed in a certain area, there was no check while reconnaissances and orders were given. Sections just made straight for the point in question and invariably found by the time they reached there, that the enemy were either waiting for them with their hands up, and grinning sheepishly, or had long since fled. Not a moment was wasted in this advance of ours onto the second battery, and we allowed nothing to delay us. If we met with a check, one section would be left to deal with it while the others continued with the movement forward.

And so for more than an hour we alternated between the dusty glare of the stubble fields, and the shady relief afforded by the walls and hedgerows. From bound to bound we advanced, clearing each building of the enemy as we passed. The procedure became monotonous in its regularity. The whine over our heads of an ill-aimed bullet, which was not even sufficient to make us take cover –

Percival and some of our prisoners near Syracuse, Sicily, 9 July 1943.

the sight of a shiny round black helmet just visible over a bank or a wall – the change in our course towards this object, while we fired from the hip – a number of green Italian backsides bounding away from us over the grass, and the ever increasing bag of prisoners. Such was our first morning on Sicily and a very pleasant form of fighting it was.

At one point Harry told me over the wireless to give Derrick a hand, as he had apparently met with slightly heavier opposition than usual. I moved towards him, but the trouble cleared just as I got up to the spot. Sergeant McDiarmid was standing there looking very businesslike, hurling No.36 grenades in all directions but not an Italian was to be seen. Apparently they had bolted into a house. Derrick seemed quite capable of dealing with this himself and so I pushed on. About 200 yards away three tubby green forms emerged from some high grass and scampered away towards some olive trees. This was the opportunity for which I had been waiting, and I quickly brought my Tommy gun to the shoulder and gave them a long burst. But luck was with them for my shooting was bad and I missed them all. However, it made no difference, for Tony's section was heading rapidly towards the spot, and a minute or so later added these three very frightened 'Ities' to the steadily increasing bag.

The battery now lay behind us, for in the course of our detour we had bypassed it. It now remained for us to bear sharply to the right, almost until we reached the coast, and then we would turn right again and enter the battery from the northern side. We now found ourselves among several houses and the going was slower as we had to clear each of these in turn. We were progressing thus when the familiar sight of a shiny black steel helmet met our eyes scarcely 20 yards away, the owner of which was ducked behind a wall. Just as we noticed him the 'Itie' got up and was met by a hail of fire from the hip. Somehow or other he was missed and he ducked behind the wall again in a flash. Then ensued a cat and mouse sort of game. We stared at the spot where he had disappeared waiting for him to reappear. We were not keen to walk over to where he was, not knowing if he had any friends with him, so we waited calmly sheltered behind a thick stone wall while we shouted insults in his direction in our best Italian. Again he bobbed up, but was down again almost before our first shots rang out. But he was just up long enough for me to observe firstly that he was very frightened, and secondly that he was trying to get his hands up. Sure enough, from the same spot as he had last disappeared came the most amusing sight of two hands waving wildly just above the top level of the wall. As we watched and waited, learning from our observation several points in the fine art of surrendering, the hands grew into two arms, which waved about in frenzy while we waited. Finally a very frightened head appeared, and the childish relief expressed by the 'Itie' at not being met on this occasion with a fusillade of shots, made us all laugh so much that we could hardly tell him to come over to us.

We had now reached a small church, outside which the priest was striding anxiously. Here I joined up with Derrick as we turned right again to make our way towards the battery. The priest came up to us and in excellent English asked us to spare his church as the women and children of the neighbourhood had come there for refuge. This of course we agreed to do and his gratitude was overwhelming. Neither he nor the other civilians whom we met seemed in any way frightened of us, which says something for the ineffectiveness of the Italian propaganda, which had run to the effect that we would act like monsters and would leave no man, woman or child alive as we passed. On the whole, they all seemed glad that we had come and that they had been liberated from the grip of Mussolini.

We made our way rapidly towards the battery across open country, and reached it soon afterwards, only to see Tony's section plus troop headquarters already in occupation. Apparently they had reached the battery some time before, but had been driven out by Alec's wretched mortars, which unaware of their presence, had decided to give the battery a short preliminary pasting.

However no harm was done, for Tony and his crowd just walked out of the area and sat down under the trees until it was all over and then returned. Alec must have been having a grand time that morning! For one thing he and his mortar section must have been pretty elated at the considerable success they had achieved the night before, with the result that they were all too eager to take on any target that presented itself. Alec told us with glee afterwards of how one of his mortar teams played cat and mouse with a small bunch of Italians for the best part of half an hour. He had noticed the 'Ities' running into a slit trench situated in the middle of a field, and not very far from where the mortar section were lying up. So he quickly mounted a mortar behind a wall, and sent a couple of bombs over onto the slit trench. As soon as they had fired, the mortar crew rushed to the wall and had a peep over to see the result of their fire. They then returned to their mortar. Things at this rate must have seemed very much too hot for the sheltering 'Ities', who decided to come out of their bolt hole and seek shelter elsewhere. But Alec, who was keeping the spot under observation, was not having any of this and at the first sign of movement, he sent another bomb over. The 'Ities' hearing its approach dashed back into the slit trench while the mortar team, revelling in this unique opportunity, were able to watch the whole proceeding from over their wall. This state of affairs continued for some little time, until the 'Ities' decided to give up the uneven contest, and to stand dejectedly in the open with their hands above their heads.

Of course the battery we had made such an energetic detour to attack was deserted when Tony's section arrived there, but there was every evidence that the occupants had left in a hurry. A short wander around the battery quickly convinced us of this! The officers' mess was still full of officers' private kit, of which, needless to say, our lads made short shrift, and I was able to replace my torn trousers with a brand new Italian pair. Some of the guns had even been left with rounds still in the breech, but the most significant thing of all was that the magazine of the battery which was situated deep underground between the separate gun positions, was found to have been mined, and in fact only needed the pressing of a time switch to have blown the whole place to pieces. This the fleeing 'Ities' had omitted to do!

It was by now around midday, and we spent a lazy couple of hours in the cool shade of the olive and walnut trees in the precincts of the battery while we waited for further orders. Our prisoners were kept busy scouring the neighbouring fields and orchards for us to bring in nuts and tomatoes, with which we could make our dry rations go down more easily. The number of tomatoes we all ate that day must have been close on fifty per head.

Round about 3.30pm we were recalled to squadron HQ which was in the same farm as when we had set out for the attack on the second battery. The whole regiment was assembled here, and after a short wait we learned that we were now going to make our way inland, with a view to joining up with the main British forces. As we waited we swapped yarns with members of other sections and troops, and had a look at the immense column of prisoners we had now collected. We learned that we had captured these two strong coastal batteries, comprising a large number of guns of all types, with only two serious casualties, one man killed and one badly wounded. Several others had received minor injuries, but nothing to worry about.

Our column of prisoners must have been a good 500 strong and was increasing all the time. In addition it was estimated that over 200 of the enemy must have been killed or seriously wounded, while we had been instrumental in the rescue or relief of well over fifty of our glider troops. Apparently one of our casualties had been the result of a typical piece of Italian deceit. He came out of a dug-out with his hands up, grinning cheerfully, and then suddenly threw down a red-devil grenade at one of our men. It exploded, severely wounding our man, while Paddy who happened to be standing by, plugged the 'Itie' with two .45 slugs, which just about blew him in half.

There were many stories of the willingness the Italians showed to be taken prisoner. On one occasion quite a large party of them were left under the sole guard of one solider armed with a Tommy gun. As they were moving in the wake of the regiment, the guard's magazine, which had not been inserted properly, fell out and for all the use his Tommy gun then was, he might as well not have had it. He did not notice his loss however until a grinning 'Itie' came running up and returned his magazine!

On another occasion, it had been decided to keep an accurate count of the number of prisoners we had under our care. And so whenever there was a period of inactivity when it might have been expected that no sections were sending in additional bodies, the guards lined up the column and counted them off. After one such count it appeared that there was one prisoner less than there should have been, so it was decided to have a recount. This of course was quite a lengthy process as it was no easy task to get several hundred gibbering Italians into some semblance of order. But eventually after about fifteen minutes the second count was completed and to everyone's surprise it now turned out that there were six more prisoners under our guard than there should have been! It turned out later that 'Ities' in ones and twos were sneaking in and joining the column, preferring certain captivity to the prospect of a very uncertain freedom, combined with a considerable chance of death.

At about five that evening we set off on our march to join the main forces. Not much care was taken in the formation we adopted or in the route we chose, as by this time it looked as though all opposition on the peninsula had been satisfactorily disposed of. Our route took us past the second battery and from then on we followed a series of hedgerows that ran along a valley until we struck a track. Just before we entered the valley the peace of the evening was abruptly shattered. All of a sudden a terrific AA barrage opened up, which made us stop in our tracks and crane our necks to search the skies. The sight we were privileged to see was certainly worth watching, and long remained a memory even after the whole campaign was satisfactorily concluded.

There they were, twelve silver specks flying at about 10,000 feet in tight formation. They looked like JU 88s and were obviously intent on giving our fleet a pasting. And then out of the clear sky there suddenly swooped down about half a dozen of our Spitfires, which immediately engaged the attacking bombers with a speed and fury discernible even to us in our position of ground spectators. Almost at once the enemy formation was scattered to the winds, and there remained for us to see and hear one after the other of them come whining down in a steady smoking curve, which ended in a puff of smoke on a hillside and a dull explosion. We must have seen five of them come down in this way, while all the while the powerful barrage dinned in our ears and the roar of high-powered aero engines circled overhead. And then suddenly all was quiet again – the barrage ceased, the aircraft were lost to view and peace reigned once more. The only sign of the battle still visible, was a number of small white dots which indicated the parachutes of certain of the enemy crews who had been able to bale out.

Shortly afterwards we came to a narrow path which we followed till it came out onto a wider track. All was peaceful once more. But we were suddenly reminded of the battle of the preceding night, bypassing the wreck of yet another glider, beside which lay the limp form of a khaki-clad soldier. It was the first dead man from our own side that many of us had seen, and once again our cheerful spirits were dampened.

Later we reached a large farm where a halt was called and we prepared to stay the night. Fires were lit, mess tins got out, sentries posted and guard rosters made out. Thankful to remove our heavy kit, we hastily ate some sort of rough and ready evening meal, and then went searching for a bed. A dry ditch and an armful of straw served admirably, and soon, rolled up in our blankets, we were fast asleep. But we could not sleep for long as the cold of that night which bit through the single thin blanket was sufficient to kill all sleep and so the early hours of the following morning found me stamping about trying to keep warm. All was quiet. It was a typical blue Mediterranean night out of which the stars shone brightly. Not a sound emerged from our column of by now over a thousand men, save for the cough of a sentry or the rustle of straw as a man tried to sleep more comfortably. What a day it had been, and here we were, sleeping by a roadside, just as though we were on one of those training schemes in Palestine. Not a sound of battle was to be heard even in the distance. It seemed incredible that only the previous night this island had been invaded by the largest force history had ever seen.

Lost in these thoughts I scrounged around for some more straw, and after I had buried myself deep into this, managed to sleep restlessly. I was wakened rudely by a terrific shindy which seemed to be taking place just overhead. The Jerry bombers were having another go at our fleet, in the hope that in the uncertain half-light before dawn they would have the advantage. The air was rent with the noise of the barrage and with the roar of diving aero-engines. We were all awake in an instant and lay in our ditch watching the show. The noise subsided as it grew lighter, and by the time the sun had risen, the enemy planes had made off, evidently considering that it would be too hot for them if they were caught by our dawn fighter patrols.

An hour was given us for breakfast and a quick wash, in the process of which we were kept busy pulling from our bodies a variety of living visitors which had chosen to feast on us during the night. I especially remember the irritating presence of a large type of sheep tick which had fastened its jaws into my shoulders and which was most difficult to remove.

We then proceeded on our way, and after about an hour's walk through shady orchards, we suddenly found ourselves overlooking the main road. Our delight was unbounded as we saw troop after troop of our tanks roaring by heading inland. The invasion must be going well for all this quantity of material to have been landed in so short a time, and to be advancing forward like this. Until then we had had absolutely no indication of how the invasion had been progressing in other sectors, and apart from the gliders these were the first of our own troops we had seen.

We crossed the road and settled in a field where we made ourselves comfortable and prepared to rest in the sun. The lads quickly explored a neighbouring farmhouse, which had apparently belonged to some rich Fascist, as it was now deserted and in the process of being looted by civilians and troops alike. By various means chickens and turkeys were caught and were quickly roasting on improvised spits built over open fires.

It was on the morning of 12 July, two days later, that we moved on again, and it came as quite a surprise to us to find that we were to return to the

Ulster Monarch, which would pick us up at Syracuse harbour. So we marched down to Syracuse on that peaceful July morning. The signs of battle that we passed seemed rather incongruous and difficult to fit in with the otherwise pleasant picture. The ditches were filled with discarded enemy ammunition, medical kit, helmets and weapons. Here and there a strange sweet, clinging and infinitely sickening smell proclaimed the presence of a corpse, already in the primary stages of decomposition. Here lay an Italian dispatch rider across his burnt-out machine – a horrible and nauseating sight with his clothes all burnt off and his skin roasted crisp like pork crackling.

We came to a large bridge which we learned had been the primary objective for the gliderborne troops. They were meant to have landed within a close distance from it, captured it and held it until our main forces caught up with them. The whole drama of that particular operation was evident to us, who had seen the shambles and chaos and the grim fate with which so many of these glider troops had met, for there within 100 yards of the bridge lay a single glider, the only one of that vast fleet to reach the objective. On a crest about 400 yards away we saw another, and that was all. Two crews out of the whole brigade had landed within easy reach of the objective. Whether they had marched on the bridge alone in their small strength and had surprised the defenders as much as we had taken by surprise the defenders of our own particular objective, we did not know. All we knew was that the bridge had been taken intact by our troops and that we were now crossing it, but of what deeds of heroism the bloody signs of battle which were to be seen by the roadside gave evidence, we never learned.

We had talked to the glider boys whom we had managed to relieve and learned from them that they had been extremely badly briefed – they had seen no photographs, and did not even know that the island was honeycombed with stone walls. They were loud and angry in their exclamations of disgust at the green American pilots, to whom they attributed the whole blame of their being dropped so far from the target. Apparently these pilots, who had never seen action before, had taken fright at the sight of the coastal flack and had cast loose their precious cargos there and then, rather than pass through the flack in such a vulnerable condition. Whether this accusation is true or not – and I suspect that like many such accusations it was only partly true – it was quite obvious to us that there had been an enormous and unnecessary wastage of life in this glider operation, and that this had largely been the result of inexperience and bad planning.

We entered Syracuse just before 10am and found the town almost deserted and in a sorry state. Already our military authorities had taken possession and were restoring order, but it was a grim and bleak sight to see the deserted streets and shattered buildings.

On reaching the harbour we were transferred onto a type of ferry craft, where we were fed and taken out to the *Monarch*, which lay some distance off the shore with the rest of the fleet.

With relief we tossed off our heavy equipment, sipped our tea, and puffed at our cigarettes. Were the events of the past few days merely a dream, to seem so remote and unconnected with us now? We might have thought so, had we not been constantly brought down to reality by the sight of a swollen khaki-clad body floating rapidly past us. Try as we might, we could not shake from our minds the glider fiasco and the terrible consequences of it.

Chapter Six

Augusta

We found the *Monarch* anchored about a mile off the shore, in the midst of a number of cargo ships, and protected by a cruiser, a monitor, and several destroyers. No sooner had we arrived on board than our attention was drawn to a red flag flying from the cruiser's mast, which announced that an air raid warning was in progress. This occurred on and off throughout the whole day although we suffered no interference from enemy aircraft. But it was obvious to us that the ship's personnel had been going through a grim and exhausting time since we last saw them, and had in all probability had to undergo a worse nervous tension than that which we had experienced. Many were not far short of being bomb-happy and all showed signs of suffering from lack of sleep caused by the persistent and worrying day and night attacks of small formations of enemy aircraft.

But the welcome which the navy boys gave us, their obvious pleasure at seeing us again, and their relief that we had had an easy time, was something we will all remember. They could not do enough for us. After we had fed and washed the majority of us fell onto our bunks and were ready to put in a period of solid and uninterrupted sleep, the first we had had since we left the ship for the initial invasion of Sicily.

But as things turned out, we were not to be allowed the rest which we needed, for round about tea time the rumour spread around generally, that we were going to be required to do another landing the same day!

The information was handed down to us in the usual way. Soon after tea Tony, Derrick and I were summoned down to Harry's cabin, and found him there looking as impassive as ever, seated on the bed with a pile of maps in his hand.

'*Take a map each of you, and find a seat somewhere,*' he said as we came in. '*As you have probably heard, they want us to do another landing this evening. I know how you all feel about it, but they consider it important and anyhow it does not seem to offer many difficulties. You see that town there,*' he asked, pointing to a funny shaped peninsula on the map, '*well, that is Augusta, an important naval port which we want to capture without delay. Well, apparently reliable reports have stated that a white flag has been observed flying above the citadel, which rather looks as though it has been evacuated. So the* Monarch *is going to sail straight into the harbour and land us in the town. We will then push through the town following 1 Troop, who will be behind 3 Troop. The object is to hold the town against any counter-attack, and if possible to push forward till we reach this road junction,* (Harry here pointed to a T-junction about a mile to the north of the town) *where we will wait till the main army reaches us. They are only 5 miles away, and should reach that point early tonight.'*

Well, that did not seem too bad, and it had every appearance of being nothing more than just a routine operation in which we would merely act as occupying troops to look after the port until our main forces reached it. If this was all there was to it, we certainly had nothing to worry about. But on the other hand, rumours of surrender had an uncomfortable tendency of being proved false, and it was not an enviable position to be in, to be the ones chosen to verify a rumour of this sort. All the more so, since we would be entering the harbour before it was even dark. We realized that there would certainly be no future in it, if there should be an active enemy battery in the vicinity.

However there was no time to give much thought to the matter, and in any case it would not have been much use, so we hurried off to brief our respective sections and to prepare our arms and equipment once more. This latter task did not take long as our equipment was lying just where we had thrown it all, and there was no need for anything to be done about it, in order to become completely operationally ready, than to fasten it on again.

It must have been an hour or so later when we were warned to make ready, and so putting on our equipment, we went up on deck to see what we could see. There, not more than a mile away lay the coast of Sicily, and ahead we could see the low grey blur of the narrow peninsula on which the town of Augusta stood. There was no sign of activity from the shore and all seemed quiet and peaceful. We were not alone: close behind us two destroyers were sweeping up towards us, followed by a larger vessel, which looked like a cruiser.

Shortly afterwards, Harry called us together again, and told us that the plan had been altered, and that instead of sailing into the harbour, we would embark in the LCAs which would take us ashore and land us half way down the peninsula on the northern side of the town; in other words, on the opposite side of the peninsula to the harbour. Embarkation would be carried out in two waves, our troop to go in with the second wave.

This was a welcome safety precaution to be adopted, and we were relieved to learn about it. Hardly had we had time to transmit the details of the change of plan to our sections, when we rounded a point and found ourselves crossing a wide bay, on the other side of which gleamed the white houses of the town of

Augusta. A silence, which always comes in early evening had descended on us, and as we steamed along towards that small tongue of land on which the town was situated, it really began to look as though the reports that the area was evacuated were going to prove true.

However, it seemed that our naval escort did not share this opinion, but had been advised to follow along and support us if and when necessary.

And so the little *Monarch* sailed into action ahead of the escorting war ships, which were more or less waiting on her orders to decide what her future action would be. Actually our last minute change in plan, which prevented us from entering the harbour, was very likely the direct result of the conversation our ship had with the cruiser.

But a few minutes later, we were very glad indeed at the presence of the cruiser and her attendant destroyers, for the peace of the evening was suddenly shattered by a loud report from shore. The tearing roar of a shell followed to burst in a vicious puff of black smoke in the air, just above the level of our masthead and about 80 yards off. It came as such a surprise to us that it took several seconds before we realized the implications of this unpleasant diversion, and then, with a numbing shock, we knew that the coast was defended, and that we would have to undertake the landing in daylight against what might be heavy opposition.

Luckily we did not have time to dwell long on this far from pleasant thought, for the first ranging airburst was followed by a few more, and then the enemy shelling began in earnest, and our whole time was occupied in watching the shell bursts and the shrapnel ripping into a frenzy the smooth surface of the water. One of the destroyers tore past us at full speed, heading straight for the shore then turning to deliver a murderously accurate broadside. Meanwhile the heavy guns of the cruiser were also in action, with such good effect that the enemy shellfire was quickly neutralized. After our ships had been firing for a few minutes, the answering fire from the shore had dwindled to no more than an occasional, and very erratic shot.

Even the little *Monarch*'s 12-pounder built onto her stern went into action with commendable accuracy; from our position above the aft well-deck, we were able to have an eye witness view of it all, almost deafened by the noise. The trouble from the shore seemed to be coming from a group of buildings situated on the top of the point which we had just rounded, and the *Monarch*'s gun was dealing with this spot most thoroughly. Anxiously we watched each puff of smoke creep nearer and nearer to the target. Now the shells were falling just short, now they were just out of sight in dead ground – and then suddenly as the smoke cleared away we noticed a gaping hole in the wall of one building, while another had practically disintegrated.

We had meanwhile come to a stop and the first wave of assault boats was speeding towards the shore. We watched them go with an intense feeling of relief as we saw them get nearer and nearer the shore without mishap. Soon they had discharged their loads and were racing back to pick us up. But while we waited for their return, we could hardly tear ourselves away from deck so anxious were we to observe the supporting fire given by our own ship and the escorting warships. The destroyers were systematically engaging any spot where they imagined trouble might be concealed and their frequent and accurate salvos were punctuated by the occasional roar of the heavy guns of the cruiser. Meanwhile the 20mm cannon shells of our Oerlikon guns were now pumping a stream of red tracer shells into the cliffside. I remember the 17-stone navigator of the ship coming out onto the deck, fairly dancing with excitement as he shouted encouragement to the gun crews. *'That's the way lads,'* he yelled, *'That's the sort of medicine they need more of: my house was bombed flat so don't mind what you do to those.'*

The navigator's enthusiasm was shared by all the other naval personnel aboard. This was the best thing they had come across in all their experience, and was a welcome change from the type of action to which they had become accustomed, where the enemy engaged were either out of sight over the horizon, or came diving down out of peaceful skies in sudden and vicious attack. Instead of getting the dangers without the compensating effect of the excitement, the ship's crew were now at last able to experience something of the excitement, without being subjected to any great danger.

'SRS second wave, stand by to embark, port side only,' the gruff voice of the loudspeaker announced, and we hastened below decks to take up our embarkation positions. There were the landing craft ready to receive us, their crews showing little signs of the considerable strain which they had just undergone.

In hardly any time at all we were in them, the embarkation operation being carried on in the shelter of the ship, which lay between us and the shore, and then with open throttles we were racing towards that narrow strip of land, and the very problematic future it contained for us.

Stacker, one of my riflemen, was lodged in the bows with a twin pair of 100-round magazine Vickers light machine guns, held at the ready to reply to any fire that might be directed at us from the area towards which we were heading. We got down as low as we could and soon distinguished the vicious whistle of small arms bullets flying overhead. But to our relief it was quickly evident that the machine guns firing at us were not on the shore where we were about to land, but were well over 1,000 yards away, for the bullets sounded almost spent as they reached us, and were far from accurate. It was established that the fire

Destroyer engaging hostile shore batteries before the Augusta landing, Sicily, 12 July 1943.

came from the other side of the bay, from the same area in fact, as that from which the enemy shell fire was thought to have come. So there seemed every possibility that there were no enemy immediately to our front, and this thought gave us some comfort.

Right down in the bottom of the boat, we hardly knew how far we still had to go, when our jangled nerves were again suddenly tensed by a long burst from Stalker's guns. It was soon obvious that he was firing at nothing in particular but was just spraying the waterfront to discourage anyone with hostile intent from looking out.

The next moment there was a bump, the doors flew open and we leapt out into about 2ft of water. Bullets were ripping up the ground around us and someone from the previous wave was yelling at us to get into single file and get out of the beach area which was under fire from the enemy machine guns across the bay. Bent low we doubled through a small gap and eventually found ourselves in a narrow street. So far there were no casualties in my section, but we soon learned that there had been at least three casualties in the first wave, two probably fatal. The two who were killed, by some strange trick of fate, turned out to be medical orderlies.

We soon found ourselves in a small back street which, after a short while, came out into a wider thoroughfare. We split up into two, each sub-section in single file on either side of the road and staggered, so that they would be in

Augusta 101

the best position to see any suspicious movement from the opposite side of the street to that in which they were. In this formation we proceeded slowly up the street.

It was a tense business. In the eerie half light we jumped at every shadow, expecting some sort of opposition from every corner, from every doorway. But a ghostly silence pervaded the whole scene. It was soon obvious that the town was completely deserted – not even a stray cat was to be seen, let alone a human being. It was a town without inhabitants and as such, exercised an indescribably spooky effect. A burst of LMG fire in the distance sent us diving into doorways like startled rabbits surprised on a summer evening, and then with faces pale with the tension we would emerge, and continue our slow journey towards the northern outskirts of the town. Many were the scares, many were the rumours of snipers at work on their insidious task, but it is fairly obvious to us now, that there was not a soul in the town besides ourselves.

After proceeding for about ten minutes in this fashion, we came to a corner where a main street branched off at a right angle to the left. In front was a sort of public garden where in better days the more fashionable elements of the community would doubtless have sported themselves on Sunday afternoons. Harry and troop HQ were established on this corner, and I could see Derrick's section spread out under some trees nearby. They had come along level with us by some parallel road.

When my section came up, Harry was on the point of going forward to contact Paddy and get a more accurate picture of what was happening. He told me to take my section round the gardens ahead to see if they concealed anything of interest, and after that we were to join Derrick's section and wait there for further orders.

So, spread out in extended order, we advanced cautiously into those deserted gardens, as the first stars began to appear overhead and the silence of the evening filled us with foreboding, through its very intensity.

A string of red tracer ripping by within inches of me made me leap into the air and then dive for some sort of cover behind a raised flowerbed. Before I had managed to get down I distinctly remember seeing the tracer bullets on either side of me – how they could have missed was an absolute miracle. The rest of my section needed no order to get under cover and when I looked round they had virtually disappeared – a pale face would peep out from behind a bush or a rifle would be seen swaying from behind a bench, and that was all. The fire seemed to be coming from somewhere on the beach behind us, and in the heat of the moment I directed a short burst in the direction from where the shots seemed to have come. But then I suddenly had my doubts – the tracer was red, and I was by this time sufficiently experienced to know that Jerry tracer was usually green. Could it be our own troops who were firing at us? I tried to remember where I had last seen Tony's section, but they had completely disappeared.

But my doubts were sufficiently strong to cause me to stop the return fire of my section and get the password shouted back. Sergeant Major Lilley who was about 50 yards behind us took up the shout, and soon to our intense relief he shouted back that the fire was coming from Tony's section. Apparently Tony had landed shortly after us and had seen these troops walking through the gardens some distance away, and mistaken them for enemy troops.

We cleared the gardens without further event and then went to join Derrick's section, which had conveniently taken up their position round a large air raid shelter. For a long while we waited in silence, while the depressing twilight deepened, and the stars shone brighter overhead. A single plane droned in the sky and now and then a solitary shell whined over, to burst in the distance. We did not know to which side it belonged, but as it landed each time a good distance away from us, we imagined that it was fired by our supporting warships. Now and then the silence of the night was interrupted by a furious burst of machine-gun fire or the crump of mortar bombs. Occasionally we saw a stream of green tracer bullets come whipping down the main road up which No.3 Troop had advanced and go soaring up into the air as they ricocheted from the house tops. Over to our left, a dull red glow proclaimed that a house was on fire – everywhere the atmosphere was sultry, oppressive and filled with suspense. What was happening out in front? If we only knew what was happening we could resist this strange dull clawing sensation in our stomachs, this reluctance to move from where we were and these fears that the sounds and indistinct shadows of the night caused us. We would rather be up forward in the thick of things where at least we would have some idea of what was happening, than to remain back here in this awful uncertainty and doubt. These were the thoughts of each of us as we lay huddled round that air raid shelter, extremely unhappy at having to play the role of reserve troop. We could hear the sounds of battle, and each time a burst shuddered through the silence, a chill shiver gripped us as we wondered what would happen next.

For we had no doubt somehow that things were not going well. Harry had told us to wait saying that he would be back in a few minutes, but he had now been gone over half an hour, ostensibly to get orders from Paddy, and had not yet returned. Tony decided to go and look for him and he too had been gone for at least half an hour. And still we waited not knowing what had happened either to Harry, Tony or Paddy.

A section formed up and silently disappeared into the blackness of the night. Who was that? It turned out to be a section of No.1 Troop which had been lying near us and which had received orders to move up. At last something was happening, not long now, and we would be able to move from this depressing place.

But still we waited with no further news. A figure came up to us out of the blackness, and to our surprise we recognized him to be one of No.3 Troop's officers. He would know all about what was happening. Quickly we pumped him for information, but when he had finished his story we felt no happier. No.3 Troop had apparently advanced up the road leading northwards out of the town, towards the crossroads which were our primary objective. But as they reached a certain bridge they ran into heavy mortar and LMG fire, and it was feared that there had been a lot of casualties. The enemy had tanks and artillery so we were told, and we could expect a counter-attack at any moment. The officer himself was now going to the beach to try and arrange for a boat to evacuate the wounded.

Still we waited but this time we were decidedly ill at ease, and we began to wonder at every shot, whether Germans or Italians would suddenly appear from behind the trees. Every shadow became suspicious, every sound a torment.

At last well after midnight, a figure came out of the darkness and announced itself to be Harry's batman. Derrick and I were to go up to Harry at the burning house, taking our maps with us. Now for it. Quickly we did up our equipment and made off towards the red glow. There were Paddy and Harry all right and their rock-like coolness had the immediate effect of calming my fears and doubts. I cannot remember any occasion when I went up to Paddy or Harry to receive orders from them in action, that I was not immediately set at ease by the calm of their manner, so that my confidence was immediately restored.

So it was on this occasion. Harry welcomed us as though everything were quite normal. He told us that we would be going forward to get into a position from which we could give No.3 Troop immediate aid, should they require it. *'Keep right to the edge of the road,'* he warned us, *'as they are sending occasional machine-gun bursts down it, and when you get to a small stone bridge crossing the road, wait there for further orders.'*

We collected our sections and carried out Harry's orders. We reached the bridge concerned without incident, even though our hearts were in our mouths all the time; but no sooner had we got there than we were ordered to return.

Once safely off the road Harry told us briefly that the enemy were holding the crossroads in some strength and that without heavy support it was hopeless our trying to attack them in the confusion of the night. So Paddy had decided not to move forward any more but to fall back around the outskirts of the town, taking up strong defensive positions against the event of a possible enemy counter-attack, which might be aimed at recapturing the town. No.3 Troop was up in front on the left, and No.1 Troop on the right, while we would form a secondary line, through which they could fall back if necessary. Derrick was given the left sector, I the centre, and Tony the right.

We went forward to reconnoitre our respective sectors and site our sub-sections. I found my task in this respect to be far from easy, as over the whole sector spread an enormous building known as the citadel, which with its courts and cloisters, its turrets and thick archways, resembled a cross between a fortress and a monastery. So, all I could do was to place my sub-section in such vantage points where they had at least 20 yards clear field of fire in front of them, and there we made ourselves as comfortable as possible, and sat down to wait.

It must have been between 1 and 2am by the time all the sub-sections were in position, and from then until dawn, I could do nothing, but visit my section posts periodically and see how they were faring. In the intervals, Corporal Mitchell and I chatted about everything we could think of to prevent ourselves

Augusta – street desolation, 12 July 1943.

A rest during enemy shelling, 12 July 1943.

from falling asleep. All activity had died down and the customary silence of night again reigned unchallenged.

About 4am we sat up with a jerk and strained our ears into the distance. What was that we had heard? Again we caught the faint sound – tracked vehicles moving along the road. The noise came in waves, sometimes loud and sometimes almost inaudible according to the vagaries of the wind. Yes, it was tracked vehicles moving all right, and what was more, we could distinguish the sound of wheeled transport also. Was this the expected counter-attack? At first we half thought that it might be, and then we considered the possibility that the enemy could be pulling out, warned of the approach of our main forces. For all we knew the transport we were hearing might quite well belong to our own troops. We listened intently, but the noises seemed to come no nearer, and soon all was silence once more.

It was just getting light, when Harry came up and told us that a patrol from the brigade with whom we were hoping to make contact had reached our forward posts, with the news that their brigade had occupied without opposition the crossroads which we had hoped to reach. Evidently the enemy had pulled out at some period during the night. The night had been a tense one for us all, and an experience we were not anxious to repeat, but it cheered us immensely when some time later we read in an English paper the translation of a cutting from a German account of that night. The main gist of what they said was that the night had '*been full of horrors and suspense for them, and it was a night they would always remember, among their most uncomfortable experiences.*'

At Harry's welcome news, we realized we could relax and set about exploring the Citadel. The place was bare and deserted, even though it had obviously been previously used for an Italian Naval officers' quarters. At any rate, beyond the interest of looking round the building, there was nothing there of military or any other kind of value.

As we were in the process of exploring this fortress, a terrific explosion seemingly from right beside us, sent us racing back to our positions and grovelling into the earth for shelter. As the explosion died away we could hear the roar of a shell, and a heavy shell at that. So now they were starting to shell us. From where we were, we could see no indication of where the shells were landing, and after the shelling had gone on for a good five minutes, we were forced to conclude, that although they sounded as though they were landing almost on top of us, in reality they must be falling some distance away and that the noise was merely being magnified by some acoustic trick of the surrounding buildings. But hardly had this thought entered our heads, than we were quickly forced to come to quite a different conclusion, for along with the explosion of the very next shell, came a shower of shrapnel and broken masonry, which came raining down all around us. Our assumed calm vanished in an instant, and we began to feel really uncomfortable.

I heard a shout behind me, and looked round to see Derrick shepherding his section back towards the centre of the town, with the behaviour of a flustered hen towards her chickens. I managed to obtain from him the news that the squadron were pulling back towards the town centre, their job having been finished, and also that the shells were falling all around his position. As he spoke another one came over, and this time I clearly saw the cloud of dust it kicked up, barely 50 yards away. With alacrity I got my section together and we made off towards the centre of the town.

There were the rest, Harry and Tony, and also the other troops. Yes, the army had made contact with us, and Jerry had pulled out. The shelling was thought to come from a gun situated in a sort of fortress built near the seaplane base in the middle of the harbour, but otherwise the strain and discomfort of the preceding night were over for us. No.3 Troop had not suffered as badly as we had been led to believe, the night before. Their sections had been scattered by accurate mortar and machine-gun fire, so that it had largely become a question of every man for himself as regards getting back to our lines. They had become separated from us by a canal or small river, the only bridge across which was so effectively covered by the enemy, that it would have been suicidal to attempt returning by that route. So, many of them had had to swim for it, and even now there were about three or four men who were still missing. (All these however turned up in the course of the morning) one or two had been wounded but not seriously and there were no further fatal casualties.

Since the main army had taken over from our positions there was nothing left for us to do, save to remain where we were until such time as we were evacuated back to the *Monarch*. The town was deserted and gradually the men started wandering off in groups to explore the area and see what they could find. There was not a scrap of food in the place, but of liquor there was plenty and soon everyone was feeling pretty merry. Someone found a piano somewhere and brought it out onto the street corner, solemnly playing it and wearing a top hat. The Fascist headquarters was found, stuffed with propaganda leaflets, but otherwise containing nothing of interest; somehow or other the safe in the bank blew up, but no one except those who were near at the time had any idea as to the nature of its contents, and even those who did would not tell!

And so we spent the rest of that day, until 4pm, wandering round the town, entering any building we chose, and depleting the town's alcoholic stocks. Casey tells the story of how he even found an army padre in one house who mildly rebuked him as he advanced towards the door with evil intent, with the words, *'What, looting?'* Undaunted by this, or so Casey's highly problematical story continues, Casey and his pal slunk round to the back door, and on forcing it open found the padre had already entered through the front and was busy rummaging through a cupboard. As he saw Casey enter, he snatched up a prayer book exclaiming, *'I was looking to see if I could find some prayer books for the boys!'*

But soon we tired of this merriment and wandered slowly back to the gardens, where, worn out by the effects of alcohol and the strain of the preceding night, the majority of us stretched out in the sun and fell asleep.

The rumour that a naval provost party was entering the town, stirred us quickly and a rapid attempt was made to cover over all visible signs that houses had been broken into. This was not so easy to do as pianos and furniture were lying in the streets and considerable mess lay all around. However we got some sort of order into the area immediately surrounding where we were, and about 4pm we learned that two destroyers were waiting in the harbour to pick us up. So our column was formed up without delay and we marched off by troops to the waiting ships.

What a procession we made – many of the more unscrupulous characters were pushing prams loaded with the junk that they had found lying around, and practically all had their equipment considerably swollen by the extra weight they were carrying. Still, they paid for it, as it was a long march down to the harbour and the sun was extremely hot, so that they were jettisoning their loads in ever increasing amounts as we covered the distance.

The destroyer on which I found myself was manned by the Greek navy, and the crew gave us a terrific welcome. Apparently they were of the opinion that we had done a wonderful job, and of course we were not the ones to tell them to the contrary.

Each man was given a hot meal and the officers were taken down to the mess where they were showered with food and cigarettes. After our meal we went up again on deck, and found conditions reigning there which must have been similar to Petticoat Lane at the height of its activity. In every corner could be seen little groups of sailors clustered around one or more of our lads, bargaining frantically for every bit of junk they had taken out of the town. The prices offered were quite fantastic, and by the time we had reached the *Monarch* about an hour later, well over three-quarters of the ill-gotten gains had changed hands, and our troops left that destroyer considerably richer in money terms than when they had come on. The most downright junk fetched sky-high prices with these souvenir-crazy Greeks, and their demand was by no means saturated by the time we left.

We found the *Monarch* in Syracuse harbour, and received as effusive a welcome as ever from our friends on board. We at once sat down to another enormous meal, while anecdotes about the past days' activity were exchanged and everyone felt greatly relieved that we were back in the comparative security of the ship once more.

But we were soon to learn that we would have been much safer on the shore than we were on that ship, for after deciding to go to bed early and enjoy a really good stretch of sleep, we were awakened by the most terrific din we had ever heard. The enemy night bombers were at it again, and from the noise that was going on it seemed that they were having a pretty determined go at us. I lay in my bunk staring at the ceiling and listening to the shattering roar of the heavy guns, and the shuddering explosions of the bombs which were landing near us. The Oerlikons situated just over my cabin then went into action and each round that they fired shivered right through the thin ceiling, so that I felt myself being shaken up and down.

I felt very frightened indeed but was too tired to get up and see what was going on. I just lay sweating in my bunk with the blanket over my head, hoping and praying that we would be spared.

The men celebrating the end of the Augusta Operation, July 1943.

At last, I should imagine just as dawn began to lighten the scene, the noise became more intermittent and then died down altogether, and I was able to turn over and put in a few hours' sleep before breakfast. Signs of strain were pretty evident on most people's faces at breakfast, especially of those who had had to remain on the ship all the time that we were ashore. For apparently the activity of the previous night was nothing unusual, and it had become a regular procedure to expect aerial attacks as soon as it got dark. The sensation of being cramped onto a floating target for bombs was by no means pleasant, and we did not look forward to the following night.

But while it was daylight we were relatively untroubled by enemy attention, and it was decided to take us over that day to Murro Di Porco and let us wander over the peninsula and have a look at all the familiar landmarks under more normal conditions.

It seemed strange to walk quietly beneath that blazing sun over an area where only a few days before, we had been tensed with excitement, and in which we had been suspicious of every building and every patch of cover. It seemed a different place now that we were able to walk where we wanted, unhindered and unafraid. Rather to our surprise we found that the place was nothing more than an attractive little part of the Sicilian countryside. Already the invasion seemed to have been forgotten. Here a peasant was working in his fields – here some ragged little children came crowding around us, with the soon familiar cry of *'Biscotti, biscotti!'* How different it all was from the time when its natural rustic charm was clouded over with the sense of danger and foreboding, which we had all experienced to some degree.

On our return to the *Monarch* we learned that another 'spot' operation had been planned for us, on which we were made ready to go at a moment's notice. Only two nights after we had come back to the ship after the completion of the Augusta operation, we found ourselves briefed to take part in a large-scale raid on Catania. The units were to be landed to the north of the town and would then sweep down into Catania to seize certain vantage points and hold them until the main army caught up with us.

Catania was a town larger than any which had hitherto been captured, and in addition was still a considerable distance away from our leading troops. The risks attached to this coming operation seemed even greater than those which we had had to take previously, and even before we knew the full facts of the situation, grave doubts milled through our minds, to the effect that an unusually tough proposition lay ahead of us from which we would be fortunate if we were allowed to return safely.

Our relief was thus considerable when at the last minute the operation was cancelled. We learned later that information had been received at XIII Corps HQ to the effect that there were far more enemy forces around Catania than had at first been estimated, so that it was concluded that the risks of carrying through with the plan were out of all proportion to the chances of a successful outcome.

Fortunate for us indeed was this change of plan, for Catania was the scene of the strongest German resistance in Sicily, and the town was not captured by our main forces until nearly a month later, and only then after some very heavy fighting. And this fact rather indicates that had we been landed there, as planned, we would in all probability have been in the unenviable position of providing the public at home with the sort of preview of what was to happen at Arnhem a year or so later!

Air raids continued that night and once again we were kept awake wondering when we would be hit. But the attacks of the following night were much more severe and it really was a miracle that we managed to come through unharmed. Quite a number of aircraft must have been used that night for from dusk until 4am, there was hardly a respite – the guns were jamming because their barrels had become red-hot, and the weary gunners were kept hard at it the whole night.

The noise of course was terrific and only served to add to our fears. Outside on deck it was as clear as day, and the fireworks that were going up were impressive enough to excite our admiration, in spite of the prevailing conditions. Tracer shells slowly and gracefully seemed to float upwards into the air, while the smaller traces from the 20mm cannon surrounded them with thousands of fairy lights. Now and then a cruiser, moored just near us, let loose a salvo from her heavy AA guns, the flash of which lit up the sky and made us jump to our feet wondering whether we had been hit.

And all the time the bombs came whistling down; a piece of shrapnel punctured our balloon and it came floating down over the deck. Until well after midnight we stood on deck, gazing into the sky, in the hope of seeing an enemy plane get shot down and loath to go to bed and thereby put ourselves in a vulnerable position should we get hit. Eventually though I went down to bed, and soon managed to sleep through the noises of the night, so accustomed to them was I becoming.

At breakfast the next morning, I heard that a bomb had fallen just short of our stern, and had set the whole ship rocking. A Belgium steamer about the same tonnage as the *Monarch*, and adapted to the same purpose, had had a very near miss, which had caused over seventy casualties among the commandos aboard. That certainly was not funny and we all felt that it was only through a whim of Fate that those seventy-odd casualties had not been inflicted on our squadron.

The news of this loss must have set the authorities thinking for that same day we received orders to the effect that we would be put ashore during the time of the raids as it would be safer for us there, and there was no reason to expose us needlessly.

So we packed up our kit as we headed back to Augusta where we were going to be landed. We arrived there and the LCAs ferried us across and dumped our kit on the landing stage. We did not bother to take all our kit ashore with us, as we thought it would only be a matter of a week or so before we would be back on the *Monarch* once more, but it turned out that that was the last we saw of her. She sailed that same morning. We heard snatches of news about her from time to time and bumped into many of her crew when we got back to England but it was to our permanent regret that we were not given the opportunity of taking a proper farewell of our many friends on this brave little ship, and of wishing them bon voyage.

She carried a very gallant and big-hearted complement of men whom we were proud to know. She ran into trouble many times after we had left her – some of her stern was removed by a bomb off Bizerta – but she was repaired from this damage in time to take part in the D-Day invasion of the continent. This ship certainly had a record of which the navy could be well proud.

Chapter Seven

Raids, Rumours, and Rest

The 'camp' which had been chosen for us was an open grassy stretch of ground about a mile north of the town, and indeed not far from the crossroads which we had attempted to attack a few nights previously. We were really quite thankful to be on solid ground again and no longer a vulnerable target to enemy air attacks. But we were annoyed at the muddle which took place over the off-loading of our heavy kit. The small amount of it which was dumped on the quay steps had been looted fairly thoroughly, while the rest was taken away in the *Monarch*, and it was not until we were in North Africa, about five months later, that we finally retrieved it.

Having established ourselves in troop areas in our field, we were free to wander where we chose, and could take a dip in the sea which lay about half a mile to the east of us. But the swimming was not good, and most of us went over to examine the stronghold on the crossroads which had given us such an uncomfortable time the night we entered Augusta. The town, by the way, was out of bounds, by order of the provost authorities who were apparently worried by the disgraceful amount of looting that had taken place there before they had arrived.

I was glad after examining the place that we had not had to attack that crossroads on the night in question, for there was every sign that it had been most strongly held. A medium field gun was still there, trained straight down the road up which we would have had to come! Under every tree, and at every point of vantage were slit trenches, and traces of machine-gun positions, while the ground was so open in all directions that it would have been difficult to have got anywhere near the place.

If we had thought that we would avoid the greater part of the unpleasantness of the nightly air raids by leaving the ship and camping on land, we were at once disillusioned by that first night ashore.

When the enemy raiders came over, with their customary punctuality, there was nothing to give us the impression that we were the best part of a mile from the target area, and we seemed to be in just as unpleasant a position as when we were aboard the *Monarch*. When it is a question of being blown to bits, one is not particular about whether one stands the risk of being buried or drowned,

Peter Davis and Ronnie Lunt, Augusta, July 1943.

as it all comes to the same thing in the end! Each flare that the attacking planes dropped seemed to be immediately overhead, and to throw out in startling relief the brilliant whiteness of our mosquito nets against the sombre background of the trees. Every bomb that we heard whistling down, could for all we knew, be coming straight down towards us. But it was the shrapnel that caused us by far the greatest worry, for this came raining down all around us, and practically each minute, we dived against the ground as we heard the vicious hiss of a red-hot piece of steel racing downwards. Many were the pieces which were found and collected the following morning within inches of where people were sleeping; the noise throughout was of course almost the worst thing about it and it was impossible to sleep while it was going on.

After a few nights of these conditions people were already showing signs of lack of sleep and varying degrees of nervous strain. This was especially obvious among those who had spent the whole time on the ship while we were ashore on Murro di Porco and Augusta, and surprisingly enough the signs of strain were most marked with the old operatives among the regiment. NCOs would shout at people to keep their cigarettes down while the raid was in progress notwithstanding the fact that the sky was filled with searchlight beams, shell bursts, gun flashes and flares, which were quite sufficient to dwarf the effect of any cigarette! We were camped on a stubble field and sleeping in the open.

With the shrapnel whistling down, we all felt vulnerable and unprotected as we lay in our beds under the stars, and one night this sensation must have become too much for a certain officer, for suddenly jumping up he wrapped a blanket around himself and made for the nearest ditch, which was about 50 yards away. But he was bare-footed and as the surface of the ground was made up of sharp corn stubble, it was soon obvious that his progress was far from easy. This retreat afforded us in consequence the amusing spectacle of an officer with hardly any clothing but a blanket, moving across the field in a series of small jumps, looking more like a young kangaroo than anything else.

Many other people must have been thinking like this officer for a day or so afterwards we moved off again. As our regiment was under the immediate orders of General Dempsey, commander of XIII Corps, it did not matter where our base camp was situated, so long as it was within a certain distance from XIII Corps Headquarters, so that the general would be able to get in touch quickly, should he require us.

Our next move was about 3 miles north of our first camp. It was a pleasant enough spot – shady olive groves, within a short distance from the sea. Troop areas were allocated and we set about choosing the particular tree which was to be our home for the next few days. My lads had procured for me an Italian naval hammock which came in very useful, as all that was necessary was to sling it between two branches and I had my bed all ready for me.

At our new camp we led a wonderfully idle life, doing a minimum amount of work and spending most of our time either sleeping or swimming. The swimming in that spot was excellent – a steep path down the cliffs took us to a narrow outcrop of low rock from which there was a straight low dive into the warm blue waters of the Mediterranean. And so despite the inactivity of the life, we were all able to keep fit and take a good deal of exercise.

To occupy the men's time and prevent them from becoming bored and discontented we adopted the idea of going out for short section marches each morning. Sections would move off independently and without formality and wander around exploring the countryside and examining positions that had previously been enemy strongholds. At some point in the morning we would stop and have a swim and then after a rest would return back to the camp in time for lunch. It was all very leisurely, informal and enjoyable. If we had thought that by moving further out of Augusta we would escape the effects of the regular nightly air-raids on the shipping in the harbour, we were once again to be disappointed, for it seemed that in our new position the shrapnel was falling around us just as thickly as before, while the noises of the barrage and of the raids seemed to have diminished to no noticeable extent. Still the flares lit up our camp with terrifying brilliance, and still the vicious whistle of the falling shrapnel kept us lying flat on the ground in an agony of suspense.

But fortunately despite many scares we suffered no casualties and gradually grew accustomed to the nightly din, and to regard it with a certain fatalistic attitude. We often had quite an eye-witness view of the raids and it was encouraging to see how, almost nightly, the barrage thrown up by the defences seemed to grow more and more formidable. Of remarkable efficiency were the searchlights which now surrounded the whole harbour. Apparently they were radar controlled for they would suddenly switch on when there was a plane caught in their beams! It must have given those pilots a fright to find themselves suddenly lit up in this way, and then, immediately afterwards to see literally tons of flaming metal being pumped up at them.

One night Jerry tried on a neighbouring airfield a trick which we had not seen before. All of a sudden the sky was lit up over a whole area. Not just one single ball flare came slowly drifting down, but a shower of golden sparks rained down over a wide area for several minutes, lighting up the whole countryside for miles around. Amazed, we watched this free show wondering what would follow it but we were too far away to see the sequel. It was not until the next day that we learned that about twenty of our fighters had been destroyed on the ground by this weapon.

How well I remember Harry Poat during those raids. He seemed completely unshakeable for he put us to shame on more than one occasion. Often as we were standing together talking and watching the fireworks, a sudden vicious whistle would send us all flat on our faces. All, that is to say except for Harry, who remained standing there and carrying on the conversation just as though nothing had happened! As we slowly picked ourselves up and resumed a more normal position, we hardly dared look Harry in the face!

No.3 Troop got themselves into trouble soon after our arrival at this camp. After the freedom everyone had had in Augusta several members of the regiment became sort of 'loot crazy' and, unless strong disciplinary measures were taken, were apt to wander off taking anything they fancied. This was of course not good enough, and Paddy passed a whole series of anti-loot legislation. Some ass in No.3 Troop chose to ignore these orders and when Paddy found out about it he was on the warpath without delay. Probably he had been on a booze-up the night before for he dealt with the matter in a manner ruthless enough to suggest this. The whole of the troop were paraded with all their kit: Paddy then went down the line, and emptied out the kit bag of each man, throwing onto a fire, regardless of its intrinsic value, any article which had not been in the man's possession before he left the Middle East. It certainly stopped the looting all right, but it also caused a certain amount of bitterness among the members of No.3 Troop for some time afterwards. However, bitterness could not last long in a regiment such as ours and soon the incident was forgotten.

In the course of our morning section walks, we were able to find out what had happened to many of the inhabitants of Augusta, which had been deserted when we first entered. Scores of people had taken to the caves with which the rocky countryside abounded, and wherever we went we were always bumping into small parties of wretched-looking civilians, who were living in this way. They were extremely dirty and obviously accustomed to a very low standard of life, for the women suckled their children unabashed before us, or else got busy de-lousing each other. One was reminded far more of monkeys in the zoo, than of human beings belonging to a civilized European country.

Even those who had still remained in their little peasant cottages were hardly living at a higher standard. From the smell which met us as we passed these hovels, it was apparent that there could have been absolutely nothing in the way of sanitary arrangements installed within. But as though this in itself were not quite enough, the occupants were so lazy and unimaginative, that they had obviously made no attempt to improvise, with the result that outside each back door one was met by the revolting sight of human droppings lying scattered all around, attracting all the flies in the whole area! And when we visited camps formerly occupied by the enemy we found all the furniture to be infested with bed bugs and the floor black with fleas.

Apart from the air-raids there were two unpleasant discomforts which we had to put up with at our camp. The first of these was the mosquitoes, which, if we had not taken the necessary precautions, would have just about eaten us alive. Heaven knows where their main breeding ground was, but at any rate, none of the local inhabitants were to the slightest extent anti-malaria minded, for in every water tub, in every bucket and even in sundry salt water pools on the beach, we saw traces of those wriggling little lava which would soon develop into annoying, disease carrying insects. Malaria, as a result, was widespread in the district and Paddy very sensibly was most particular from the first to enforce all the anti-malaria precautions as laid down by the military authorities. One hour before sunset every man had to change into slacks and roll his sleeves down while some sort of sticky yellow paste was rubbed into the skin of any parts of the body which were then left exposed. Section officers had to inspect their sections each evening to see that this was done. In addition we were dosed with Mepacrine tablets twice a week, and it was compulsory that we should sleep under mosquito nets. These precautions were certainly effective, even if they were considerably annoying, for we did not have more than three malaria cases the whole time we were on the island, while other units lost a large proportion of their strength through this cause.

The other curse was, of course, the flies, and it was these which, far more than even the air-raids, drove us out of one camp after another. Once we realized how rapidly and in what numbers they collected, stringent measures were adopted to ensure that our sanitary arrangements were as perfect as they could be and the latrines and the cookhouse were inspected daily by Phil Gunn the MO. But despite all our efforts, and despite a vigorous anti-fly campaign launched by Phil, in which every man was urged to make, carry about with him and use, a fly swat, we were unable to keep the menace down, and it was found that we could only spend a limited period in each camp, before being driven off by the ever increasing number of flies to find a new one. Naturally little else could be expected with the prevailing filthiness and unsanitariness of the civilians who were living around there, but the curse of it all was that this plague of flies, brought with it a troublesome sort of dysentery which put us out of action for stretches of several days. In spite of all our precautions, this state of affairs continued, and so the only thing for it was to move our camp, and keep on moving at least once a fortnight.

The officer sent out to our new area as advance party met us as we marched in, with a most pathetically gloomy look on his face. *'What's the matter?'* we asked, *'what is the new camp like?'* He looked us up and down pityingly for a moment or two and then replied: *'You poor fools! You think you are getting away from the air-raids by moving further out of Augusta don't you? But take it from me, it is far worse here. Last night was dreadful. Just take a look at this!'* Whereupon, he held up a large and jagged piece of metal which must have landed near his pitch during the previous night. *'Oh, and by the way,'* he called after us, as we proceeded to our area, *'if you look down by that gap in the wall, you will see an unexploded shell which arrived to cheer us up last night.'* This news was disconcerting and we wondered if we would ever get a decent night's sleep on the island.

We were soon rudely reminded of our gloomy words of welcome about getting no more peace in this camp than in the last, for we had just finished lunch, and I was settling into my hammock for a short nap, when the roar of diving aero-engines immediately followed by the explosion of a bomb, gave me such a fright that I nearly fell out of my tree. Ronnie Lunt, the padre, was clutching his arm looking rather pale, and produced quite a nice bruise where a thrown-up stone had hit it. Apparently one of those cursed enemy fighter bombers had sighted our water cart filling up the cook's water containers and had loosed a small bomb at it. No harm was done as the bomb landed in the middle of the wadi about 200 yards from the camp, serving merely to scare the wits out of the civilians who were living in the nearby caves.

One day we found an enormous ammunition dump, abandoned by the enemy, and persuaded the RE sentries to let us take some of the explosive back with us for the purpose of fishing, although of course we did not tell them that this was the reason we wanted the stuff. We had managed to find several boats at our last camp and so our time was kept fully occupied cruising around in these, swimming, and chucking explosive charges into the water in the hope of bringing some decent sized fish to the surface. In this last activity we met with some success and on several occasions were able to supplement our dry army rations with the fruits of our labours.

During all this time our army was held up just in front of Catania, and while this condition lasted we knew that it was unlikely that we should be required for a further operation. But one night we noticed that the sky to the north of us was lit up by the flashes of the guns. We walked to the top of a small rise and watched this terrific bombardment and nothing was necessary beyond this sight to tell us that Monty was attacking Catania.

Sure enough, a few days later we heard that Catania had fallen and that the army was now racing down towards Messina – the invasion of Sicily was almost a thing of the past. At the same time the rumour spread that we were going on another job. The first we heard about this was that our squadron was ordered one afternoon to march to the docks and board two LCIs which we would find there. These Landing Craft (Infantry), or LCIs as they were called, were something quite new to us then. At a guess I suppose they must have weighed about 200 to 300 tons, and they could hold about 250 troops in their four holds. They were well-built mass-produced little ships with a cruising speed of about 10 knots: for protection they had two 20mm Oerlikons, and their normal crew was about ten men. Each ship had only two officers, both lieutenants, one the skipper and the other the number one.

Naturally, on account of their larger size these craft did not have quite such a shallow draft as the much smaller LCAs, but even so, it was quite remarkable that they only required 2ft 6ins of water in front and a depth of 4ft 6ins at the back. The landing operation was effected by means of two long ramps which were pushed forward to a distance of about 25ft in front of the ship's bows, and which were then dropped onto the shore – at least that was the idea, though if the beach was of a shallow gradient they would drop into about 2ft of water.

About 5pm we set off to march back to our camp, feeling pretty depressed at having such a long march ahead of us in the heat of the afternoon. Just as we were leaving the northern outskirts of the town of Augusta there was a sudden roar of engines, a whistle and an explosion about 50 yards to our left, and three enemy fighter bombers streaked over our heads at a height of scarcely 500ft. As they disappeared from view one of them let loose another small bomb, which we saw land about 200 yards to our right – and then the planes were gone out to sea, just as fast as they could go.

In the silence that ensued we all felt rather sheepish. The whole thing had happened so quickly, that Harry had not even had the time to yell at us to take cover, while none of us officers desired to be the first to break ranks and dive into the enticing shadows of a nearby ditch. Much the same feeling must have gone through the minds of the men, for in the absence of any word of command not one of them broke ranks.

The net result of it all was that we kept on marching just as though nothing had happened, and so quick had the whole event been, that we had not even lost step!

The next day, 6 August was my birthday, and to celebrate it we learnt that the job was definitely 'on', with the result that the whole day was spent in the by now well-known routine of briefing, issuing equipment and ammunition and preparing weapons. We were to land on the coast about 9 miles south of Messina and the same distance north of our forward troops, to blow a tunnel through which the main coastal road ran, and thereby to cut off one of the main lines of the enemy's retreat out of Sicily. Only our troop was to take part in the operation and we were to provide the necessary protection for the engineers as they carried out their demolitions. It was hoped that both the tunnel and a large chunk of the cliff would be brought down, and as the coastal railway ran parallel to the road at that point, only slightly lower down the cliff-side, it was our intention to block the railway as well.

The plan of the operation was a very simply one – too simple it seemed to us! One section would protect the left flank, another the right, and another would keep the beachhead open. We were to avoid fighting as far as we could. But as the engineers would need well over an hour before they were ready for their demolitions, and moreover in the course of that time, would have to make several minor demolitions to prepare for their main charge, it seemed unlikely that we would get away with it without attracting enemy attention, and we felt that we would be lucky indeed if we could do the job without some tough fighting. Jerry only needed to sit on the top of the cliff above us, and roll down bombs and grenades, and we would have had a very unpleasant time.

About 5pm, just as we had completed all of our arrangements and were sitting around waiting for the order to climb into the transport that was to take us to our LCIs (for we were to do the job that same night), word was passed down that it was all cancelled. This news was hard to take quietly and a certain amount of discontent and restlessness was shown. After all, this was the second job which we had been meant to do, and which had been cancelled at the last moment, and we were beginning to wonder if we would ever serve a useful role again in this campaign.

So instead of fighting for our lives we spent that night drinking from a cask of red wine that Ronnie Lunt had managed to procure, and chatting and joking among ourselves until dawn came to disperse us, and to encourage us to freshen ourselves up by a swim in the sea. Apparently the operation had been cancelled because it was feared in corps headquarters that by blowing the tunnel, we might delay our own forces in their pursuit of the enemy than prevent the enemy from escaping. Be that as it may, the Germans blew the road at that very spot a couple of days later which showed that not much could have been gained by our doing so.

It is of course impossible to guess what would have happened had we attempted to do the job. A machine-gun emplacement was found to have covered the whole area of the intended operation when we visited the place later, but it is not known whether this would have been manned or not. If it had been, it would

John Tonkin and Paddy Mayne, Catania, August 1943.

have been the end for a lot of us, as being cut into the face of the cliff, the aerial photographs had shown nothing to lead us to expect its presence there.

A few days later the squadron was shaken by the news that both Richard Lea and Mick Gurmin were leaving. Paddy had decided that there was no place for them in the regiment.

We were sorry to see them both go, and I was particularly grateful to Richard for the way he had stood by me in getting me into the regiment, and no one could deny that he had done much useful work in getting his squadron pulled together from the days way back in Chekka when the future had seemed so futile and uncertain.

Harry Poat was promoted to major and made second in command under Paddy, although he still kept the operational command of our troop. Everyone welcomed this change, as no one could have been more suitable for this job.

A day or two after our operation was cancelled, we saw one evening a formidable looking fleet of about twenty-five LCIs sailing northwards about 3 miles out to sea. From watching them, we calculated that a brigade at least must be in the process of being landed, and even at the time we thought it rather funny that we were not on the job with them. But the next day the whole story came out. Apparently it was all a ruse to try out our new rocket guns fitted on special ships. The fleet sailed quite brazenly towards Messina, and naturally the Germans could not help spotting them, with the result that they collected their forces and prepared to give the invaders a hot reception. But instead of discharging troops the ships did a dirty trick. They just sat back about half a mile from the shore and pumped in high explosive as hard as they could go. The Germans were there in force waiting to deal with any troops landing, and must have had quite an unpleasant experience as a result of these very explosive rockets that were blasting the rocks all around them. Meanwhile the Americans were taking full advantage of the new disposition of the enemy forces and pushing in their attack from the west.

Tony, who was always busy fiddling about with something, had managed to procure a 20mm Besa gun from a nearby ex-enemy battery, and had set it up as the regimental aircraft protection centre. He and his section were just itching to fire it at something but alas, they hardly ever got the chance.

One day we were suddenly roused out of our customary stupor by the sound of our anti-aircraft guns opening up. At the same time we heard a plane slowly pass overhead and this time Tony really believed that he had a chance of showing what his guns were worth. So he immediately pointed the guns at the plane and let fly. The plane in question turned out to be nothing more than an old 'Walrus', a plane whose outline is characteristic and unmistakeable, and moreover a plane much in use by our own navy. Also from watching the position of the AA bursts we soon realized that our guns were not firing at the plane, but several hundred feet below it, presumably to inform it that it was flying too low over a defended area. But Tony, jumping immediately to conclusions, was firing straight at the plane and continued to do so until it was out of range.

The same thing happened some days later when an enemy fighter did streak overhead to drop a bomb in the vicinity of a destroyer we could see a mile or two out to sea. Tony was waiting there, quite ready for it. But this time his gun fired five rounds and then jammed so thoroughly and effectively, that his section were kept busy most of the afternoon trying to put it right again. Poor Tony! It was a long time before he lived down the story of the 'Walrus', and the fact that despite it being just about the slowest flying aircraft in our possession, he still missed it!

Catania had now fallen for over a week and with XIII Corps on the far side of the town, it was felt that we were too far behind and so we were to be moved up to Catania.

The sappers had just finished repairing the railway from Syracuse to Catania, and so we were to go by rail. Thus one morning we packed up and marched down the dusty hill to Brucoli station. After a considerable wait the train snorted in, and our disgust can be imagined, when we found that the Italian railway authorities had allotted to us a few goods waggons on one end of the train, whilst the ordinary passenger coaches at the other end were crammed with Italian civilians of all shapes and sizes. Needless to say we soon remedied this and travelled to Augusta in comparative comfort.

At Augusta we changed lines and proceeded on our slow journey to Catania. Slow indeed it was, for we did not get to our destination until nearly six hours later. The distance was not much over 20 miles and so we could have walked it almost as quickly.

Once arrived at the other end, we were taken by transport to our camp. Signs of battle were pretty evident along the route and the town of Catania seemed to be in a sorry state. But in view of the terrific bombardment to which it had been subjected, this fact was not surprising!

The site for our new camp proved to be the most pleasant in which we had yet been. In addition to the fact that air raids in this locality were few and far between, we found ourselves now in shady lemon orchards with an abundance of fruit all around. The ground was terraced and irrigated with a primitive sort of culvert arrangement and the sea was only a few hundred yards away.

But there was one serious disadvantage about our new site. It was so dusty that it was utterly impossible to keep clean. The ground, through extensive cultivation, had powdered-up to the finest type of dust, which blew about at the slightest breeze and when anybody passed. Our beds, our clothes, our food, everything was covered in it, and it was only for an hour or two after the bi-weekly irrigation, that we were able to get some measure of relief from this curse.

We were not the only ones to be stationed in this spot. The whole of the Special Service Brigade to which we belonged was centred around the area about 3 miles north of Catania, in the neighbourhood of the village of Aci Castello. No.3 Commando and No.40 Marine Commando were our companions and on the whole we lived on good terms with our neighbours.

Our life was spent in the same way as before, save that because of the enclosed nature of the country, the section walks had to be suspended and PT was re-introduced with compulsory swimming parades. Also we started a mild form of training programme again, with a daily inspection to keep the men up to scratch. All this just sufficed to keep the men from becoming slack or unfit. They reacted immensely well – in spite of the filthy conditions in which we were living. They would go down to the sea daily, and wash their clothes with their small piece of issue soap, and then spread them out to dry on the rocks. The result of all this was that when they went out in the town, they soon won for themselves the reputation of being the smartest troops in the area. With a reputation such as this, they were able to get away with sundry misdemeanours which a soldier less well turned-out would have been extremely rash to do. They soon realized this for themselves and took a great pride in their turn-out and bearing whenever they left the camp area.

We had been in this area about a week when rumours of another operation once again began to go the rounds. The enemy was evacuating the island rapidly and Messina was on the point of falling. No one doubted that we would be needed in the next step of the campaign, the invasion of Italy. So it was not a great surprise to me, when Harry sent for me one morning, and told me that I was to go up to a small village on the north coast of the island, about 10 miles west of Messina. Milazzo was the name of the place, and I was to accompany Major Franks of No.3 Commando, in order to recce a squadron area. The squadron apparently would be following-on in a day or two's time.

So off Brian Franks and I set for our 60 mile run which took us the best part of five hours. As the situation around Messina was still by no means clear, we had to make a wide circuit over to the western side of the island, the American area. The narrow, dusty, mountain roads were jammed with transport, which caused us delay after delay. However, after numerous stops and inconveniences we were able to reach the main road which ran along the north coast, and from then on our journey was comparatively easy.

Milazzo was a small harbour and a very delightful spot. Brian Franks, who proved to be a charming and amusing companion, told me that it was because of this harbour that the town had been chosen as the brigade base, and it seemed that we would be embarking from here for our next operation.

We found a suitable house which was to be squadron HQ, which Brian entered by the simple method of blowing the lock out with his .45 automatic, and then left me on my own to make all the necessary arrangements, saying that the unit would probably be arriving the following day. I hung around there completely on my own, for two more days being completely chewed by mosquitoes at night and bored to distraction during the days. The owner of the house we had taken over came back and put me on to a much better and larger house, which had been owned by an Italian general who had fled to Germany. So I installed myself there and waited patiently for the unit to arrive.

I was left on my own in Milazzo for two days and then a 15cwt truck from the unit arrived to fetch me back with the information that the intended move and operation had once again been cancelled.

So the following morning we went off through Messina and down the coast, a truly wonderful run, and well worth the trouble and the distractions of the

Harry Poat and two Australian pilots of 450 Squadron. Hotel on Mount Etna, 25 August 1943.

whole trip. At one point, just before we descended into Messina, we were able to look over extensive folds of tree-clad hills, and suddenly on coming to a crest we saw there below us the Straits of Messina, shining like a narrow blue ribbon through the intervening heat haze. It came as a very great surprise to us to realize that for the past five minutes we had been looking at Italy, at a country still in enemy hands!

The roads were crammed with civilians, all of whom were most anxious to obtain lifts from the few service vehicles which were passing that way. But there were several security posters, and even road-blocks, with the express purpose of preventing this.

We arrived back about 3pm to find my troop area deserted; they had all gone off on an excursion up to the top of Mount Etna. Apparently about two thirds up, there was a large tourist hotel, which they had taken over, and where they were having a roaring time. Naturally I lost no time in joining them. The hotel was a magnificent place – great spacious marble halls, heating and baths, and gleaming modern furniture. What a contrast it formed with the squalid and shabby houses of the neighbouring villages.

It had been 'discovered' by some Australian airmen, pilots of a Kittyhawk squadron, who had taken it over complete with all its cellars. Apparently the place had been used as an officers' mess when under enemy occupation, and its cellars were well stocked. The Aussies were grand types and only too glad to welcome us, even though we were butting-in on a private party of theirs.

An enjoyable evening was spent listening to the piano and the racy Australian flying talk, and drinking down the watery German beer as fast as possible. After a good night's sleep on a real bed, (the first I had slept on since I left England, except for one or two short leaves in Cairo and Tel Aviv), I decided the next morning to climb to the top of Etna, since the rest of the troop had already been up the previous day.

That morning some of the Kittyhawk pilots came to beat the place up, and there was talk of them landing a small 'spotter' aircraft on a narrow strip beside the hotel – and all the time we were drinking and yarning, yarning and drinking, so that by the time I was due to start on my climb I was anxious to forget about the whole thing.

However, I had told too many of my intentions, with the result that they all kept me to it and packed me off immediately after lunch. Rose, Tony's batman, and Kit Kennedy, a blond Scotsman, who was always smiling with a flash of gleaming white teeth, made up the party. If I was a bit 'mellow' when we started, it did not take me long to sober up, and at the end of half an hour I was dead cold sober, feeling very unhappy and wishing I had never started on this fool's venture.

Peter Davis on summit of Mount Etna, August 1943.

For the first fifteen minutes we went along the road up to its end, and we then had to branch up a track to the left, which wound itself painfully upwards. I was just about beginning to feel completely worn-out, after we had been struggling along for well over an hour, when we came to a small alpine type of hut. Kit Kennedy who had done the climb before, glibly informed us that we were now not quite halfway to the top. At these words, Rose and I flung ourselves down on the ground in despair and refused to proceed further until we had had a rest. Our morale was very low, especially since we had met a major in the Highland Division coming down, who almost ordered us not to proceed further, saying that we would never get down before dark. However we decided to 'press on', and after we had had a cigarette by the hut were in more or less a fit state to proceed.

The surface over which we walked on the next stage of the climb consisted of fine ash, into which the feet would sink, so that for every yard forward we progressed, we would slip back a foot. There ahead, about three-quarters of a mile away, lay a building called the observatory at the end of this smooth, gradual, but infinitely exhausting slope. Step by step we struggled on – at least Rose and I did; Kennedy was having no difficulty – and we had to stop to ease our cramped muscles every 20 yards or so. After a climb of about two and a half hours we reached the observatory. There was nothing remarkable about this building, save for the visitors' book which was left there to sign, and after a short halt there we proceeded on the final stage of the climb. The top of the volcano was not more than 300 yards away from us now, but the slope of the symmetrical cone rose up steep and sheer, sprinkled with large black rocks, which caused our route to wind helplessly between them. It was a good half hour's climb still – as we went up, here and there we would find the ground hot under our feet – white sulphur smoke would seep through cracks and fissures in the rock and we were almost stifled by the pungent sulphur fumes.

At last we reached the top and were able to look down into the enormous crater, which seemed to be about 400 yards in diameter. Most of it was dead, and only here and there out of relatively tiny openings the thick white smoke gushed forth fouling the air with sulphur fumes. One crater in particular seemed especially active that afternoon and great crashes and explosions would emerge from it together with several ominous rumblings.

Our journey down took us less than an hour, while it had required just on three hours to reach the top. It was quite a relief to get back to the hotel and sit comfortably resting my aching feet. There was another big party that night, and we left early the following morning for our camp at Aci Costello, sorry indeed to leave those crazy parties and that crowd of open-hearted genuine and sincere Australians. From that day we had a soft spot for 450 Squadron, and when, as sometimes happened we met up with any of them at a later date, it was a good excuse, wherever we were, to try and emulate those carefree hard drinking days which we had spent together on Mount Etna.

But we were not given the time to settle down to our old life once more. For we had scarcely been back five days, when rumours began to circulate about another operation, an operation which was to coincide with the invasion of Italy. In spite of the previous false alarms to which we had been subjected, somehow we all knew that this coming job would certainly come off, and in this we were not disappointed. Except for a couple of brief visits, it was henceforth farewell to Sicily and on to the mainland of Europe.

Chapter Eight

Bagnara

This time briefing was quick and to the point. Aerial photographs, and excellent ones at that, were issued of a little town just north of the toe of Italy, about 10 miles from Scylla. This town, by the name of Bagnara, was to be our objective. The procedure was as usual. Our squadron would be landed there during the night, would capture the town and hold it until the arrival of the main army, which would then be about 12 miles away. The plan was essentially simple. We would embark in Catania on two LCIs, which would drop us at an easily recognizable point just south of the town. Once landed, No.3 Troop would push through to the north side of the town, we would clear the inland half, and No.1 Troop would clear the beach and coastal area. Not much was known about the enemy resistance, but it was not thought that it would be great.

We embarked on the two LCIs in Catania harbour on 1 September, two days before the actual invasion of Italy. Without hurry we proceeded northwards, to drop anchor at a point on the coast about mid-way between Catania and Messina. Here we disembarked and were free to do as we pleased for the rest of that day and to spend the night in comparative comfort, sleeping on the beach.

We embarked the next morning to the news that our troops had landed on the toe of Italy during that night, and that all was going satisfactorily for them. But things certainly were not going satisfactorily for us, for we had only been aboard a few minutes when we realized something was wrong. Our anchor cable had fouled the propellers, with the result that we could not move an inch until it was cleared. This was not an easy job to do at the best of times, but, judging from the way in which several of the naval crew seemed to think that it was all a terrific joke, there were not many signs that the crew were really trying their hardest to clear the obstruction. A pair of them were actually overheard saying that they were in no hurry to get the ship in running order again, especially as they would have to go on a landing operation that night! It all seemed so nicely arranged, and there we sat helpless, getting more and more angry watching the futile attempts of the crew to get our ship moving again.

The other LCI, which was quite all right, remained behind also, and we spent a lively afternoon transferring from one ship to the other, as plans were altered, and as decisions were made as to how our weight would best help to free the obstruction. The trouble was at last remedied at about 6pm, by one of the sailors diving down fitted with some sort of diver's mask and untangling it by hand.

This unexpected and irritating delay need not have had any effects on the operation plans, for even though we had been held up for the best part of a day, we were not more than three or four hours sailing from our objective. Thus as night came down, in all its ominous intensity, and in its shielding blackness, we were able to slip away at full speed towards the coast of Italy, and the original plans for our landing remained unaltered.

Operational lighting was installed and in the dull red or blue glow, which gave a sinister and grotesque twist to our faces, we groped around making the final preparations. Around 2am we began to feel restless, knowing that we should be there any minute now. I went down to visit my section who were in the forward hold, fully equipped and merely waiting for the word to disembark.

As I entered the hold, the dull murmur of conversation ceased and I was met with a barrage of questions – *'What's the griff, sir?'*, one would ask, *'When are we due to land?'*, and *'Is it true that those naval types are making a hash of things?'* – these and similar questions fired at me with such eagerness, only served to show that the strain of waiting was beginning to tell on the men.

I found myself a seat, lit up a cigarette and endeavoured to tell them all I knew, which indeed, was not much. We should have landed half an hour ago, and although the Italian coast could clearly be seen, we could not yet recognize the large dry river bed, which was to be the main landmark to guide us into the right spot. To help pass the time away, I once more went over with my section all the details of the briefing, and they listened intently ready to grasp at anything which would help take their minds away from the painfully dragging minutes, and the strain of this uncertainty of waiting.

When I had finished I left them, in search of more news. I had hardly left the hold when I bumped into Harry, looking considerably more ruffled than usual; in fact he was in a fuming temper.

'Oh,' he said gruffly, *'tell your section that we will be landing within the next few minutes. God knows what the navy think they are doing – I've never come across a more clueless lot in all my life! Look! There's the river bed and the bloody fools have gone right past it.'*

With these words Harry pointed to a thin white ribbon which we could just see cutting the blackness of the coastline way back in our rear. *'Tell your section,'* Harry went on, *'that in all probability we are being landed in the wrong place, and that we have not a minute to waste, as it will be light in less than an hour.'*

Harry strode off, with this parting remark, to pass the news on to his other sections, while I went down to give my section this latest, and rather forbidding piece of information.

A few minutes later we were called on deck to our respective disembarkation positions, and after a further wait we touched the shore. With a terrific crash and rattle of chains and pulleys the ramps fell down onto the beach, making sufficient noise, or so we thought, to awaken everyone within half a mile radius. Immediately the disembarkation began; in complete silence it was carried out – nothing could be heard save the sighing of the wind and the lapping of the water against the sides of the ship. We waited patiently, as we were to be the last troop to disembark, and as we waited we could see one dark shape after another glide noiselessly down the ramp and disappear into the darkness.

At the end of the ramp stood a figure, which could have been none other than Paddy – occasionally he stopped someone and whispered a few words – then the column would move on again.

Just as we were about to disembark, a sudden shout from the bridge rent the silence of the night and caused us to freeze into our positions. *'Get a move on, army'* the voice shouted, *'we don't want to be here all day!'*

It took us sometime to overcome our initial amazement that anyone could be so outright foolish shouting like that in the middle of a landing operation behind the enemy lines, and after our apprehensions brought into existence by this piece of stupidity had died down, we found ourselves seething with fury. I noticed a general fidgeting and muttering behind me which gave evidence of the feelings of at least my section. We realized that the first signs of dawn were beginning to light the eastern sky, and that this had obviously given rise to fears on the part of the navy, of being caught in a vulnerable position when the sun rose. Wretched people, how we swore at them for getting restless solely through consideration for their own skins, when they would be safely out of it all in less than half an hour from now – by which time, who knows what would have happened to us.

But we were too busy disembarking to let our anger affect us as greatly as otherwise – we were only too ready to obey the naval officer's orders and get off the wretched ship, just as quickly as we could. After all, we had already been on it quite against our will for a matter of three hours or so more than had been planned, and moreover it was a great relief to us to get our feet on dry land again and to be able to strike out on our own, no longer having to depend on others.

As I stepped off the ramp, Paddy came up to me and told me where I could find Harry and where to put my section. I noticed at once that we were in completely the wrong place. From the vivid memory of the area which I still retained in my mind as the result of a detailed study of aerial photos, I was able to recognize certain landmarks. It was almost as though I had been there before, so easy did I find it to pinpoint the spot where we had been landed. We were literally a good two miles out of position. Instead of being landed just under the dry river bed at the point where the coastal road went through a sort of tunnel, a point about 2 miles south of the town of Bagnara, we had been landed on the northern outskirts of the town, just by a little cluster of houses. These were isolated from the main part of the town by a sheer spur of the mountain which jutted out right to the water's edge. What a complete and utter mess-up, and I had no idea what would happen next.

I found Harry with no difficulty. He was sitting on the beach leaning against a low stone wall. He seemed by now to have completely regained his composure, for his voice was calm when he addressed us, and his orders were clear and to the point.

'Look here, chaps', he began, as soon as we were all three present, 'as you have probably realised, we have been landed miles out of position. Paddy has completely altered the plan. We have not time to clear the town now, and we certainly do not want to be caught in it in daylight, so we will go straight through the town and hold the bridge over the wadi bed, which is at the foot of the main road leading northwards out of the town up the mountain. No.1 Troop will be pushing ahead of us to seal off the northern approaches to the town while No.3 Troop will be doing the same at the south end. Now get cracking, and tell your sections what I have told you, but for heaven's sake don't delay.'

We left him hurriedly, marvelling at the speed with which the whole plan had been altered. Apparently, Paddy had made his new plan, before he had even left the LCI for he saw at a glance where we would land and what would be necessary. It was in moments such as these that Paddy showed himself to be not only the born leader, but the born soldier as well. The ability to make split-second decisions, which later proved to contain equal wisdom as decisions that are normally hammered out over a period of days, is certainly not common to many people, but it was a marked characteristic of the real genius of Paddy – genius seems the only word to apply to this man, so completely inscrutable himself, and yet so astute in his unfailing ability to anticipate the decisions of the commander opposing him, and to act accordingly.

A few hurried commands to our sections and we were off, just as the stars began to fade and the first chill rays of dawn came to throw their unwelcome light upon our activities. Hell! Because those navy boys had landed us two hours late it looked as though we would be at a considerable disadvantage if the town should prove to be strongly occupied, for we would not even have the blessed cloak of darkness, in the use of which we had been so well trained and on which we had come to rely so strongly, to give us the full benefit of the element of surprise.

We rounded the steep rocky spur which jutted out seawards, by keeping to the beach for a few hundred yards, while we headed for the main part of the town. We then branched off inland up a narrow street which led straight up the hillside. Here we adopted our usual street-fighting formation, with one sub-section on either side of the road, each scrutinizing the windows and doors on the opposite side of the street.

We proceeded thus for a short distance while the murky indistinctness of dawn gave way to the pale light of the budding day. Suddenly loud cries of *'Inglesi, Inglesi, bono multo bono,'* caused us to turn our eyes upwards, and there we had the pleasant opportunity of seeing an elderly gentleman, clad in a long flannel nightshirt, standing on a balcony and clapping his hands for all he was worth. Above him, hanging from a large flagpole, there waved lazily an enormous white flag, consisting of at least a double sheet.

'You're playing safe, aren't you, Antonio?' one of the lads shouted up at him good-naturedly, as we plodded past. But the elderly gentleman only grinned all the more, repeating even more lustily than before, his shouts of *'Inglesi, multo bono!'*

We left him there without further word, safe under the protection of his immense white flag, and pressed on up the hill. It was now full daylight, but at such an early hour, the town was absolutely deserted. At length we came to the main coastal road, which was cut into the mountainside, and ran about 200 yards inland from the beach.

We turned left down this towards the bridge we were aiming for. All seemed quiet and the peace of that beautiful autumn morning slowly began to reassure us. It looks as though the place is unoccupied after all, was the thought that now entered our heads.

'Is that No.3 Troop on the road behind us, sir?', Johnny Hair my runner asked casually.

'I expect so,' I replied equally unconcernedly, *'they should be somewhere around there, but I'll just have a look.'*

I had hardly troubled to follow Hair's pointing finger so sure was I that any troops marching in single file up the road, a bare 300 yards behind us, would be some unit or other of our squadron. But to be on the safe side, I had a squint at them through my binoculars. *'Yes, they're ours,'* I announced, and was just about to put my glasses down, when I noticed something unusual about their headgear. Where had I seen those peaked caps before? Those close-fitting caps with long peaks, which sat snugly on the head and shaded the eyes. Sergeant

Cattell had one, but that was a German one. In this slow fashion it dawned upon me that the file of troops following us up the road were GERMANS!

'Watch out, lads, they're Jerries', I shouted and we made a frantic dash up a little alleyway leading up the hillside. At the same moment, Derrick's section who were immediately behind us, became aware of the enemy following them, and his Bren gunner swung round and began blazing away from the hip. It would have been an easy matter for us to have slipped up the hillside and taken up a vantage point overlooking the road, and to have let the oncoming Germans walk straight into the trap thus formed. But this Bren gunner, by not waiting for the fire order, spoilt all that for us. Once he had fired, the Germans knew that something was up and dived for the nearest cover. Other Germans in the vicinity must have heard the firing, and realized that all was not so peaceful as the original calm of the morning might otherwise have suggested. As it was, some of the Germans in the party concerned, made their escape and the information they were able to give may well have been a partial cause of the trouble into which we later walked. Had we been able to capture this party to a man, not a shot need have been fired, and it might well have been possible for us to continue up that road and exercise an equal surprise on any other enemy troops in the vicinity.

I took my section up a series of rough steps and narrow alleys which brought us out into an ideal position – there below us stretched the road, up which we had come. We could cover with our fire every inch of it and observe the slightest movement. Quickly I placed out my section in favourable positions and there we waited, with eyes glued on the spot where the Germans had gone to ground.

Meanwhile considerable firing had started all around, entirely coming from our troops and apparently directed at the unfortunate Germans who had been so much taken by surprise. Probably some of the other sections could see more than we could, as from various sounds it became evident that there were some of the squadron even further up the hill. But we did not wait in vain – every now and then a bush would move, or a white face or hands could be picked up from the dark green undergrowth of the vines. Lance Corporal Little was having a wonderful time trying to pick off anyone who was unfortunate enough to show himself. Occasionally Sanders and his Bren gun got busy and sprayed the area pretty thoroughly, letting the wicked red tracer bullets dart in and out of the foliage like live things. Correspondingly streams of tracer were also being poured into the position from another angle further to our left, by a section of No.1 Troop who happened to be there.

Naturally this state of affairs could not go on much longer, and I observed Pat Reilly taking his section back up the road towards the point where the Germans lay. I ordered the section to hold their fire and to lie there ready for any trouble. But the Germans felt far from giving trouble and surrendered meekly, extremely thankful at thus being freed from a position which, I should imagine, must have been an absolute hell while it lasted. How little did we know then, that in the space of less than an hour, my section would be in a situation very similar to that in which these Germans, now our prisoners, found themselves. They were Germans this time all right – no more of those fawning childlike little men, who made such a show of things when there was no enemy near, but who forgot all about their Duce as soon as it meant fighting – altogether about thirty of them were roped-in, and these turned out to be the first German prisoners taken in Italy. They were engineers and had been concerned in preparing demolitions in order to hold up the advance of our army.

Harry's runner came to me then and told me to report to troop HQ. Harry was situated on the road, about 50 yards up the hillside. It was hardly believable that this was the same road along which we and the Germans had come, and I found it difficult to make it out until I realized that the road was climbing the mountain in a series of sharp hairpin bends, and we had just cut-off a long chunk of it by going straight up the hillside. Harry seemed very pleased with our initial success. *'Yes we've got them all right,'* he said with satisfaction, *'but look, we've got to press on quickly so don't waste any time. I want you to take your section up this road. You will see Derrick and his crowd at that very steep hairpin bend at the edge of the town. Go past him to the next bend and find a position for yourself there and then wait until I come up and tell you what we will be doing next. Hurry now, and get your section off.'*

Johnny Hair, my runner, had meanwhile been sent off to fetch the section up without delay, and as I turned away from Harry I found them waiting a few yards off. We started up the road at once feeling considerably reassured at our initial good fortune, and not a little flushed with this success. Maybe it was this sentiment that inspired in us a feeling of confidence and carelessness, which, when considered in the cold light of reason, could certainly not be justified. After all, we did not know where the enemy was, what was their strength, or how long it would be before we were relieved by our main forces. But in the heat of the excitement we contrived to forget about all this, and marched up that road in single file, feeling happier than we had felt for the last 24 hours.

Soon the houses began to thin and we were able to see the road wriggling round the side of the mountain above us and to our left front. An Italian civilian, standing in the doorway of one of the houses, caught my eye and beckoned me over. With the air of sharing a great secret with me he pointed up towards the mountain, to a certain little culvert which broke the regular outline of the low wall flanking the road, saying the one word, '*Tedesci*'. I did not speak Italian but I knew that *Tedesci* meant Germans – but what was this fellow doing, giving me information about Axis troops? Surely it was in his interests that the Germans should throw us back into the sea? I could not imagine an Englishman behaving likewise in the event of a successful German landing in England, so felt very inclined to distrust the voluntary information given by such means. So I thanked the Italian politely but continued on up the hill, regardless of his warning. What a fool he must have thought me, as later events proved him to be completely correct about the German positions and he must have been genuinely anxious to help us.

We soon came to the hairpin bend where we were expecting to find Derrick's section, but to our surprise found No.1 Troop in occupation. Their headquarters were there, for I could see Bill Fraser bending over a mess-tin by the side of the road, having the usual brew-up. He greeted me cheerfully, with the information that Derrick had pushed on up to the next bend.

'*There does not seem much on,*' he informed me, '*so I don't see why I should not have some breakfast. No, except for a bit of sniping we have not seen any signs of the enemy,*' he said in answer to my request for information.

Bravely disregarding the temptation offered by that appetizing piece of bacon frizzling in the mess-tin, we left Bill, who seemed quite at home and unconcerned, and carried on up the road.

There was Derrick at the next bend, as we had expected. His section were all under cover and in fire positions, and Derrick himself was crouching by the wall looking worried. His concern made a marked contrast to Bill's nonchalance, and it was thus most difficult for us to decide which of the two to believe. I placed my section under cover, and then went over to see what I could find out from Derrick.

He greeted me like a long-lost friend, and with a great show of caution pulled me down behind the wall, under the cover of which he was crouching. '*Don't stand there, you fool,*' he hissed, '*don't you realize that they're sniping this road like fury?*'

'*Where? I didn't notice anything on the way up,*' I replied tending to take Derrick's words with a pinch of salt, since I knew him to be always rather inclined to exaggerate.

'*You may not have yet,*' he replied, '*but you soon will if you go on much further up this road. Where do you think you are going to? I honestly do not recommend you to go beyond this point.*'

'*But I have had direct orders from Harry to take up a position on the bend above you,*' I protested '*and I can't disobey those orders unless I am actually forced to by opposition. And I can't see much sign of that yet.*' I added, rather scornfully.

'Well push on then, but for the Lord's sake keep your eyes skinned,' were Derrick's parting words as I left him to collect my section and carry on up the road.

Watched anxiously by Derrick and the rest of his section, we rounded the bend, hugging the steep rocky side of the mountain, and ready to dive for cover at the slightest sound.

'Blast!' I exclaimed, as I noticed that the road ran dead straight for another 300 or 400 yards at least, *'It looks as though we shall have to park ourselves somewhere around here!'* And with these words I began looking around for a good position. To my dismay I found that there was not a scrap of reasonable cover in sight. The whole area was under the complete observation of that small culvert ahead, for the road apparently turned sharply at some point in front and then ran, rising steadily at right angles to us, away to our left. Derrick had partially confirmed the information given me by the Italian civilian, by stating his suspicions that the sniping to which he had been subjected had come from that self-same culvert.

So I watched the spot anxiously, ready to dive out of sight of that point as soon as any trouble started. But where could we go to? That was indeed the question. The road had been cut out of the mountainside, with the result that to our right we would be faced with a sheer cliff to climb, while to our left the ground dropped away in bare parched terraces, sprinkled here and there with vines, and affording no cover at all from the area where I had reason to believe the enemy might be.

Hell, what a nasty position to get caught in if they should open up on us, I said to myself. We would not be able to leave the road at all, and would provide a perfect target – pray God that we can make that next bend without trouble.

Turning over these chill thoughts in our minds, we pushed forward as rapidly as possible, thankful that so far we had been left unmolested. How peaceful the scene seemed in that clear sunny air. How lovely was the dark green of the mountain vines in the rays of that friendly sun, and the mirror-like surface of the sea far down below us. Who could think of fighting on a day like this, when everything seemed to suggest peace, happiness and friendliness.

I was interrupted in pleasant thoughts of this nature by the venomous whistle of a single bullet passing close overhead. *'So Derrick was right after all,'* I had just time to think as I urged my lads to make full use of the scant and available cover.

A second later all hell seemed to have been let loose. I hardly had time to digest the ominous warning of the swish-swoosh, swish swoosh of a falling mortar bomb, when a terrific explosion shook the ground. A shower of debris and stones fell around us and on looking back, I was able to see a column of black smoke and dust rising from the edge of the road, barely 40 yards behind.

'*God that's where Corporal Mitchell's sub-section were,*' I murmured. There was no stopping to see what was happening to them. If they were all right, they would follow, if not – too bad!

'*Follow me!*', I shouted and we doubled like mad things down that road, in a vain search for cover from those murderous and seemingly all-penetrating eyes, on the hillside above.

The sharp wicked roar of a fast-firing Spandau gave us yet further incentive to get under cover. We rounded a slight right-hand bend as the bullets started to whip around us, and there, about 50 yards ahead on the left side of the road, we observed with relief, something which might afford some degree of shelter. A small peasant cottage of one room lay invitingly ahead of us. If only we could make it.

'*Come on! Make for that house,*' I shouted, and we covered the remaining distance at record-breaking speed. The fire was becoming not only more accurate, but also more intense with every yard we progressed, and I marvelled that so far no one had been hit. At first it had been spasmodic and wild, just as though the enemy had been taken by surprise, and were still in doubt as to whether they should be firing at us or not. But from the way we saw it, it soon become clear that any initial doubts that they may have had were being quickly dispelled, for bullets seemed to be kicking up all around us, and the terrifying, vicious r-r-r-rip of the light machine gun dinned in our ears, and tensed our nerves as we ran for our lives.

'*In here quickly.*' We had come to within 15 yards of the house towards which we were aiming, and Sergeant Storey and I, who were in front, fell flat on our faces in the protecting shade of a tall cactus plant. But we were still exposed to the merciless observation of our hidden enemies and our way to safety was barred by a strong wire fence.

'*Give me your wire-cutters,*' I yelled to Storey over the din, '*come on hurry up.*' For Andy Storey, the solid but infinitely slow Yorkshire man was acting in a dazed, stupefied sort of way. I caught at his arm and shouted furiously into his ear for the wire-cutters, while the bullets bounced off the road or tore through the nearby cactus bushes.

'*Oh, wire-cutters,*' he said numbly, and started fumbling around in helpless fashion. After what seemed an interminable period, but which could hardly have been more than a couple of seconds, I had the wire-cutters in my hands, and with a couple of quick strokes, had cut a way through the wire, and at last we were in the shelter of the house.

'*What the hell was the matter with you back on the road?*' I enquired of Sergeant Storey once we were safe. '*Were you deaf?*'

'Oh no, sir,' he replied, *'I heard you the first time, but you know, they were firing at us pretty thoroughly up there. I was taking out the wire-cutters when a bullet made a furrow in the road about an inch from my hand! And that made me start thinking you know!'*

Now Andy Storey was one of the most unimaginative persons I have ever met, and in that quality lay his bravery, for not being able to imagine the implications of certain sounds and occurrences, he would venture to accomplish feats which a person with more imagination would have trembled at. So for him to start thinking was a serious business and I quickly set him the job of collecting the rest of the section, who were arriving in trickles by the route along which we had come.

Thank heavens, here they came, all apparently none the worse for their experience. There was McNinch, and Hair, Telford, Ashurst, Sandy Davidson, Eddie Wilson, and Smith with the Bren gun. Close upon them came Charlie Tobin and Stalker, and finally, almost after I had given them up for lost, John Stone and Tunstall, who had arrived by another route.

'Is there anyone else, Lance Corporal Johnstone?' I asked the last arrival.

'No, Sir, I think Corporal Mitchell kept his sub-section where they were, as that first mortar bomb landed plumb in front of his sub-section.'

'God, what a piece of luck!' I exclaimed, for the sub-sections had advanced up that road in single file at about 25 yard spacing, and the first bomb had just happened to land between them. *'But do you know if anyone was hurt?* I then asked him.

'I couldn't say, Sir, I don't think so, but there was such a cloud of dust around that I could not see much. But I heard Corporal Mitchell shouting to his men to get down and under cover.'

So it seemed that Corporal Mitchell had got the situation well in hand, and had hoped to get his section into a position from which he could give us support. Still, I could hardly expect to see him now.

I looked round to see who had been able to arrive at the spot where we were. Yes, all HQ and all McNinch's sub-section were there – there was Tideswell, whom I had not noticed before, sitting calmly beneath the cactuses, scooping the earth out of his rifle muzzle.

Well, now that we were here, what had we to do next? We were a mere thirteen men and in none too comfortable a position. The first thing to do was to get the men in some sort of defensive position, but this was by no means easy. We were certainly off the road, but the area seemed to be just as exposed, and all movement had to be carried out extremely carefully, or else the bullets would start whipping around us again. Except for the small space immediately behind the house, the ground was most uncomfortably bare. We were on the left side of the road, and the side of the mountain fell away in a series of small terraces at a very steep gradient. Each terrace was about 4ft wide and about 4ft below the other, so movement downwards or upwards was difficult, especially since we were still under the eyes of the enemy. But somehow we contrived to get our few men spread out, and in reasonable positions, though the vines and cactuses which provided the only cover were small and scattered, providing little protection from view and none from fire. I did not dare keep all the men in the close vicinity of the house, in case an accurate mortar bomb should wipe out the lot of us.

Having got my section in position I had a peep through the window of the house towards the direction of the enemy.

The cunning devils – the road bent sharply, less than 200 yards ahead, at the point where it crossed a deep wadi. From there it doubled back to the left at an acute angle to the stretch of road from which we had come. Rising all the time, it ran dead straight along the far side of the valley, almost parallel to us, until it disappeared from view round the shoulder of the mountain away over to our left. It was very obvious that the enemy had chosen this stretch of road as the central point for their defensive position, for from there they were in a position to cover every inch of the road from the point where it left the shelter of the houses on the outskirts of the town. They must have been watching us all the way of our painful advance up that cursed road, and waiting with their fingers curled around the trigger until we had moved within so short a range that it must have seemed almost certain that they could mow us down at the first burst.

So there we found ourselves in the scanty shelter afforded by the house and its surrounding vines and cactuses. Barely 250 yards away, across the valley, and considerably above us, lay the Germans in well-prepared, camouflaged positions, so situated that, unobserved themselves, they could watch every movement we made.

At first we did not realize the danger of the position. Once we were under some sort of cover, the machine-gun fire died down almost completely. Only occasionally did the sharp, ripping, and infinitely wicked burst of that Spandau ring out, but the fire was not directed at us. Apparently they had spotted some movement further down the road, caused by our troops vainly trying to find in that bare and exposed mountainside some sort of cover that would protect them from the watchful and murderous eyes above.

Meanwhile, the mortaring continued in earnest and in fact the bombs had continued falling, in monotonous regularity from the time when that first one had so narrowly missed my section. They seemed to be passing straight over our heads and to be directed into the town itself, over which the enemy must have had an equally close watch as over our own position. We did not like it at all.

The Germans knew that we were in and around that small house, and any moment we expected to be welcomed with a hail of deadly HE bombs. But for some reason or other no bomb landed near us during the whole course of that day. Maybe we were too close to the enemy positions for them to consider it safe to try and bomb us out in case some of their bombs fell short. Maybe, we might have been just out of view of the mortar OP, which seemed to be situated further up the hill than the remainder of the enemy positions. Or else the very nature of our position helped us. It would have needed a very lucky and accurate shot to have knocked us out. If the bomb fell short on the road it would have been above us, and it is unlikely that it would have caused much damage; on the other hand, the slope on which we were, was so steep that even if the bomb had only been 10 yards beyond our position, it would have fallen right down into the valley and exploded a good 50 yards below us. Maybe the Germans realized this difficulty, but the fact remains that we were spared from mortaring during the whole time we were in that position, which is something for which we had every reason to feel grateful.

Now that the enemy's attention seemed to have been diverted from us, temporarily at least, our confidence slowly began to return, our excitement to abate, and our normal instincts and emotions to regain their customary position. We sat up in the brilliant sunshine of that cloudless morning, eating breakfast from our 24-hour ration packs. Soon we discovered we could walk about fairly openly without calling forth that vicious stream of bullets. Even the swish of the mortar bombs passing overhead failed to worry us after a while, as we realized they were not aimed at us. But I did not want to take any risks so gave orders that no one should move unnecessarily or fire without the direct order from me.

A mortar bomb landed on the small church tower in the town below, cracking the bell and setting it tolling furiously. The harsh discordant clang of it, rising on the peaceful morning air, contained a sound suggestive of something grim and ominous – something that reminded us of desolate bomb-shattered cities, deserted and putrid, forbidding and repellent in their very desolation.

We shuddered as we heard that sound. It brought the terrors and discomforts of war, which were even then being experienced in the small town below us, right up beside us as we lay on our peaceful mountainside, beneath the warm caressing rays of the sun, and lulled into a false security by the gentle rustle of the vines in the morning breeze and by the rich odour emanating from the grapes.

After breakfast, McNinch and I decided to try and pinpoint the enemy positions. We entered the house and peeped cautiously out of the window, raking the opposing hillside with our glasses. But not a movement could we detect – not a sign or sound of activity. We were near enough to have discerned even the blue haze of a cigarette had one been burning. But the opposite hillside seemed motionless, deserted, and wonderfully peaceful.

'*What do you make of that pile of brushwood, below the road, just to the right of that culvert?*' McNinch asked me, lowering his glasses and rubbing his strained eyes. I had a peep at the indicated spot. On close examination, we found that the innocent pile of brushwood served to conceal a concrete position of some sort, for through a small gap we were able to make out the grey gleam of a concrete block.

'*I think I've found another one, sir!*' McNinch's sharp eyes were now penetrating the rough attempts at camouflage and one by one, we detected several spots which looked as though they concealed some sort of activity. Altogether we recorded seven 'possible' enemy positions. Of none could we feel definitely sure they were defensive points, but all of them betrayed something suspicious, for it was this which had at first focused our attention on them. But still there was no sign of movement to reveal to us, as we watched which, if any, of the points we had noted were occupied by that cursed machine gun.

Eventually, after about forty minutes of the most intense scrutiny of the mountainside opposite, we gave up. Although we now had several alternative points to choose from at which to direct our fire, we were still as completely ignorant as before, as regards the point from where the main opposition was coming.

'*Look, sir, there's a bloke up there having a dekko over that wall,*' Telford shouted at me. I quickly examined him through my glasses, yes, there he was, apparently quite unconcerned looking out over the wall which flanked the road, eating an apple. But I could just not make out whether he was a soldier or a civilian. The sun was behind him and his outline was in shadow. I was defeated, and could come to no definite decision.

'*Let me have a go at him,*' pleaded McNinch quickly moving over towards the Bren gun.

'*No, not with that,*' I said, with reference to the Bren, '*you can have a bang at him with a rifle, if you think that would do any good.*'

But by the time McNinch had found himself a rifle, the inquisitive apple-eater had again bobbed down behind the wall, and although we waited patiently, with our eyes fixed on the spot, he did not reappear.

'*Never mind, you wouldn't have hit him anyway,*' came the mocking taunt from Charlie Tobin, who was sitting on the terrace below us.

'*Let's have a bang at them, sir!*' he continued, after I had explained the approximate area where I thought the enemy were lying concealed. He fingered his EY rifle lovingly, and started screwing the grenade discharger onto the muzzle. '*Look, just let me put a couple of grenades over there with this*,' he pleaded, '*I am sure I can wake them up and give them something to think about.*'

I was quite sure that he could, but in not quite the way he imagined, and doubted whether the Germans would be worse off from being woken up, than we would, after they had reacted in the way I expected. Moreover the maximum range of the grenade discharger was only 200 yards, which meant that even by the widest stretch of the imagination, we would be unable to do more than send the grenades falling harmlessly into the valley below. So I persuaded Tobin to postpone his murderous inclinations assuring him that his opportunity would come soon enough.

Alas, how was I to know that poor Charlie Tobin's opportunity never would come.

As the sun rose higher in the sky and the minutes fled by, I began to wonder where our other troops had got to. I looked back hoping to see some sign of them, but the road bent fairly sharply about 60 yards behind us, and nothing was to be seen. Strange fears then began to worry me. We seemed to be all alone. We were the only post of our troops that could be seen and yet there we were, scarcely 250 yards from the enemy. All of a sudden we felt utterly alone. What if our troops could not see the enemy from where they were, and we were left to fight a pitched battle with vastly superior forces. And where had my second sub-section got to? Surely Corporal Mitchell, encouraged by the quiet of the last hour, would have tried to bring his men up to join us. I would have felt much happier with a few more men and an extra Bren gun.

I let these thoughts turn over in my mind for a further half hour, urging my wireless operator to try like blazes to get through to Harry at troop HQ. But although the set was working correctly, not a signal could be received from it. Apparently the mountains interfered so much with reception that it was just about impossible to pass messages by that means.

I started to wonder what Harry was doing about things, and sincerely hoped that he had decided to climb the mountain above the road, and was even now moving forward to take up a complementary and supporting position above us, in the cover of the young pine trees that were growing there in a quite appreciable density.

But as the minutes went by, and there was still no sign of any activity on the part of our troops, I decided that I just had to get a message back, to let Harry know where we were, that we had had no casualties, and also the approximate area where we knew the enemy to be situated, in the hope that Alec and his 3-inch mortars could be called in to give them a spot of trouble.

So, encouraged by the continued lull, which had been uninterrupted for the last ninety minutes, and motivated by the growing restlessness among my men at the constrained inactivity, and moreover, genuinely anxious to get word back to Harry, I called Johnny Hair over and gave him a verbal message. Only later did I realize that it was a great mistake not to have sent a written one.

'*Look here, Hair,*' I began, as he approached, '*I want you to go back and take a message to troop HQ.*' Hair looked dubious. '*No, I think it will be all right,*' I continued, reassuringly, guessing his thoughts, '*there has not been a peep from up there for the last ninety minutes, and as long as you keep off the road and use all the available cover, you should manage it fairly easily. If things get too hot for you, just choose a nice spot and lie up there until the trouble has eased off a bit. Tell Major Poat where we are, and also tell him that the enemy opposition seems to be centred around those caves on the hillside over there, and that we would appreciate a bit of mortar fire on that area to enable us to try and find a better position further up the hillside. Get Corporal Mitchell to climb the mountain across the road, until he gets under cover of those pine trees, and then to come along with his sub-section until he is level with us. If Jerry gets up there above us, before our own troops, we will have had it with a vengeance.*'

Hair seemed to have grasped the gist of these orders pretty well, so after a final repetition of them, I dismissed him, not without some considerable apprehensions, lest I had incorrectly interpreted the apparent quiescence on the part of the enemy, and was as a result, sending my runner on a very risky mission.

We watched him set off jauntily enough, his rifle at the trail, and apparently ignorant of the torments he was causing in my mind. Hugging the bank of the terrace immediately below the road, and using to the full the all too scarce cover that was available, he reached the bend in the road, and disappeared from view, without the slightest indication being given from the slopes above us that the enemy were aware of his progress. With a sigh of relief, I settled back to wait, happy in the knowledge that Hair had at least accomplished successfully the first and most dangerous part of his journey to Troop HQ.

But about five minutes later my blood went cold at signs of renewed activity from the direction of the enemy. Isolated rifle shots began to ring out and a couple of short bursts from the Spandau. Somewhere behind us the reassuring slow rattle of a Bren opened up. Probably the attention of the enemy had been attracted by some movement of one of our other sections which had promptly retaliated. I told McNinch to spray the area in front with his Tommy gun, in the hope of making the enemy keep their heads down and cover Hair on his way. A few minutes later the normal peace of the morning reigned once more, and we settled down to wait patiently, confident that Hair had accomplished his perilous journey all right, as the fire from the enemy had not seemed very intense or to have been concentrated anywhere in particular. While this brief exchange of fire had been going on, Telford, lodged in the window of the house, was once again striving to discover from where the enemy fire was coming. But no tell-tale smoke betrayed to us the position of that Spandau, no movement was observed on that bare mountainside opposite us, to help us narrow down the area in which the enemy could be located.

As soon as everything was quiet once more, and we were able to relax, we sat back to wait, hoping to hear signs on the hillside above us, that Corporal Mitchell had arrived and was getting his sub-section into position. But close on an hour went by with no sign of movement either from the direction of our own troops or of the enemy. The firing had ceased completely and we were left to 'enjoy' that fragrant scene to the full.

Word passed round that somebody was coming up the road. I looked back and saw that a civilian, an old shabbily-dressed peasant, was rounding the bend and coming towards us, unmolested. We lay low and let him pass without seeing us, as we did not want the Germans to find out our position from interrogating him when he reached them.

Intently we watched him as he approached the enemy positions, hoping that by some movement, evoked by the sight of this approaching civilian, the position of those cunningly hidden Jerries might be betrayed. But to our amazement, no figure came to cross the gap in the cactuses about 25 yards ahead of us, since this was the first point where we expected to see the civilian again after he had passed us. How strange! He seemed to have disappeared completely. Either he had stopped somewhere by the road, about 20 yards ahead of us, or, as was almost certainly the case, he had turned up the mountainside by some small track which was invisible to us from where we were lying.

We did not like this. What if he were working for the Germans by passing onto them information about the positions of our troops? We decided that we should at all costs try to rope him in.

Sergeant Storey pointed out to me a wide culvert that ran under the road about 10–15 yards ahead of us, which seemed reasonably easy for us to reach, and at once the idea entered my mind to take a patrol of two men up to this culvert and see if we could get under the road by means of it. From here we could call the civilian in, without being observed by the enemy, and we might well be able to reconnoitre a concealed route to a better position among the inviting pines on the slope above us on the far side of the road.

Once I had made up my mind to this effect, I called for a couple of volunteers to come with me and see what we could see. Sergeant Storey and Charlie Tobin immediately jumped up, extremely anxious to be able to do something after the long period of enforced inactivity which they had undergone. So I quickly gave them their instructions, and leaving them in the shelter of the house, turned back to give some last minute orders to McNinch who was left in command of the position.

Just as I was turning towards the patrol to lead it out of the shelter of the house towards the entrance to the culvert, a long, wicked burst from that murderous Spandau which had remained quiet for so long, once again shattered the silence, causing our hearts to race madly and the chill sweat of fear to prick out on our brows.

The feeling of relief that surged through me at the thought that the Germans had started their nonsense again before I and my patrol had left the shelter of the house, was interrupted by the sensation of numb horror, when, on looking towards the spot where I had left Storey and Tobin, I discovered that they were nowhere to be seen.

Something akin to panic seized me. God! Had that long and vicious burst been directed at them? Had they wandered out in front of the house without waiting for me? This was the thought which flashed through my mind, and it soon became obvious that that is exactly what had happened.

Vainly we called after them, shouting at them to stay where they were but to let us know if they were all right. But our shouts were drowned by the roar of the Spandau, and no answering voice was heard to soften the anguish in our hearts.

After a short period, the firing again died down, and once more all was silent. Once more we shouted to Tobin and Storey. What was that? I was sure I had heard something. Yes, there it was again and with a feeling of indescribable relief I recognized Storey's voice.

But my relief was only short-lived. After the silence had been completely restored, we found that we could converse with Andy Storey with ease. He was in the culvert beneath the road and was talking to us from a hole we could see on the far edge of the road, about 10 yards ahead of us.

'*Are you all right?*' I shouted.

'Yes, I think so,' he replied, '*But they were pretty close!*'

'*Where's Tobin? Is he with you?*' was my next question.

'*Tobin? No, he's not here. Why? Did he follow me out?*' Sergeant Storey shouted back, amazement and anxiety clearly evident in his voice.

So they had got Charlie Tobin. After we had shouted his name in vain for a further five minutes that was the only answer to the question of his disappearance. I felt frantic at the frustration of not being able to move freely and find out where he was. I attempted to crawl along the side of the house in order to see if he was visible round the corner. But I had hardly started moving when a devilishly accurate burst from the Spandau sent me sprawling back again to the shelter of the house. It was sheer suicide to attempt going forward by that route and so the project had to be abandoned, and I sat disconsolate, overwhelmed with grief and the feeling of utter helplessness.

My feelings must have been the same as those of all sensitive young officers at losing the first of their men. Bitterly I reproached myself for having conceived that hare-brained plan of sending forward that patrol. Were it not for my inexperience perhaps Tobin would be living now. I was the one to blame for his death, and I felt that all the men were looking at me accusingly, with the same thought in their minds.

Another shuddering burst from that Spandau threw me out of these morbid thoughts, as Storey, pale and breathless, came tumbling over the wire fence, landing almost on top of me. I could hear the bullets whizzing off the road a few inches from his swiftly moving heels.

I was at least glad to see him again, apparently none the worse for his adventure. He had waited in his culvert until all had seemed quiet again and had then made a dash across the road to the safety of the house. But that ever-watchful and fiendishly accurate gunner was ready for him, and let him have it as soon as he emerged from his hiding place. But in some miraculous fashion he was unscathed, and such was his stolid Yorkshire calm, he did not even seem to be especially perturbed, at the events of the last few minutes.

We now felt bitter, angry and deeply sorry at Tobin's death, and these emotions rose strong enough within us to make us cast all cautions to the winds and retaliate with all the strength we could muster. Without delay, and with hatred in our hearts, we opened up at those scattered positions, in any one of which that deadly Spandau might be. Tunstall and McNinch were by the Bren gun, sending streams of wicked red tracer into one position after the other. With malicious pleasure we saw a flicker of red flame spring up in the brushwood which served to conceal the largest position and the one most probably containing the Spandau. Tunstall then switched his red tongues of death-dealing tracer to a small cave whose mouth was visible as a black dot on the smooth hillside opposite. With perfect accuracy, the bullets streamed in through the opening.

A sudden movement in the entrance to the cave attracted our attention. A man was there. We gave him a burst just for luck and he scuttled inside. A few seconds later, to our intense pleasure, we observed a white flag being frantically waved from the cave-entrance.

But our jubilation at this welcome sight was not allowed to last for long, for with an angry roar the Spandau again came into action, still completely invisible to our straining eyes. And once it came into action, the uneven contest was over. All too easy was it for the German gunner to spot the exact point from where our fire was coming. The tell-tale tracer, so invaluable for night firing, which was the use to which we had imagined it would be put, gave our position away as completely as if we had run across and told the enemy gunner ourselves. In a very short space of time the bullets were churning up the parched earth around us, kicking up stones into our faces, and ripping the cactus over our heads into shreds of pithy green. It was futile to carry on engaging this unseen enemy and we crouched down in our exposed position, while the bullets whipped around us, and wondered when our last moment would come. Only too obvious was it then that it had merely been some civilians sheltering in that cave who had been waving that white flag so frantically.

This time the enemy seemed determined to finish us off for once and for all. A second Spandau opened up from a position further to the left and all we could do was to try and bury ourselves in the ground, hugging the wall of the terrace on which we were. To our eternal good fortune this wall was very slightly convex (from the point of view of the enemy), and by going back a few yards and keeping as close to it as possible, we were able to escape from the line of fire of those spitting bullets. Try as he might, the Jerry gunner could not bring his fire sufficiently round to hit us, without striking the wall about 5 yards in front. His fire formed a tangent to the curve of the wall, and mercifully we were behind the point of contact. If the enemy gunners were to move about 20 yards to the left, they would be able to hit us again, so we kept our fingers crossed not daring to move from our cramped spot, and praying that it would not occur to the enemy to move into the better position.

Most of our trouble seemed to be coming from that second Spandau, not from the one which had troubled us at first and which had killed Tobin. The bullets were passing really close, despite the fact that they could not hit us. Sandy Davidson soon got so cramped that he tried to stretch his legs, but shakily he pointed to his trouser leg. The moment he had stretched out his leg a bullet had made a neat little hole through his drill trousers. That warned us to hug the wall even closer than before.

After this situation had lasted for close on ten minutes with the enemy gunners pouring in magazine after magazine into our position, churning up the ground and sending the cactuses tumbling down around us, Tunstall got impatient. His face was pale with fury, and his eyes glinted as he started to crawl forward with his Bren gun.

'*I have had enough of this,*' he muttered '*I am not going to let those bastards do this to us,*' and with these words he went back to his previous position. He found a stout piece of board, behind which he crouched aligning his gun over the top. To the shouted orders of McNinch and myself to the effect that he should not be a bloody fool and should come back, he paid no attention whatever. With a muttered curse at his foolhardiness, McNinch sprang up and went to join him. Once again our Bren gun sent its deadly stream into the enemy positions. It gave us joy to see this, and yet we all knew how it would end.

Suddenly, before we had time to realize what had happened, McNinch and Tunstall were hurled back upon us by what seemed an almighty force. The stout piece of board behind which they had been crouching was tossed aside like so much matchwood and the Bren was rolled over into the open. Partly by the force of the impact, and partly by their instinctive recoiling, the two gunners came tumbling down upon us, Tunstall emitting the most dreadful dry gurgling sounds and moaning in gruesome fashion. Blood streamed from his mouth.

We got him into the shelter of the wall and McNinch, heedless of his own exposure, started patching-up his wound, while all around the murderous hail of bullets continued to fly, and we could do nothing in the way of retaliation save lie pressed against the wall of the terrace, our hearts oppressed by a variety of fears and torments.

Tunstall had had a lucky escape. The burst must have struck the ground a few inches in front of him, sending up a shower of dirt and stones into his face. A splinter of the bullet had passed through his cheek as it bounced off the ground, but his teeth seemed all right and after our initial fears, we soon discovered that his injuries were not so serious as we had first imagined. But they must have been very uncomfortable nevertheless, and there was certainly no moving him while this deadly fire continued, so that he had to lie out in the blazing sun, in a cramped position, while the flies, quickly attracted by the smell of blood, buzzed around him, aggravated him by their persistence almost to the point of complete desperation.

For a full half hour the bullets continued to rain around us, while we did not dare move. My binoculars had fallen onto the terrace below, but try as I might, I was unable to retrieve them, as each time I exposed myself to do so, another vicious burst sent me scurrying back to the shelter of the wall. The Germans had been wakened with a vengeance, for in addition to the machine-gun fire directed at us, they were also sending over bomb after bomb into the town below, increasing our fears each time as the dread rush of the bomb passed overhead.

Eventually things quietened down sufficiently to enable me to make a dash for the Bren gun and gain the comparative shelter of the house. Telford and Storey followed, and soon there were three of us in the house, peering through the window in the hope of being able to spot the smoke of those wretched machine guns. But we were not allowed even to look through the window for long, as isolated rifle shots started coming through it at us, forcing us to bend below the level of the sill.

I examined the Bren gun. It had been hit on the bipod, and was completely choked with dirt, but we rapidly got it clean again. It was a comfort to have it within reach once more, in case the Germans should take it into their heads to come down that road, with a view to putting in an attack on our position. We hoped fervently that some of our other troops were in a position to give us support if the enemy tried to emerge from their hiding place, with hostile intentions toward us.

Gradually things grew quiet again, and to a certain extent we were able to regain our composure. What next, we wondered? Would the Jerries put in an attack or would they be content to pin us down in our present position, unable to move an inch without bringing down that hail of bullets?

We did not have to wait long for the next item on the programme. Shaken, and extremely worried at the situation in which we had found ourselves, I happened to look back, just as a figure appeared coming towards us round the bend of the road behind us. To my horror I recognized Corporal Mitchell followed by his sub-section. Oh my God! To see them walking calmly up that road, just after the Germans had shown their sting to the full, was as much as I could bear. Obviously the gunners above were trying the same trick as they had tried with us, namely to let the oncoming troops continue right up that road, until they were in certain range, when it was hoped that a single deadly burst would wipe out the lot of them.

I could not sit there and watch that happening, but why oh why, had Corporal Mitchell come up that road, instead of making use of the cover that was abundant on the hillside above?

Obviously Hair had got back safely, but what had happened to my message? 'Look out, Mitchell,' I shouted, 'get down, they've got every inch of the road covered. Get down and find some cover and for God's sake get off the road, and don't try to reach us.' The anguish in my voice must have conveyed to Mitchell the seriousness of the situation and the urgency of my message, for in a flash his men were scattered in search of cover; but their search was in vain, and Mitchell had to lead his men back down the road at breakneck speed.

At once, realizing that they had been cheated of their prey, the enemy gunners opened up, with all the fire power they could muster. Helpless we watched those vicious bullets chipping fragments off the cliff face, and off the wall by the road, and with every second getting closer and closer to the swiftly running men. It was like a bad dream to have to stand there and watch – they had now reached the bend again, and to our relief all were round it except for the last two men. One of them staggered as he reached the corner and just toppled over, the other also fell. But although hit, they managed to pull themselves round that corner with incredible rapidity and soon to our anxious eyes, there was nothing left to remind us of the horrible drama that had just been enacted.

But it was soon clear that although round the bend and out of view, Corporal Mitchell's section were still under observation from that second gun, situated somewhere further over to the left. Furiously it continued firing, sending a shudder through us at each burst, as we thought of those poor devils haring down the road.

Soon there was a short pause, and then it was our turn again. For a further twenty minutes the bullets whipped around us, subjecting us to all the mental tortures that could be imagined. Eventually the fire died down, the Germans obviously well satisfied that they had wiped us out completely.

If that was their opinion, I was certainly in no way inclined to alter it by showing them that the majority of us were still alive, so I shouted down to McNinch to give orders that no one was to move unnecessarily and that not a shot was to be fired; we did not want to have to go through that lot again. The men certainly did not need to be told twice, and they lay quietly, thankful that the cactus bushes were no longer being torn to shreds above them, and that the dust and stones were no longer being kicked into fury within a few inches of them.

I tried to collect my numbed and scattered senses and to come to some decision as to the best course of action we could now take, in view of the recent events. We had already tried to move to a better position and had been driven back. In vain had the other sub-section tried to reach us, and we greatly feared that they had suffered heavy casualties in the attempt. It was useless for us to try and fall back to a less isolated position, for had we attempted this, we would have undoubtedly suffered the same fate as Corporal Mitchell's luckless sub-section. To go forward was impossible, and indeed it was just about impossible to move more than a yard from our present positions. Thus the only remaining alternative for us was to remain where we were, lying absolutely doggo, so that we would not attract any more of that unwelcome attention down upon us.

This we therefore decided to do, but each one of us wondered if we would ever survive the eight hours that separated us from nightfall, for only under the protection of darkness would we have our first opportunity of making contact with our own troops again. We sited the Bren along the edge of the road, ready to take on any Germans who should attempt to come down it towards us. That was our greatest fear, and I could not avoid the thought that it would indeed be a sorry time for us should this possibility materialize – we would either be killed or taken prisoner, with very little chance of fighting back.

My other fear was that the Germans should move round the hillside, protected by the cover to be found on its upper slopes, until they had reached a point immediately above us. From here they would be able to overlook us completely and deny us the use of even the scant amount of cover we were then utilizing. If they got there I realized there was no hope for us.

And so we lay there for those eight long hours, scarcely daring to move for fear of those deadly guns aligned on us. The quiet of that peaceful valley returned once again, and indeed, so quiet was it that we could even hear the Germans shouting at each other from the other side of the valley. It grew blazing hot, and Tunstall was suffering the acutest discomfort through the heat and the flies. It was feared that he had been blinded as his eyes were so full of dust that they were completely blocked, and looked dull and lifeless. Carefully McNinch tried to sponge them, but this caused Tunstall so much pain that he was unable to do much to make him more comfortable.

In the middle of the afternoon, a sudden sound reawakened my fears and worries. Straight above us, a few rifle shots rang out from the very point from which I had the most to fear should the enemy reach it. Soon the rifle shots were reinforced by long bursts from a carbine or short-range automatic weapon of some sort. But after a while, I discovered to my relief that the shots were going nowhere near us, and were more than likely aimed at the direction of the enemy. Maybe after all, one of our sections was up there, in an effort to give us some help – at any rate no unpleasantness developed from the signs of activity above, and gradually our fears subsided.

The agony of that afternoon is hard to describe. Never have I felt quite so miserable. To have to give up one of my best men as dead and to have another one wounded on my hands, without hope of getting him medical attention before evening – to know that at least half of my other sub-section must have been killed or wounded in trying to reach us, and to know that we were powerless to do anything to improve our positions before dark, were sufficient thoughts to send my spirits to the lowest level. If only we knew where our troops were and what they were doing. We felt wretchedly alone on this bare mountainside, except for that well dug-in enemy detachment above us. How dearly I would have loved to have been able to pass this burdensome responsibility that rested on me alone, into the hands of someone more confident and more capable. After a while I gave myself up completely to my gloomy and morbid thoughts. I bitterly reproached myself, not only for having been the direct cause of Tobin's death, but also of the casualties inflicted on Corporal Mitchell's section. With these feelings uppermost in my mind, I must have set a very bad example to my men, for I did nothing to help them bear their unpleasant lot more cheerfully.

I think they sensed my feelings, for Telford and Storey did their best to set going some sort of easy and light-hearted conversation. But it was all to no purpose – after a few minutes the gloomy silence descended once more upon the scene, and nothing could be heard save the groans of Tunstall, punctuated by the occasional swoosh of a passing mortar bomb on its way to the town.

Storey discovered that by standing on a box, set back from the window, and looking down through the window from this angle, he could just see Tobin's body lying beneath the front wall of the house. He was very obviously dead. He lay there, stretched out peacefully, just as he had first fallen, his rifle by his side, and the dust and foliage mingled in his dulled hair.

And so the hours dragged by – with the aid of our small solid-fuel cookers, we managed to brew up a mess-tin full of tea, with the small remaining amount of water left in our water bottles. This we were able to pass to Tunstall and McNinch, who were by now feeling their cramped position terribly. The sun began to sink in the cloudless sky and the shadows to lengthen. Maybe the seemingly impossible would happen, and we would be allowed to make our way to a more secure position under cover of darkness, but we did not dare allow ourselves to hope too much.

About an hour and a half before dusk, we were horrified to see a figure once again rounding the bend, where a few hours before Corporal Mitchell had met with that murderous rain of fire. It was Sylvester, one of the mortar section, advancing slowly and carelessly up the centre of the road, as though he did not have a worry in the world. Again I shouted my warning to him, but he seemed to disregard it completely, and still come on towards us. Was he mad? we asked ourselves. With bated breath we watched him continue his carefree climb, shouting warnings at him all the while, and wondering just when those machine guns would open up once more. But to our extreme surprise he came on unmolested. At the beginning of the bend, about 50 yards behind us, he stopped and started to talk to someone who was apparently lying in the road, sheltered from the view of us and the enemy by a low 2ft wall that flanked the side of the road. He then came up to us.

'*Message from squadron headquarters,*' he announced pleasantly and casually. '*You are to remain in your present positions throughout the night. Further orders will be issued in the morning.*'

With these words, he turned to leave us. He seemed surprised to learn what we had been through that morning, and not very concerned about the danger to which he was exposing himself, by walking so openly along that road. Obviously it had not been intended for him to make contact with us.

'*By the way, one of your men, Lowson, I believe his name is, is lying in the road beneath that wall, on the bend,*' he carelessly mentioned. '*No, he's not wounded,*' he added in answer to our anxious question, '*but he refuses to move and told me that I was mad to come up to you.*'

Silently we agreed with Lowson, and watched Sylvester stroll down that road again, still without exciting the slightest activity from the direction of the enemy. I began to wonder if they had pulled out, but remembering the sudden way in which Tobin had met his death, was not anxious to investigate. Lowson had certainly shown some sense, for instead of exposing himself by moving back along the entire length of that bare stretch of road, he had lain all afternoon out

Action position, Bagnara, 3 September 1943. Showing shredded jacket and cacti.

in that baking sun, just concealed from the view of the enemy by the curve of the low wall beneath which he lay. He told us afterwards that he had tried to move, but the slightest movement had brought down such a mass of fire upon him that, like us, he had decided that the only thing to do was to lie doggo where he was.

At last the shadows deepened, and the opposing hillside grew blacker and more indistinct in the growing darkness. The first stars shone palely above us, and I decided that it was time for us to move back. We did not relish the idea of lying in that exposed position, allowing the enemy to make full use of the cover of darkness to creep up on us and surprise us.

So softly the word was passed round and silent figures assembled in the shadows of the house. Widely dispersed, we set off down the road, thankful for the darkness which protected us from the watching Germans.

Tony's section, the nearest of our troops to us, was easily found a good 300 yards down the road from the position we had just left, McNinch and Tunstall went straight on to the Aid Post which Phil Gun had set up in the town. Tony and his lads were extremely pleased to see us and were fully aware of the ordeal to which we had been subjected throughout the preceding day. They could not do enough for us and were soon busy cooking us a meal and a hot brew of welcome tea. I fully expected to hear all sorts of recriminations against me, both from Tony himself and from his men, but instead, all I met with was sympathy and understanding. It was just bad luck, they said, and we had done in their opinion, remarkably well to be able to come out of it with so few casualties.

It can be understood how these remarks and sentiments cheered me for I was taking Tobin's death and the other casualties very hard.

Anxiously I asked after Mitchell's sub-section. *'They were amazingly lucky,'* Tony replied, *'for although they were nearly all wounded, we have got them back and there is every chance that they will all recover quickly. Glacken and Corporal Mitchell seemed to have got it the worst. Paddy Glacken was shot in the back, but luckily the bullet went in at an angle, and came out without breaking anything. Corporal Mitchell was hit under the arm, in his side, and I am afraid he lost a lot of blood before we were able to get to him. Kirk got one through the leg, Squires through the wrist, and Little in the arm. Clarke was wounded in the arm by that first mortar bomb.'*

Thank heavens they were all right and that there was every hope that they would recover from their wounds shortly, and would suffer no permanent harmful effects. As it turned out, all of them, except for Kirk were back with me by the end of three months, medical category A1 and operationally fit again. Kirk's leg gave him a lot of trouble owing to the nerve having been severed, and it was thought that it might take two or three years before he was completely all right again.

I gathered also from what Tony said, that some of his section had been terrific getting my wounded lads back. All of Corporal Mitchell's sub-section, except for Sanders and Lowson (who had remained behind), had been wounded in some way or other, and Corporal Mitchell, Glacken and Kirk, had not been able to move from the shallow drain gully by the side of the road, in which they had been able to find some sort of temporary shelter from the enemy fire. Several of Tony's section, without thought for the danger to which they were exposing themselves, had succeeded in getting across the road to them and dragging them safely in.

Tony's section also had had a pretty rough time of it that morning, for the cover they had been able to find was scarcely sufficient. The section lay in a shallow dip among the vines sheltered from the machine-gun fire if they kept low, by the bank of a small wadi running down the mountain side. But though they were able to avoid the bullets, they were still under the observation of the enemy, who would send down a mortar bomb on them every now and then just for luck, and a veritable hail of bombs if any movement were observed from that area. The strain was evident with everyone, but the relief at seeing our own troops once more, and at knowing that, all along, they had been in a position to help us had the enemy tried to attack us, was a very great comfort. Our fears of a few hours previously up by that house where we had seemed so isolated and so helpless now seemed unreal – thus, slowly we began to get over the experience of those past hours and to find our tongues again.

Tony told us what had happened that morning. It had been almost impossible to move in the town during daylight under such close observation from the overlooking heights. Every movement had brought down a bomb from those clear skies, every careless exposure had meant the threat of death. Paddy's HQ situated right in the centre of the town, had had a bad time, for every time a runner approached or left the place, it had been the signal for a few bombs.

Alec had had difficulty in retaliating to this source of trouble, partly because it had been impossible to pinpoint the position of the enemy mortars or of their OP, and partly because of the lack of suitable mortar sites in the area of the town. There was only one decent position but this was right in the centre of the town, and was sufficiently obvious to the enemy for an answering rain of bombs to be brought down on that spot, as soon as he started firing. He therefore chose a small garden, and in spite of difficulties of observation, managed to fire off a few rounds. He then packed up his mortar in double quick time and got under cover to wait for the reply.

It was not long in coming. As Alec had anticipated, a rain of bombs came back on the one position in the town really suitable for mortars, and which for that reason alone Alec had discarded.

Bill Fraser's breakfast had been rudely interrupted. It may be remembered that he was cooking in an open space off the road by the last houses, as we went up the road past him. Almost simultaneously with that first bomb, which had so narrowly missed my section, another bomb had landed fair and square in the middle of the space where Bill's cooking operations were taking place. Two signallers of his headquarters were killed instantly. But Bill, with all the characteristics of the usual Fraser luck, had at that moment just moved off through a gap between two houses, and was unhurt.

Tony told us also, that the rest of our troop – Derrick's section and Harry and his HQ – had managed to climb further up the mountain, into the cover of the young plantation of pine trees and were playing about somewhere up there. More than likely it was they who had been responsible for the disconcerting firing above us on that previous afternoon. If only we had known, what a relief it would have been. Harry had had a remarkable escape. He was carrying a wad of maps in this thigh pocket, and as he was giving orders out to someone, a tracer bullet passed right through his pocket, setting it on fire, and also the maps which it contained. In truly characteristic fashion, Harry calmly patted out the smouldering flames with his hand and went on talking. The bullet passed right through his pocket killing a signaller who was standing nearby.

Thus the unit casualties had been surprisingly small, as apart from those killed or wounded in my section, only three others, strangely enough all signallers, had been killed.

A runner came up breathlessly to Tony's position from squadron HQ with the welcome news that the army, whose job it was to relieve us, had arrived and that the forward elements were even at that moment in the town below us. In all our landings of this nature the moment when we heard that the army had been able to reach us as planned was always cause for jubilation and afforded the biggest relief of the whole operation. The longer our small unit remained behind the enemy lines, and separated by several miles from our main forces, the greater was the risk of our being engaged and probably overwhelmed by some powerful enemy counter-attack.

As soon as the forward patrols of the relieving brigade had contacted us, stretcher-bearers were sent up, and our wounded were immediately evacuated to the base hospital at Reggio Calabria, far to the south of us. No one who saw these men at work has anything but the highest praise to offer at the magnificent way in which they got the wounded away. Again and again they would toil up the

Charlie Tobin's grave, Bagnara, 3 September 1943.

steep hill to the dressing station, carrying their heavy loads several miles back to the ambulance, (for the bridge which had been our primary objective, had been blown a few hours before our landing – we had actually heard the explosion of the demolition from the LCIs), and always returning without wasting a second, cheerful, confident, and soothing to the wounded who were delivered up into their care. These men may have been non-combatants, but they had the guts, the bravery and the endurance of first-class fighting men.

We settled down to sleep that night, wrapped in some old blankets that had been appropriated from a nearby house. It was a long time before we could sleep, so on edge were our nerves after the ordeal of that day. Again and again I would hear that vicious burst that had sent Tobin to his death, and wake with my heart racing and a cold sweat on my brow.

Eventually, worn out as we were, we fell into a fitful sleep. We were woken rudely by the sharp explosion of a mortar bomb, falling only 30 yards or so below us. Hell! They've started again, was the thought as we unrolled ourselves from our blankets, and started to get up. I looked at my watch – it was 6am exactly. Surprisingly enough, that was the Germans saying goodbye to us for we heard nothing more from them the rest of that morning, and it soon transpired that they had pulled out. The news of the arrival of the army in the town below them, made them realize that if they did not get out quickly, they would not be able to escape at all. There is no doubt that the troops opposing us were good soldiers. Their shooting had been most unpleasantly accurate and never by a rash movement did they betray to us their exact position. There could not have been many of them, and I doubt if their number exceeded 30. But there was no denying that they had done a good job, for they had held our whole regiment up for an entire day by the skilful choice of their positions; but of course they were considerably helped by the nature of the ground.

Towards 11am the order came down to us that we would be pulling out within the hour and that the infantry brigade who had relieved us would be taking over our positions. McNinch and I quickly got together and decided that before we went we must bury Charlie Tobin, and so, taking about three other members of the section, we again marched up that stretch of road which held so many dread and vivid memories for us.

But the conditions were different this time. As we slowly dragged ourselves up the steep gradient, we were not troubled by the thought of a watchful enemy above us. It had begun to rain – the first rain we had seen since we had left Palestine – and the lowering clouds and heavy mist gave the scene a very different appearance from that of the previous day, when the sun had blazed down out of a cloudless sky. We reached the house without incident, and there, in the barren rocky soil, we laboriously dug a shallow grave among the vines, into which Charlie's body was gently laid. A couple of the lads hacked out a rough sort of cross, which merely consisted of two sticks bound together. Roughly they scrawled on it the number, rank and name of the dead man and placed it at the head of the grave.

Then after a minute of silence, during which each of us was left to his own thoughts we sadly trooped down the hill to re-join the rest of the regiment.

I found Sergeant McNinch by my side, and was surprised to see this hardened and usually so cheerful soldier overcome with emotion. *'You know, sir,'* he said, as though to himself, *'it's funny that it is always the best that catch it. Charlie Tobin was the kindest-hearted man in the section – he would never say a hard word about anyone – and they have to go and kill him. And here am I a drunken old reprobate, and am still alive.'* In Tobin's pay-book had been found a pathetic will leaving various of his pals in the regiment a few shillings here and a pound or two there.

As if to bear out Mc Ninch's words, that the best always seem to go first, it was scarcely a month later when he too met his death – a cheerful and brave soldier and a born leader, he was the idol of the section who would do anything for him. Possibly, if there should be any truth in his theory, it was just because of these qualities that he had to go. But why waste our time wondering? We shall never be in a position to know what influences the wandering hand of Fate as she cuts a thread of life here, and another there, leaving a multitude untouched in the middle.

We marched down the hill into the town again in that depressing rain, our hearts heavy within us at the thought of death. There was a long march still ahead of us to the south, until we came to two LCIs moored close in to the beach. The sea was rough and the shore was shallow, so we had to wade out to the ships. It was a tricky business as the wind was continually trying to turn the ships broadside to the coast, and it was feared that if the anchor failed to hold, they would be dashed onto the shore. But we got on board without mishap, and were soon speeding towards Messina, which was our immediate destination.

Thus ended the operation at Bagnara where I can say that I first received my baptism of fire. Many useful lessons were taught me on that operation, and thereafter I was no longer the green and inexperienced young officer that I had previously been. A closer bond was formed between me and my men, and thereafter I was able to feel for the first time that they would all follow me anywhere.

From the point of view of the squadron as a whole, the operation was considered a great success. Paddy had pulled the rabbit out of the hat once again, in spite of the fact that the navy had landed us far too late and moreover in the wrong place. But maybe even in this glaring error, Fortune had been smiling favourably upon us, for we later learned that the Germans, who were expecting an attack from our main forces advancing from the direction of Scylla to the south, had taken up strong defensive positions almost exactly on the point where we had planned to land. There is no judging the roundabout and seemingly meaningless ways of Destiny!

As it was our casualties had not been heavy. We had landed behind the main defences of the enemy and had forced them to retire into the hills. Our occupation of the town had greatly facilitated the advance of the main army, up the coast, and had enabled them to move forward 12 miles in a single day. Once again, Paddy had good reason to feel pleased with himself, and the prestige of the regiment was even more firmly established in the opinion of General Dempsey, under whose orders we worked.

But for me personally, it was an experience that I was never able to forget, and which I was not anxious to repeat.

Chapter Nine

Italian Holiday

It was already late in the afternoon when we found ourselves winding through the rambling offshoots from the main harbour of Messina, passing through narrow channels and bays before we eventually tied up in a small dock apparently reserved for LCIs only.

At the best of times the craft were too small to allow any degree of comfort to the numbers they were carrying, and so we were all too ready to go ashore and spread ourselves. But such was the damage that Messina had suffered that it was an incredibly difficult task to find any building in the dock area which even had a roof on it, and so we were not able to find much greater comforts ashore than we would have enjoyed had we remained aboard the LCIs.

However, we settled down in a sort of factory or garage, the roof of which was not completely down, and since the floor was of concrete, there was a mad scramble in search of beds and bedding, in the course of which, with singularly little success, the whole area was ransacked.

Occupied with this many of us visited a nearby Italian barracks which was of course now empty, and laboriously man-handled down to our billet the heavy double-tier wooden beds which we found there. But we were all badly disappointed with the results of our efforts. No sooner had I erected my bed, and with a sigh of relief, cast myself down upon it, than I started scratching. At first I thought it was mere imagination, and made the brave determination not to give up my comfortable bed without a struggle. But it was no use. Eventually the itching became so intolerable that I had to sit up and carry-out a thorough examination, and to my disgust I discovered a stream of flat, brownish bed-bugs scuttling off to shelter as fast as their small legs could carry their bloated bodies. A thorough scrutiny revealed that every crack, every joint in every bed, was teeming with these unpleasant creatures, and so it was with reluctance that we consigned our beds to the cookhouse fire, and resigned ourselves to sleeping on the concrete floor for the next two nights.

Two days were spent quietly at Messina, during which we did nothing but rest and laze around at will. Not many of us ventured far afield, being quite content to chat with each other about the events of a few days previously and to read any books or magazines on which we could lay hands. Franco arrived

'Monty's Highway' – Main road at Reggio Calabria, Italy, September 1943.

with a bag of mail from home, which we were overjoyed to receive, as it was the first batch to come through since we had left Suez, two months before.

The only place of interest that we found in Messina, was a former Italian Fascist headquarters, stacked high with propaganda leaflets, posters and postcards. The entertainment with which these provided us was better than any cinema show, and my whole section spent many amusing hours there collecting these souvenirs as proof of the childish Italian mentality, and the lengths to which Mussolini had to go in order to cajole the Italian people to support him.

But we were not given the time or the opportunity for a thorough examination of Messina, for, late in the afternoon, two days after our arrival there, we found ourselves aboard our craft once more, and steaming towards the white cluster of houses which shimmered on the coastline the other side of the straits, and which we recognized as being Reggio Calabria.

As we sailed out of the harbour and looked towards the receding coastline, we realized that in all probability we were seeing the last of Sicily – that island which held so many memories for us, and which, with a special attraction all of its own, had won its way to a varying extent into the heart of each of us. But not many of the attractions of the island were visible to us as we took our last glimpse of the bomb-shattered houses of Messina as they slipped behind us and faded into the distance. For it was a paralysed, empty town, the former beauty of which was now stamped with the indelible impression of war. Gaping holes and dangling beams were now all that was left of buildings which had previously attracted and welcomed the tourist from afar. And as if symbolic of the catastrophe into which Mussolini had led his country, on the largest and highest building which rose up above this scene of desolation, we could trace the word DUCE painted in enormous black letters.

As we crossed the Straits of Messina, I found myself automatically thinking of the old Roman legends I had heard as a child – of the rock of Scylla and the whirlpool of Charybdis which, between them contrived to send any ship to its doom that attempted to pass through those dangerous straits. And now, man had so far succeeded in conquering or controlling the forces of nature, that we were able to make the crossing in so small a vessel as an LCI, and indeed could have managed it safely in even an LCA. But nevertheless, as I looked over the side of the ship, or listened to the conversation of the naval personnel aboard, it was easy to discover the origins of the old legend. For the straits were only 3 miles wide, and through them the waters of the Mediterranean poured in a fast and capricious current. It was as though this narrow passage formed a bottleneck through which the water had to rush.

We were not bound for Reggio Calabria as we first thought, but for Gallico, a typical small Italian coastal town about 5 miles north of Reggio, and merely consisting of a small cluster of white houses at the foot of the mountains, by the water's edge. Here we were met by the advance party and allocated billets. Even an officers' mess had been picked, and we arrived there to find Paddy and the rest already sampling the cellars of all the houses in the vicinity. Corporal Corps, Paddy's batman, was at the moment I entered, being briefed to reconnoitre a wine store that had only just been discovered somewhere in the vicinity.

I shall always remember that night. It was warm and clear and we sat on the balcony with our glasses in our hands, watching the crowds in the streets below. There was something in the air – the church bells were ringing and all the civilians were running about excitedly, shouting and singing. Obviously they were making rather a pitiful attempt to celebrate something. We wondered what! Small bands of youths and young girls waving the Italian flag paraded through the streets, holding hands. Here and there a bonfire sprang up in the twilight around the flickering glow of which little clusters of black silhouettes collected. In the distance Very lights soared through the air, stabbing the blueness of the serene sky with lazily-moving balls of coloured flame.

Italy had capitulated! And these poor devils were running around madly, trying to force into their dulled hearts, so long stunned and duped by Mussolini's rule of iron, some semblance of happiness, of which they had so long been deprived. Only when the glorious hypnotic veil with which their beloved Duce had shrouded himself, and with which he had invoked their adulation and blind loyalty, had been so roughly torn aside by the landing of our troops in their native country, was their illusion shattered, and they were forced to realize that the essential consideration in their type of war-making was to make sure that they were on the winning side.

'*The war is over – peace, peace, at last!*' The shrill Italian cries rose into the clear night air arousing in us as we watched and listened, not only a feeling of healthy scorn, but also one of pity. Poor fools, we thought, the war may be over for them, but not quite as they think. So long as the Germans carry on the struggle, they will not be allowed to turn their attention to the reconstruction of their overturned regime and the conversion of it to a law-abiding peaceful one, in place of the militaristic one they had formerly fostered so ardently. They will be kept down and bled by our occupying troops who will not easily forget their previous underhand and treacherous behaviour. And if the Germans do not feel inclined to withdraw across their northern frontier, their country will undoubtedly be ravaged by the horrors of war; their fair cities blasted into destruction and their vineyards soaked in the blood of soldier and civilian alike.

Such were our thoughts as we watched the Italians celebrating their peace so joyously. The future for them was grim and frightening: whichever side won in the end, their nation would be held in ridicule, and would have to suffer heavy penalties. And yet in their naiveté, these people were able to celebrate their country's capitulation, with no feeling of shame or foreboding, and with nothing in their hearts but real relief and happiness.

But we were never slow at finding some excuse for a celebration, and so, despite our more realistic thoughts on the subject, we too joined in the general jubilation at Italy's surrender. Barrels of wine were procured from nearby wine stores, and glasses were kept filled until late into the night. Signal cartridges and Very lights were sent shooting into the quiet sky, to the frenzied delight of the watching civilians.

I had a bed to sleep in that night! John Tonkin had found it for me in a neighbouring house, and so pleased was I at this unexpected piece of good fortune, that I made a point of leaving the celebrations early, so that for a change I could have a long, undisturbed night's rest.

But it was the same old story! Hardly had I put the light out and settled myself comfortably among my blankets than trouble began. It was not Paddy this time, who, although drinking heavily, was adopting that night the rather unusual policy for him of 'live and let live'; the torments to which I was subjected were far worse than any which Paddy could devise. An infuriating itch on my arm set me scratching wildly, almost drawing blood so great was my desire for relief. And then it started all over my body. Bed-bugs again! Just my luck when for once I actually had a bed in which to sleep. In vain did I try to let my mind conquer matter by concentrating on sleep and attempting to ignore this torturing itching. I was determined not to give up this bed without a struggle. Time and time again I lit the candle and went on a careful round of inspection, flattening with an angry blow those repulsive little brown creatures, which crushed with a pop leaving a bright red stain of freshly sucked blood. But the contest was too uneven and eventually I had to withdraw to a less vulnerable spot, and even then my sleep was restless and disturbed, for I had taken along several of the wretched creatures in my blankets. Perhaps the most annoying thing about it all was that John Tonkin who was sleeping in the same room on another bed, slept through the night without receiving a single bite.

The next day I learned that Phil Gunn was going to Reggio to see how our wounded were getting on, and I was glad to accompany him, in order to find out the state of my own men who were reported to be in the hospital there.

What I saw cheered me immensely. Little, Squires and Clarke all had minor flesh wounds and were remarkably active and cheerful, while all the more serious cases were doing well and were in high spirits. Only Kirk seemed to be in pain and worried about the future, and it was not easy trying to cheer him up. I never saw him again as his wound took a long time to heal, through the nerve being severed, and he was the only one who did not eventually return to me.

Also in the hospital, in the same ward as most of my lads was a German corporal who belonged to the party we had surprised at Bagnara, and who had been wounded in the arm. I could not resist going up to him and airing my German on him. After the necessary introductions I asked him a few questions. He was a young fellow, speaking with a strong Rhineland accent, and certainly did not seem to be one of the arrogant, fanatical Nazis about whom we had heard so much.

'*Were you surprised when we opened fire on you?*' I asked rather brutally.

The German nodded vigorously. '*Yes indeed, even after you had been firing at us for some time, we still thought you were Italians.*'

'*Are you glad that you are now a prisoner and safely out of the war,*' was my next question.

'*Yes, very glad,*' was the astonishing reply. '*At least I can feel safe now, which I was never able to do before.*'

'*And what do you think are Germany's chances of winning the war now?*'

'*Impossible. We have no hope of winning,*' replied this most sensible and un-fanatical corporal.

'*How long do you think the war will last now?*' I then asked. '*Another year?*'

The German shook his head, '*Scarcely,*' he muttered. Although aware that I was decidedly hitting this man while he was down, I could not resist having another crack at his expense. '*And what do you think of your wonderful Luftwaffe?*' was my final question.

An eloquent exclamation of disgust was the only answer I received. Quite obviously this particular German did not think much of his precious Luftwaffe.

After that, I took my leave of this surprising German. The interview worried me. Why were we fighting decent people like that? There was no hatred in his eyes as he spoke to me, indeed he even seemed pleased at the opportunity of talking to someone in his own tongue. He was no ardent Nazi with puffed-up ideas about the master race. He was just a simple country boy, stolid, unintelligent and good-natured. He did not want to fight us any more than we wanted to fight men like him. It all seemed wrong somehow, to think that only two or three days before I had been crouching behind a bush with murder in my heart, frantically encouraging my section to kill this very man.

We left Gallico the next day. The same two LCIs which had landed us at Bagnara took us off. We had come to Italy because XIII Corps had been sent over to take part in the invasion of the mainland. Apparently the invasion of Italy was progressing so well, that we were already far behind General Dempsey's corps headquarters, and now had to move up to a new base further north.

So we lay on the deck of the LCI making the most of the friendly autumn sun, and watching the green Italian mountains slowly glide past our starboard rail. Sicily faded behind us and was soon no more but an indistinct smudge on the horizon. On we went, past Bagnara, all the time hugging the coast; the rocky, vine-clad mountains, falling steeply to the very water's edge and towering over us, completely dwarfed us. Here and there we passed a small cluster of white or pink houses which sprawled along the narrow shore, or made half-hearted attempts to scale the neighbouring heights above. And all along the coast ran the little single-track railway, winding round the mountains like a child's model, and occasionally disappearing into the heart of a mountain, to emerge again from the other side. Away out to sea numerous small islands broke the straight line of the horizon. Barely more than single rocks, they jutted sharply out of the blue water, radiating pearly pink lights in the afternoon sun. And then they too were behind us.

At last we rounded a bend and turned in towards a small bay. The mountains drew back from the coast, leaving a mile wide strip of flat green orchards broken occasionally by the gentle undulation of a foothill. Around the bay the usual collection of brightly coloured houses met the eye. But this was no fishing village such as we had been passing throughout that day; it was a small town by the name of Pizzo and it was here that we made our next temporary base before we continued northwards once more.

Pizzo was half way up the foot of Italy and was situated on about the narrowest part. The railway station was taken over as billets for our troop and No.3 Troop and very comfortable billets it made. As for the officers, they were very comfortable. Tony who had gone off ahead as advance party had managed to take over for us a charming little house right by the water's edge. For a change, it was clean and comfortably furnished, and the majority of us even had beds. We merely had to step through the French window and we were on the fine, silvery sand of the beach, and then a 20 yards run took us unto the clear warm water into which the beach disappeared steeply.

We spent a very pleasant few days at Pizzo, with no thought for the future, but enjoying the present to the full. But we also made use of this opportunity to digest the lessons we had all learned at Bagnara. Thereafter we determined we would keep away from roads like poison, only advancing up them, when no other alternative was possible. And then again, if only we had had a 2-inch mortar with us at Bagnara

Scalea – 13 Corps HQ officers' shop, September 1943.

we might have been able to make those Germans opposite us feel considerably more uncomfortable than had been possible with our available weapons. And so a 2–inch mortar was issued out to each section, and for two or three mornings we went out to a neighbouring small hill and practised the various ways of getting the best effect from this invaluable little weapon.

Our next holiday resort was Scalea, another small town, this time well up the ankle of Italy. We were taken there by our LCIs in the same way as before, and found on arrival that the whole Special Service Brigade comprising No.3 Commando, No.41 Marine Commando and ourselves, were to be based at this spot.

Scalea was a picturesque but dirty little town built on the top of a hill, and descending by a maze of mean and narrow streets to the water's edge. The beach was broad and sandy, in the midst of which, right opposite the centre of the town rose up a massive rock, dwarfing the neighbouring houses as it raised its bulk like a small hill above their rooftops. A small German landing craft had been sunk by our aircraft about 100 yards out to sea, and its masts and some parts of its superstructure were still visible sticking forlornly out of the water.

Johnny Wiseman and 'Franco' Francis, Scalea, Italy, September 1943.

At Scalea we were only a mile or two from XIII Corps HQ and so had to behave ourselves. General Dempsey came to see Paddy and it was soon obvious that the two of them had formed a real friendship based on mutual admiration and agreement in ideas. This seemed strange as on the surface the two seemed so different, but it is quite probable that the difference was not so much due to different characters but rather to the respective positions which they each held.

Possibly the same qualities – determination, shrewdness, a quiet and calculating common-sense and a real brilliance in anticipating the thoughts and actions of the opposing commander – were, in the main, those which had caused each of them to progress so far in his own special sphere, and which now allowed them to find pleasure in each other's company.

Paddy was in a great festive spirit during those few days we spent at Scalea and on several occasions the sergeants came up to the officers' mess to join in a social evening. Glasses would be kept filled, tongues would loosen, and differences of rank would be forgotten. There would be serious discussions, anecdotes at someone or other's expense, light-hearted banter punctuated by loud and numerous peals of laughter.

And then Paddy would think that it was time to sing. He would sit back in his chair, gaze fixedly in front of him with a wicked grin on his face, and holding a glass of whisky precariously in one hand would launch forth into 'Eileen' one of his favourite Irish songs.

Paddy knew he could not sing and he would not try to. Occasionally he would strike one note, tremble on it for a fraction of a second, only to lose it again. Nine-tenths of his song was spoken in a high-pitched monotone, but with some sort of queer timing and cadence about it, as though in the singer's ears he was being accompanied by a mighty orchestra imported direct from the Emerald Isle. The music was obviously in his mind, but not in his voice! Thus we never knew the tune of this song 'Eileen' as, with the exception of Corporal Taggart, the mess cook, Paddy was the only one who did, and he could

'Franco' Francis and Peter Davis, Scalea, Italy, September 1943.

not reproduce it. Neither did we learn the words beyond the opening line, 'Eileen, beautiful Eileen, Won't you come walking with me', (or something like that, for Paddy would never sing the song unless he had plenty to drink, and by that time his brogue would have become so pronounced that it was well nigh impossible to make out what he was saying. And added to this, his voice whether he were talking or 'singing' would be so low, as to be almost inaudible.)

Once Paddy had started off on 'Eileen', we knew that this was the signal for the party to begin. Corporal Corps, Paddy's batman would be summoned, and was made to sing to the gathering. Not that Corps minded really, for by this time he had become all too well accustomed to this form of treatment, but he always felt it necessary for his own self-respect to resist for a time the CO's arbitrary demands upon him. Corps had a lovely rich tenor voice, typically Irish, which he knew how to use, and the way he rendered the sad, haunting air of 'Kevin Barry' (one of Paddy's favourite rebel songs about the ruthless way the hated English stamped out the Irish freedom!) was sufficient to move a company even in such hilarious spirits as we were.

Then Sergeant Bennet would stand up and in a rather slushy tenor voice would croon out some popular sentimental song, or would give us a few tunes on his mouth-organ, at which he was a master. He would be followed by Casey who in a rough, tuneless voice would come out with a version of 'Down in the garden where the Praties grow'.

As a break and relief from all this singing McNinch would be called upon to reel off some of his monologues. He was a past-master at the game, for without a flicker of an eyelid, and with a face completely devoid of expression, he would sit back in his chair, glass in hand, letting the mirth-provoking words roll off his tongue with a facility which implied much training before many an appreciative audience. And although his long, rambling stories, certainly not fit to be heard in any drawing room, kept us all convulsed with laughter, he allowed nothing to disturb his granite-like expression and his slow, regular delivery.

As a rule Paddy was disgusted with any of the bawdy conversation with which one usually meets when a number of men get together, and it is probably for this reason that the parties we had were really surprisingly clean. To this, McNinch with his monologues was the exception, but he got away with it simply because he was able to put his story across so well, and because he did not merely rely on smutty remarks in order to raise a laugh.

After McNinch had run through a selection from his very ample repertoire, the star turn was called out, namely Sergeant Major Rose whose full, rich and well-handled voice was always much in demand. The room was completely silent as he sang 'Mother Macrea' which would be followed by something more lively such as 'The green-eyed yellow Idol', and then, without fail, we would have our regimental song, our own version of 'Lili Marlene', based on a chorus which we had picked up from 450 Squadron back at Etna. It did something to us to hear these words so gaudily describing the sort of work for which we were trained to do, and yet set to the sad music of the well-known German song.

As Rose sang, the haunting notes seem to hang in the silent air. Conversation would cease and men would listen intently as they tapped time to the music with their toes or fingertips, soaking in those typical words which came from us and belonged to us so completely.

There was a song we always used to hear,
Out in the desert, romantic, soft and clear,
Over the ether came the strain, the sweet refrain, each night again,
With you, Lili Marlene, with you, Lili Marlene.

Check you're in position, see your guns are right,
Wait until the convoy comes creeping into sight,
Now you can press the trigger, Son, and blow the Hun, to Kingdom come.
And poor Marlene's boyfriend will never see Marlene.

Forty thousand rounds of tracer and of ball,
Forty thousand rounds of the stuff that makes them fall,
Finish your strafing, drive away, and live to fight another day,
And poor Marlene's boyfriend will never see Marlene.

Creeping into Fuka, fifty planes ahead,
Belching ammunition, and filling them with lead,
A flamer for you, a grave for Fritz, He's like his planes, all shot to bits,
And poor Marlene's boyfriend will never see Marlene.

The Afrika Korps has sunk into the dust,
Gone are its planes, its tanks are turned to rust,
No more do we hear that soft refrain, that lilting strain, each night again,
With you Lili Marlene, with you Lili Marlene.

As the last note of the song died away in the smoky air, there was a momentary silence, as though each of those old campaigners who had originally made the name of the regiment widely known through their hard and daring desert battles, were far away, reliving the past, and were only able to return gradually to the present life.

Then the talk, the jokes, and the laughter would begin again, glasses would empty and fill more quickly, and the party would continue until the morning sun streamed through the windows. Paddy was in his element. He was never so happy as when he was able to drink amid a crowd of his officers as eager to drink as he. He would always think up some new subject for conversation or some new diversion to keep everyone active. Trials of strength would be started and strong men would lie on the floor facing each other with their right hands clasped and their elbows on the floor, trying, with the beads of sweat standing out on their brows, to force their opponent's wrist and forearm down onto the ground. Or there would be cock fighting, in which two opponents would try to catch each other off-balance, and 'throw' each other. And when all had tired of such exertions, there would be competitions as to who could drink a pint quickest, or who could balance a full glass of wine on his forehead and, keeping it there, sit down and eventually lie horizontal on the floor, and then get up again without spilling a drop.

Such was a typical party that we used to have in the regiment. Many of course were not so harmless or so friendly. For instance, Corporal Taggart, the old Irish mess cook, who had seen too many of his countrymen succumb to liquor and in consequence would never touch a drop of the stuff himself, confided in me one day how he was always able to know which way the developing party would turn.

'It's like this, sir,' he said. *'If the CO starts off by singing "Eileen" I know that everything will probably be quiet and peaceful. But it's when I hear him singing that song "And he trod on the tail of my coat" that I know there is going to be trouble. For that is a fighting song, and the CO will bring his fist down with a crash on the table at the appropriate place in the song, sending the glasses flying. And once he does that, that sort of puts ideas into his head, and he will then go around wanting to have a crack at anybody he sees.'*

I don't know how much truth there was in Taggart's theory, but thereafter I was always careful to step very warily when I heard Paddy start up with 'On the tail of my coat', for when Paddy became awkward, chaos was let loose. No one would be safe. Everyone, whether he wanted to or not, had to come in to drink. Glasses and bottles would fly and raids would be made on neighbouring billets and rooms. No one in the house could hope to escape from the 'party', with the result that as soon as it became apparent that the party was going to be a rowdy one, there would be a scuttle of mess staff down the stairs and out of the house into a safer building, where they could hope to spend the night without disturbance. But even this was only a hope, and not always realized, for if Paddy took it into his head that he wanted someone's presence, distance would be no deterrent to him, and the unfortunate victim sought out and forced to present himself!

We were hardly allowed to spend any longer at Scalea, than we had spent at Pizzo, for after only a week, we found ourselves on the move once more. A rumour of an impending operation flickered into life, smouldered for a day or so, and then went out. We were surprised to find that we were not continuing our trip northwards up the west coast of Italy. The LCIs were taking us all south again, through the Straits of Messina and back to Catania. Why? We asked ourselves this question, time and time again.

On arrival back at Catania we installed ourselves in our old camp among the lemon groves. Once settled, the prospect of an impending operation seemed more and more certain, for stores were collected and issued and we were made up to fighting strength once more. The buzz of excitement began to spread among us and would not be stilled.

Catania bore a very different appearance from that which had met us when we first saw the town. Now, it was clearly a Line of Communication area. Small notices proclaimed that here lived such people as the Claims and Hiring's personnel, the Pay Corps HQ etc. and in front of the main barracks two impeccably dressed kilted sentries stood guard, as smart and shining as any guard outside Buckingham Palace. There were officers' clubs, troops' theatres and cinemas, and an immense NAAFI. The trams were running once more, most of the shops had re-opened, and a busy throng of shoppers was filling the main shopping centres, although there seemed little enough for them to buy.

We only spent two nights at Catania, the second of which was somewhat disturbed. Paddy had felt the urge to celebrate. I do not know whether he sang 'The tail of my coat', but at any rate he was in a very wicked mood that night. All the officers were sleeping on the balcony of the small house which had been used on the occasion of our first visit as the squadron head-quarters. A terrific din awakened us, as though a large-scale air raid were in progress. But it was only Paddy. We could hear him stumbling through the rooms of the house, like the proverbial bull in the china shop. Every now and then there would be a mighty crash followed by the tinkle of broken glass. We pulled the blankets over our heads

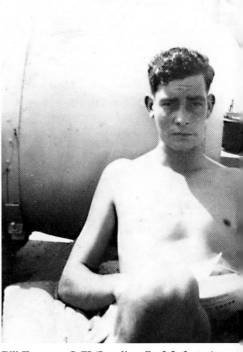

Bill Fraser on LCI (Landing Craft Infantry), Italy, October 1943.

LCI Squadron at Manfredonia, 2 October 1943.

and lay where we were, feigning sleep, and wondering how much longer we would be left relatively undisturbed.

We had not long to wait, for shortly afterwards flower pots came hurtling out of the French window of Paddy's room, to burst with a crash and disintegration on the hard paving stones beside us. No one moved, though each moment fearing that one of those flying flower pots would land on some recumbent form. Soon, to our relief, Paddy tired of the pastime of trying to make the flower pots or glasses land as close to us as he could without actually hitting one of us. Then, terrific crashes and the scurry of feet below proclaimed that things, and large and heavy things at that, were being toppled over the balcony. The mess staff sleeping below were beating a rapid retreat. Immense earthenware bowls full of earth, each of which must have weighed 2–3 cwt, went crashing to the ground in this manner, to burst with a sickening explosion on the paving below.

The next morning revealed a scene of incomparable chaos, despite the fact that a squad of men was busy cleaning the place up. So bad did it look that the damage was easily passed off to the Claims and Hiring's officer who visited us later that day, as bomb damage.

After spending two free days we set sail again. Our little fleet of six LCIs each towing two LCAs set off northwards once more, carrying besides ourselves, No.3 Commando and No.41 Marine Commando. Was it another job we

Paddy Mayne, Manfredonia, 2 October 1943.

wondered. But the persistent rumour was squashed. We were told that we were still fulfilling our previous role of following up behind XIII Corps. They had been transferred from the west coast of Italy to the east coast, and we were merely following them. While the change had been taking place, we had been sent back to Catania to re-equip, and we were now going up the east coast, until we came up with XIII Corps headquarters again.

This explanation seemed logical and satisfactory, and successfully killed the rumour.

For one night and two days we sailed northwards. We saw the lights of Brindisi flickering out to sea, despite the black-out, and then towards evening of the following day, we pulled into a small harbour that lay nestling below a long mountainous tongue of land that jutted out to sea. It was Manfredonia, a small town which had somehow remained untouched by the war. As we drew into the quay, we saw a vast crowd of civilians waiting there to receive us. Somehow they had obviously heard of our approach. As we drew nearer, a ragged cheer from the quay interrupted the silence of the evening. And then they began to cheer and wave wildly with an enthusiasm which was difficult to fathom. Here were we, the invaders of their homeland, being treated as liberators. It all struck us as being peculiarly false, especially since the first question the civilians asked us was invariably, *'When will the food ships be arriving?'* That evidently was why they were so enthusiastic. What a funny war these Italians were having, when they thought that once they had changed sides, everything would at once be all right for them, and that their past sins would be speedily forgiven them.

Suddenly the rumours of a coming operation rekindled and spread like wildfire. General Dempsey was here, and even now he and Paddy were in conference. This was at least true, for in the middle of the afternoon, we saw them pacing slowly down the quay in earnest conversation.

Before even the general had taken his leave, the rumour about the operation was confirmed by Harry summoning his officers and giving us a rough preliminary briefing. We were on our way to Termoli, where the whole Special Service Brigade was to do a landing on a larger scale than any of the preceding ones. Manfredonia lay on the south side of the large hump which formed the top of Italy's boot. Just on the north side of this hump lay the small town of Termoli, which we knew to be of considerable strategic importance, because of the fact that it lay on the eastern end of an important main road running right across Italy from west to east.

Because of this we felt that the Germans would not easily be persuaded to relinquish their hold upon the town, and we were therefore filled even more than usual with forebodings that all would not go well with us in the coming landing, and that there would probably be hard fighting and many casualties in store for us.

It was not a happy prospect as we sailed through the blackness of that moonlit night towards our objective, scarcely 40 miles away.

Chapter Ten

Termoli

It was a dark night, and we had hardly started on our journey towards Termoli, when black clouds began to blot out the stars and the rain to fall softly. There was a feverish activity aboard the small craft, as we made every effort to find out for ourselves, and to pass on to our waiting sections, any detail which might prove to be helpful.

As usual our briefing consisted of an essentially simple plan. This time the plan was so vague, in fact, that we were hardly told anything, and realized that our actions would have to be decided for us by the way future events developed. As it was, Harry was able to tell us the following.

The whole brigade would land at a point about three quarters of a mile beyond the town, and there No.3 Commando would stay, to clear the beach and form a strong beachhead. No.41 Commando would attack the town of Termoli itself and attempt to capture it before dawn. Meanwhile we would push on rapidly inland to try and capture, and prevent from being blown, two important bridges which ran across a small river that flowed about 2 miles south-east of the town. No.3 Troop would deal with the bridge which carried the main coast road across this river, while No.1 Troop was responsible for the bridge further inland, by which the main lateral road crossed it. If we could capture these two bridges, unblown, and hold them until our main forces arrived, we would have done a useful job indeed.

Overlooking the town and the two bridges was a ridge of high ground which it was essential for us to take if we were to hold on to our objectives once these were won. This then was No.2 Troop's task and, avoiding the roads, we would make our way across country to these hills, clear them, and take up good defensive positions upon them. Harry, with troop HQ together with Derrick's section and Tony's section would be responsible for overlooking the bridges, while I was to be behind them, overlooking the small country track which connected the village of Castel Benito with the town of Termoli, and thereby ensuring that our west and south-west flanks were covered.

And that is all we were told. No information about the probable enemy strength had been given and thus once again, the job was no more than a gamble. If the place turned out to be strongly held, we would have a very tough time, while on the other hand, if it were only lightly held, we would hardly be able to say that fighting for it had been necessary. Which would it be this time we wondered? Murro di Porco had been a walkover, Augusta, rather more tricky, Bagnara really rather unpleasant, and now Termoli?

Several pointers made us feel that this time we would not be so lucky, and that this would be just the spot that the enemy would be likely to want to defend strongly. For one thing, as already mentioned, an important lateral road, running across Italy reached the Adriatic coast at this point. The country was much flatter than we had hitherto found in Italy, and thus the enemy might well decide to make a stand for it here with his armour. And finally the presence of that river which ran 3 miles or so south-east of the town, and which was the first decent sized stream that had so far been encountered in Italy, seemed very ominous to us. If the enemy were looking round for a temporary defensive line, it seemed likely that this river would immediately attract them, and they could therefore be expected to be found in the area in comparatively strong numbers!

That was the worst thing about these landings we had to do. The mental strain which went with them was intense, and was often far in excess of what the job warranted. It was all such a gamble. Even though we carefully weighed up all the pros and cons in our minds that we could think of, the ultimate outcome and success of the operation depended so much on luck, that it was well nigh impossible to make a satisfactory prediction. We might capture all our objectives without firing a shot. Or we might take a small enemy by surprise and polish him off. Or we might be met by an expectant and alert enemy and have to fight for every inch of the way. And worst of all, and what we all dreaded more than anything else, was the grim possibility that the enemy might be able to mount a powerful counter-attack upon us and wipe us out before our main forces had caught up with us.

Before every operation we prayed that we would be able at least to get ashore under cover of surprise. And once we had a secure footing on the shore, the thought of a possible counter-attack was never far off. How lucky in some ways it is, that we cannot foretell the future, for had we known then, as we prepared for this landing at Termoli, that that little town was to be the scene of one of the bitterest battles many of us were ever to experience; that a very powerful German counter-attack was indeed to develop, but by the grace of God a few hours after the leading elements of the main forces had reached us; and that even then the situation would be extremely critical for the following 48 hours; we would have gone ashore on that landing filled with all manner of fears, which would probably have adversely affected our fighting qualities.

Through the blackness of the night we were just able to discern the blacker line of the Italian coast, as it slowly unwound itself past us. There we waited with our equipment on, completely ready for the slight bump that was to tell us that we had landed. All was silent, save where a rifle accidently clinked against the side of the superstructure.

We looked towards the shore. There over on the port side was the little outcrop of land on which we knew the town was situated. We were being landed in the right place this time. Although we were in the same landing craft which had landed us at Bagnara, and which had then come in for so much criticism from us, we had nothing but the highest praise for the way the navy were carrying out the job on this occasion.

In complete silence we edged our way in towards the low cliffs of the shore. The ship shuddered and was still. We were there. Nervously we hitched up our packs and prepared to go off. But there was some delay and the disembarkation seemed to be being carried out with ominous slowness. We had touched down on a low sandbank about 20 yards from the beach and the ramps were not long enough to span the gap. This was where the LCAs which we had been towing came in useful, for as quickly as possible, these were made ready, and soon they were ferrying us speedily and silently over the intervening stretch of water.

At last we were ashore, and I quickly got my section together and struck off inland until we came to a railway cutting. Here we stopped in the friendly shelter that this afforded, while Harry sorted out his troop, and checked that all were present. I looked at my watch. It was 3am: only two hours before dawn.

The railway cutting seemed full of troops, as No.3 Commando and No.41 Marine Commando were also there, and a fevered ten minutes was spent in sorting out this mass of men into their respective units and sub-units. Many were the challenges whispered tensely through the darkness, as a sub-unit of marching men came upon another. Brian Franks of No.3 Commando, was busy getting his unit together and happened to come across John Tonkin's section. The password we had adopted consisted of the usual challenge and answer. This time the challenge was 'Jack Hobbs', the answer to which was to be 'Surrey and England'.

Brian Franks wanted to establish the identity of the section of troops he could vaguely see in the darkness ahead of him, so he approached and whispered the password challenge to John Tonkin. '*Jack Hobbs!*' '*Sorry sir,*' came the immediate reply from John who had quickly recognized the challenger, '*he's not in this section. This is the S.R.S. here!*'

Meanwhile Harry had got all our troop together and without further delay we set off on our journey inland, towards the ridge of high ground which we knew to be 2 or 3 miles away, and which we had to reach before dawn.

The going was bad; the light rain which had fallen earlier on in the night had made the ground very slippery, and the loose soil was quickly churned up into a sticky mud by the countless stealthy feet that passed over it. We were wearing rubber soled boots, to ensure that all our movements were carried out as silently as possible, and it was with considerable dismay that we found that these afforded absolutely no purchase on the slippery, muddy ground over which we had to go. Under the weight of our heavy packs we struggled up the far slope of the railway cutting. There were many delays as one man after another found himself slipping down that treacherous incline, and it was only with considerable difficulty that we were able to reach the top at all. Each man, once he had reached a suitably secure position had to help the next man up to it, before he could again proceed.

Thus, when we had all eventually reached the top of the cutting, a good forty minutes had elapsed from the time when the LCI had first touched the shore. In scarcely an hour and a half it would be light, and the one thing we did not want, was to be revealed by the light of the rising sun plodding across the 2 miles of open ground that separated us from our destination.

So on we struggled, the urgency of our position lying heavily upon us, as with the sweat pricking out all over our bodies we fought our way forward step-by-step up the gentle slope of the open country we were crossing. Continually a man would slip and fall headlong. He would be helped up by his neighbour, and then with increased exertions would strive to make up the gap that had grown between him and the man in front.

We came upon Alec's mortar section who were suffering even worse difficulties than we, for they were loaded to capacity, and even under favourable conditions would not have made easy progress. Each of the 'carriers' was loaded with twelve 10lb bombs, so that with over a hundredweight on their backs they found that the treacherously slippery surface was almost too much for them. But they struggled on, realizing that if they did not reach cover before dawn, there would be little hope for them and the utter urgency of the situation gave them added strength. How pathetic it was to see one man in particular, who was small and slight in build, bent double by the weight of the enormous load he was carrying, and almost with tears of desperation in his eyes straining every muscle to try and accomplish something that he was physically incapable of doing. But he had guts and nothing would make him say no. Every minute he would slip and fall, to be helped to his feet by Tony, to stagger on a few yards again and then repeat the process.

The strap of the pack belonging to a mortar bomb carrier broke and as I brought up the rear with my section I found this dejected man standing by his now useless load, wondering what to do. I bade him leave the pack behind and attach himself to my section.

As we plodded on, we began wondering how our other two troops were faring. For even if we did consider ourselves to be having a rough time of things, we realized that they were certainly worse off. For the two bridges which were their objectives lay almost twice as far from the point where we had landed, as the ridge towards which we were bound. We knew that they had started off before us, but fervently hoped that they were making better going, for otherwise they would never reach their objectives under the protecting cover of darkness.

We crossed a road and realized that we were about half way towards our ridge. At that moment a few ragged shots rang out from the direction of the town to our rear. They were followed immediately by a wild burst of firing, which continued spasmodically for the next fifteen minutes. Obviously the marine commandos had run into some sort of trouble, but from the sound of the firing it seemed that our side were holding their own without trouble, for the quick-firing bursts from the German light machine-guns were rare, and were almost drowned in the rattle of the Brens.

We had now lost our precious surprise and had to proceed with more care than ever. The eastern sky was rapidly paling, and already our range of vision was being uncomfortably extended. But to our good fortune, there was a light ground mist which we knew would remain until the heat of the sun had grown sufficiently to dissipate it. But it was an uncomfortable sensation to find it getting brighter every minute, and yet no matter how much we strained our eyes, nothing could be seen all around save the monotonous flat plain of grassland over which we were passing as quickly as our tired legs could carry us. Not a tree, not a hedge, or small wood loomed up to give us a feeling of security against the ever increasing brightness of day, which left us feeling exposed and vulnerable as we scurried forward towards the cover which we knew lay somewhere ahead.

Eventually, just as it was becoming most dangerously light, we topped a small rise, and there to our joy, right in front of us we saw that the country had taken on an entirely different aspect. For 200 yards, an undulating scrub-covered stretch of rough country rolled away in front of us, its outline broken here and there by sparse copses of dry, aged trees. We entered this welcome cover just as the golden rim of the sun rose up over the horizon to our left. Straight in front we could see, indistinctly looming through the mist, the vague form of the ridge towards which we were aiming. The presence of this high ridge in the hitherto flat and open country seemed rather unnatural, as though it had been arbitrarily placed there by some almighty creative hand.

And even as we rapidly covered the intervening space which separated us from the welcoming, vine-clad slopes now clearly visible in the light of the growing day, a shower of sparks seemed to rise into the air from the crest and in a graceful parabola slowly curve down towards us. They were tracer bullets and the sound of the firing reached our ears a few seconds later. We dived for the nearest available cover and with thumping hearts glued our eyes to the spot, in an endeavour to sum up what was now happening.

It did not take us long to realize that although the bullets were scattering all over the area, they were not being fired at us. Indeed so dispersed and unco-ordinated were they that we soon concluded that the bullets were ricochets off the top of the ridge. What is more the tracer was red. Obviously one of our troops, almost certainly No.1 Troop, whose objective we knew to lie somewhere on the other side of this stretch of high ground, had bumped into a detachment of the enemy, and their fire was passing high onto the ridge and falling in a cascade of red sparks into the area in which we were. We learned later that Bill Fraser's troop had ambushed a stretch of road and caught a half-track and motorcycle combination, which they had succeeded in blowing off the face of the earth.

Doubling through the hail of spent tracer bullets, we reached a sunken track down which we proceeded until we came to the point where two tracks crossed. We had a field of fire of several hundred yards from this spot, and since these tracks would very likely form the route along which the enemy might possibly come, this junction seemed the obvious spot in which to take up a temporary defensive position.

So my section dispersed and took up their various concealed positions, and we sat down to await further developments while the growing heat from the rising sun gave warmth to our bodies and comfort and confidence to our hearts. All was now quiet; not a shot was to be heard – not the slightest sign of battle broke the peacefulness of the pastoral scene.

Soon my radio operator informed me that he was in contact with troop HQ. They had reached the top of the crest without incident, and had been busy rounding-up several surprised and rather dazed Germans who had offered little resistance. They had now cleared the whole eastern half of the ridge of the enemy and were firmly established along the top, in excellent positions. I was told to remain in my present position, and in the meantime to make sure that the valley in which I was, was clear of all enemy.

It was scarcely possible to believe that we were still technically behind enemy lines, so peaceful was the surrounding scene. The Italian peasants were carrying on with their normal daily tasks, just as though nothing unexpected had occurred that preceding night, and as though our presence were completely taken for granted.

Soon after 10am I took out a small reconnaissance patrol with which I wandered round the area to see if anything was developing. We made for a white farmhouse which was situated on the top of a slight knoll, which looked as though it might be in a dominating position. The farmer was in the middle of his yard busily crushing grapes with some type of primitive wine-press. Mostly by sign language we obtained from him the information that there were no Germans within 4 miles of us, and so were able to proceed towards the road with some degree of confidence. An Italian came rushing up to us and confidentially pressed into the palm of my hand a small round brown loaf of bread, not unlike that made by the Arabs, together with a piece of strong smelling farm cheese. He also confirmed the report that there were no Germans within 4 miles, and moreover informed us that on the road junction which lay about 400 yards away, over the crest, a detachment of British troops was installed.

We quickly made our way over to the spot in question and made contact with a section of Marine Commandos who seemed to be having a lovely time. Concealed in the ditches, they covered not only the main coastal road with their fire, but also the minor road leading to the village of Castel Benito which lay somewhere beyond the ridge of high ground in possession of No.2 Troop. Every ten minutes or so, a small German car or motor-cycle would be seen approaching. The ambushers waited until the last moment and then opened up on it. They had already captured several vehicles in this way, and those which were no longer serviceable after the rough treatment they had received, were quickly manhandled into a small dip in the ground that lay nearby, from where they would be invisible to the next unsuspecting Germans who approached. Apparently, as the officer in charge gleefully told me, the Germans seemed to be very slow in realizing that something was up, for the ambushing party had been at their game ever since dawn, and still the German vehicles came along singly or in pairs at regular intervals. Even as we were speaking, the cry was raised that another motorcycle had been sighted coming down the main-road, and a few minutes later its battered remnants were being dragged onto the refuse heap, while its riders were led over to the dejected group of prisoners that were sitting nearby.

They were having a roaring time, those Marines, and how we envied them, when we compared their lot with the relatively dull position in which we had found ourselves.

Eagerly I asked the marine officer how the general operation had succeeded.

'*Oh very well,*' he replied. '*I believe that over 300 prisoners have already been taken! Our lads found that elements of a parachute battalion were occupying the town. Actually, just as it was getting light they heard a lot of shouting and found a company of Germans neatly lined up with their sergeant major calling the roll. They lost no time in opening up on them and managed to put nearly every man of this particular company in the bag. Other odd parties were mopped up here and there, and we have had very few casualties. There was some pretty stiff fighting round the station though, for some of those Jerry paratroopers were billeted there, and it took us quite a time to dislodge them. However, the town is in our hands all right now, and Jerry seems to have pulled right out, for there is not a sign of him anywhere in the area. It was rotten luck about that section of yours though!'*

These last words cut short my jubilation at the excellent news the commando officer had given me.

'What section?', I stammered in amazement.

'Oh didn't you know? I don't know myself how true it is, but I heard that one of your sections, complete, walked straight into the bag. Still, don't take my word for it, as I only heard it by chance.'

I could get no further information on this point, and so slowly took my patrol back to the section position, pondering over the information I had received, and wondering which section could have suffered the described fate. It certainly wasn't one of our troop sections, and all I could conclude was that either No.1 Troop or No.3 Troop had been caught by the all too early arrival of daylight, in a vulnerable position still some distance short of their objective.

When I arrived back at the spot where my section was established, I was greeted by a grinning Sergeant Storey.

'We've found a prisoner, sir,' he shouted. *'Some "Itie" kids came up and told me where he was hiding, so I took a couple of the lads and followed them. They led me to a farm shed, and there we found young Fritz hiding. He wasn't half mad at those kids for giving him away. Spat something out at them in German real nasty like. Must have said that he'd do them if he got half a chance.'*

I looked around for young Fritz and found him sitting sadly about 20 yards away, all by himself. I went up to him and questioned him. He was very young, nineteen and a half he said, but I doubt if he was much more than eighteen. He had the long eyelashes and the finely modelled features of a girl, and a pretty one at that. But for all his good looks, he was without a doubt one of the Nazi brood. At first he kept himself arrogant and haughty, answering my questions with an unwilling monosyllable. But where he differed from the British soldier was that after I had been working on him for about twenty minutes, asking him friendly questions about where he came from, where his family were, and all that, and telling him of the parts of Germany I had visited before the war, he suddenly opened up and in a torrent of speech, far too fast for me to be able to understand he poured his heart out.

It seemed as though he was so surprised at finding someone willing to talk to him in a friendly way that his natural reserve and suspicion fell away from him on the spot. He talked like one unaccustomed to much speaking, as though this outlet to his mind had been suppressed for many years, so that now once the floodgates were opened, out the torrent came.

On he chatted in his boyish voice, his words blurred and clipped, and made almost incomprehensible by his excitement. His home, his parents, his fiancée, his army training, his parachute course, were described at length. He told how he and a friend had been surprised in the town when the Marine Commandos attacked it, how they had made their escape and swum across a river, he carrying the magazines and his companion carrying the machine-gun. They had been fired upon and he feared his companion was dead. Eventually he landed up in the farm where we caught him.

I also learned from him that there had been about 800 troops in the area that morning, that he was not at all happy at the idea of being taken prisoner, and that Russia had invaded Germany!

I gave him a short pep-talk about German aggression in general, trying to convince him that Germany had invaded Russia as well as most of the other European countries. But I might as well have saved my breath.

'*You must in any case admit,*' he said proudly, '*that the German campaign in Poland was a model feat of military skill. Why in merely 21 days we had conquered the whole Polish army.*'

I couldn't control my disgust, and called out to the lads telling them of what this cheeky young devil had said. He was greeted with a roar of derisive laughter.

'*Shoot a line at him, sir; tell him about Sicily: it hardly took us more than 21 days to conquer that!*'

So I let young Fritz have it, telling him that any country that prepares for war over six years will have an initial advantage over one that did not. I reminded him that there were no Germans left in Africa or Sicily, and that even now we were nearly half-way up Italy.

'*Do you really think that Germany will win the war?*' I asked at the end.

He hesitated a moment. '*It's possible,*' he said dubiously. That coming from a young and arrogant Nazi paratrooper was in our opinion a sure sign that the German morale was becoming dangerously low.

I contacted Harry on the wireless and told him that I was changing our position to the farm we had passed when I had taken out the patrol. This was on slightly higher ground than the neighbouring valley and offered a more commanding position over the immediate vicinity than the low-lying and rather too sheltered spot in which we were at present.

After we had moved there, and chosen the best possible defensive posts, I reported having contacted the Marine Commando road-block, and mentioned the rumour about one of our sections having been captured.

To our great disappointment Harry confirmed this report. John Tonkin's section had been surprised by strong German forces and had been compelled to give themselves up. It was only later that we learned in greater detail exactly what had happened. Following the lessons learned at Bagnara, they had been at great pains to avoid moving along the road, and as far as possible had kept to the open country. But in view of the fact that they were pressed for time they kept close enough to the road to be able to use it as a rough direction indicator towards their objective. They came across a small party of Germans on or near the road and opened up on them. But it was no small sub-unit they engaged, but a whole company spread out along the upper side of the road as it wound its way up the hillside, and almost before they knew what was happening, they were meeting with fire from all sides. By the most extraordinary ill fortune when they bumped into these Germans they could not have been placed in a more unfortunate position. For they were on the lower side of the road, in a sort of shallow valley. In the darkness they had not realized that the road, climbing in a series of sharp hairpin bends, surrounded them on three sides. Thus the Germans only had to seal off the entrance to the valley in which they were, and the section was trapped.

From their positions above the road, the Germans were able to pour into the small area of that shrub-strewn valley a murderous volume of fire from three sides. After trying to get out by the way they had come, and finding that the Germans had effectively sealed this off, there was nothing left for the section to do but surrender. John Tonkin himself, with one of his men, was in the process of laboriously crawling along a ditch in an effort to get away, when a guttural voice behind him said softly, '*Come out you naughty boys,*' and there scarcely 2 yards away from him and above him he became aware of a section of grinning Germans.

All the section were captured with the exception of two or three who with extreme bravery lay doggo in the undergrowth ignoring the warning shouted by the Germans that they would spray the whole area with machine-guns unless they gave themselves up immediately. It must have been hell for them as they lay there, not daring to make the slightest movement, and watching the twigs and shrubs being torn to pieces around them and wondering if there was a slight chance that they could be missed by that tornado of fire. Two, I believe, did survive it, but a third, Lance Corporal Fassam, was not so fortunate and was killed instantly.

Towards three that afternoon, my signaller came up to me with a wireless from Harry.

'Take patrol up western end of high ground near Castel Benito and push southwards to try and contact our main forces advancing from that direction. Keep in wireless communication and report if you can see our forward troops. Derrick patrolling the ridge to the east of you. Keep clear of Castel Benito, as enemy possibly in vicinity.'

That was all, but we welcomed the chance of being at last able to do something more active, and quickly made ready. I preferred to take a small reconnaissance patrol of four or five riflemen with me, which would be easy to control and which would have more chance of being able to move about undercover, than would a stronger force, such as my whole section, which might prove to be too large and cumbersome.

It was not hard to pick four good men, and within ten minutes we were at the road-block to inform the Marines of the route to be taken and to ask about the whereabouts of our nearest troops in the area.

From a youthful and friendly officer whom I later discovered to be Lieutenant Colonel Manners, CO of the Marine Commando, I obtained all the information about our own troops' positions I required, along with several amusing stories about the fighting that had taken place that morning. Brian Franks had had a brainwave. He wanted to know the strength of the enemy forces in Pescara, the next town up the coast, and started questioning an Italian he had found in one of the houses. The Italian surprised him by picking up the telephone and ringing-up a friend of his who worked in a hotel in Pescara, from whom he was able to obtain the required information, despite the fact that there were Germans sitting in the lounge of the hotel the other end, according to the veiled remarks to that effect coming over the wire. Brian Franks was so elated at his success in tricking the Germans in this way, that he entirely ignored the fact that the Germans would be able to try out exactly the same dodge, as regards finding out our strength. In all probability that 'Itie' rang through to his pal and told him how strong we were, as soon as Brian had gone!

Colonel Manners gave my patrol a lift up the hill in a truck his unit had captured at the road-block. We went up the little country road that ran inland to the village of Castel Benito, and my section got out at the crest, about half a mile short of the village and from this point started our patrol.

We passed a small detachment of No.3 Commando who had a 3-inch mortar position up on that high ground, and from then on we were alone. Keeping in single file, we made full use of the plentiful cover and headed eastwards along the ridge until we came to a small white farmhouse standing high on that peaceful hillside.

From the farm we took out our glasses and scanned the neighbouring countryside. Behind us was the broad coastal plain, which we had crossed so laboriously the preceding night, while to our front the ground rose gently to a smooth crest which cut off our view scarcely 200 yards ahead.

The ridge on which we were continued over to our left, and it was somewhere over there that we knew the rest of our troop to be. But it was divided at the point where we stood by a deep and densely wooded valley which, cutting it at rightangles, ran away to the south. Across this valley we could discern another ridge, as smoothly undulating and as bare as the one on which we stood, and running parallel to it, which also rose gently to the south in a gradual, uninterrupted curve.

Suddenly we became aware of three little black dots which broke the regular line of one of the crests on the opposite ridge. That they were men, and furthermore troops, we could not doubt, but the question was were they enemy or were they some of Derrick's patrol which we knew should be somewhere in that area? Soon the figures moved, and this was just sufficient to allow me to recognize through my binoculars the blue-grey Indian shirts with which our unit had been issued. They were Derrick's section all right, and for the next few minutes we watched with considerable amusement the great show of caution they exercised when they caught sight of us. The three figures suddenly bobbed back into dead ground as soon as we moved into the open, and then proceeded to study us through their binoculars with the utmost suspicion. Meanwhile we had contacted them over the radio and introduced ourselves formally to each other with such words as '*Peep-bo! I can see you!*'

Our route now lay to the south and led us across completely open ground. Always about a hundred yards ahead of us ranged a crest, beyond which we could not see, and as soon as we reached this point, it was only to find our vision blocked by a similar crest just ahead, and so it went on. It was heart-breaking as the purpose of our patrol was to reach a point overlooking the main road which we knew to be somewhere in front, and up which our main forces were approaching.

It was a great comfort to have Derrick on our left flank, for while we scanned his ridge, he was covering the one on which we were, and in this way we were both able to know much more about what was going on around us.

Once Derrick told me over the wireless that a section of unidentified troops was digging in just above us, but as the slope on which we were was convex, we could not see them. I imagined they would be some party from the No.3

Commando mortar section we had passed about half an hour previously, so did not let the news worry me unduly. Derrick told me later that they were definitely Germans.

Somewhere to our front and over to our right the tearing burst of a quick-firing machine gun rudely shattered the silence. How well we knew that sound! Our experience at Bagnara had permanently drummed it into our minds. A Spandau or an MG 15. We looked at each other significantly. So there were Jerries somewhere in front of us, and within half a mile at that! The willpower that was necessary to look over each crest as we came to it became more and more of an effort.

But nothing occurred to justify our fears, and as the red rim of the sun touched the horizon to our right, we realized that we would have to think about returning, if we did not want the rest of the section to report us as missing.

So I contacted Derrick on the wireless telling him that I was packing up, and with relief we turned about and made our way back to the section position. When we reached the farm that we had passed on the upper slopes of the ridge, we descended straight down into the valley below, and by this shortcut were able to reach the others just as the first stars were beginning to appear in the sky overhead.

We decided to spend the night where we were, and Sergeant Storey got busy arranging the sentry roster while I went off to let the Marines know where we were sleeping, and to arrange for us to be fitted in with their general defence system.

Young Fritz was sent over to re-join his comrades who were safely out of harm's way on an LCI, and after we had fed, we established ourselves in a barn full of fresh, clean straw. We spent a comfortable night, undisturbed by any unpleasant interruptions. The straw in our barn gave us good protection from the cold, and most of us were able to sleep soundly. Sentries with Bren guns had been posted in what were considered good positions, where they lay quietly with ears pricked for any sound. They handed over automatically at the end of their two hours' stretch, while the rest of us slept as soundly as was possible in our communal bed of straw. All of this shows that we did not take very seriously the possibility that the enemy might be up to no good that night.

Once or twice during the night I woke up – probably on account of the cold – and went out to see that the guards were acting properly as had been arranged. It was a clear cold night, with no moon to aid the straining eyes of the sentries. Just before dawn, I was on one of these rounds when I lost my footing in the darkness and came rolling down into a clump of brushwood, setting up sufficient noise to waken the dead. Any doubts I may have had about the sentries doing their work properly were quickly dispelled, for at the noise, Stalker swung round in a flash, his rifle at the hip, and pointing straight at my stomach. I do not know which of us was the more scared – Stalker by the thought that some marauding Germans might have stumbled on our positions, or I, at the thought that Stalker might be a trifle 'trigger happy'! Needless to say, I lost no time in introducing myself.

We awoke to find the sun streaming through the chinks in the walls and roof of our barn, and to our joy we found the coastal road covered with a stream of transport pushing past our position westwards up the coast. The army had arrived, and our worries were over, or so we imagined. Carriers, 3-tonners, PUs and ambulances all went past us in a steady stream, while we stood watching, filled with relief.

'*Well, that's just about the easiest operation we've ever had – almost beats Murro di Porco,*' commented one of the lads.

'*Yes! If all operations were like this one, I wouldn't mind fighting at all,*' answered another.

We threw all caution to the winds – we moved about openly and without attempt at concealment, and lit a huge fire over which we cooked our breakfast. Singly or in pairs, we roamed the neighbouring countryside in search of eggs and other foodstuffs which would make a good meal.

Since there was obviously no point in our staying where we were any longer, for the army were by now all around us, I decided to move out about 10am and make our way to the coastal road, where we would be most likely to contact Harry.

No thought of war was in our minds, as we moved about unconcerned, collecting our kit and putting on our equipment. We never dreamed that we might be being watched by unfriendly eyes from the very slopes up which we had climbed that previous evening. The Germans had been at least four miles away then, and were by now probably over twice that distance from us – or so we thought!

But even as we were completing our preparations to leave, we were amazed to hear the whine of a shell interrupt the silence of that morning, in which all thoughts of battle were so far from our minds. A second later a shattering explosion shook the ground, and a column of dust rose up no more than 75 yards from the farmhouse. The women in the farm screamed and the civilians who, until then had been working so peacefully on their normal daily tasks, were all of a sudden gone.

We certainly could not explain that shell away as being one of our own. But where had it come from? That shell had been so obviously aimed at us, but how?

Our own troops were all around us, and our patrol of the previous afternoon had established beyond doubt that those overlooking heights were completely clear of the enemy. No! We just could not be under enemy observation. That shell must have been fired blind from a range of several miles and had probably been aimed at the road junction behind us. This was the only solution which presented itself to our dulled and over-confident minds, for so secure did we feel that we never even contemplated the possibility that the enemy may have moved since that preceding afternoon.

Even as we looked at each other aghast, and wondered what lay behind this unpleasant diversion, there it came again. Once more the tearing, roaring whine of a shell compressed the air over our heads and sent us flat onto our faces. This time it burst further away, almost out of sight in the valley immediately below the steep wooded slopes of the ridge.

'*Never mind,*' I shouted, '*they are probably having a crack at shelling that road junction, from miles away*', and these words were no attempt to mislead, but were the real expression of my true opinion.

So we decided to disregard the shells, and as soon as we were ready we moved over towards the road, in accordance with our previous plan, in a formation only slightly more extended than it otherwise would have been. But we had hardly

TERMOLI · NUOVO SEMINARIO E GIARDINO PUBBLICO.

Public gardens, Termoli and monastery forming regiment's billets, 3–5 October 1943.

ventured out into the open, when something which sounded very like a mortar bomb, tore a hole in the earth barely 50 yards behind.

We could not understand it. If the Germans were firing blind as we imagined, their shells were falling uncomfortably close to us. It seemed almost as if we were being followed by the wretched things.

It did not take long for these doubts to materialize, for when two more bombs landed immediately behind us, even my confidence began to be shaken and I was forced to admit that this was no coincidence, and that we were actually being shelled or mortared. So we spread out in extended order, and doubled across the remaining few hundred yards which separated us from the road, as hard as we could go.

We reached an orchard on the roadside and here, panting from our exertions, we settled down to discuss this extraordinary occurrence. We looked around – our troops were everywhere, going about their normal tasks entirely unconcerned. As we arrived breathless at the edge of the road, a section of Marines lying beneath the trees looked at us with surprise and barely concealed amusement. Traffic streamed along the road, groups of men were cooking around smoking fires, and, in short, no one seemed the least concerned about the shellfire of a few moments ago.

The shells were not aimed at them though, we thought bitterly. But it did seem so incongruous. It was as though, despite the fact that the army had relieved us, we were still on our own, and still had to fend for ourselves!

We moved off to a group of farm buildings near the road, and here in the clean cool cowshed we had our lunch, washed down with a brew of tea made with fresh milk we had obtained from the farmer.

A small German truck came up and stopped just by us. Out of it stepped Harry Poat, looking as spick and span and as emotionless as ever. He told us that the rest of the squadron had been relieved the previous evening, and had spent a comfortable night back in the town in billets which they had taken over. He would arrange immediately for a truck to come out and pick us up. Eagerly we asked him for news about the landing operation and from the account he gave it seemed to have been most successful. Of the 800 enemy troops who were in the area when we landed, over 50 had been killed and more than 300 taken prisoner. They were the remnants of a parachute battalion stationed in Termoli, and had been taken completely by surprise. Both No.1 and No.3 Troops had reached the bridges which had been their objectives without too much trouble, but unfortunately these had been blown before they had been able to reach them. Except for the unfortunate loss of John Tonkin's section, casualties had been extraordinarily low among our unit, although the Marines had had a rather tougher time of things.

We were most sorry to learn that Bob Merlot, who in spite of his age and value had stubbornly insisted that as intelligence officer he should go forward with the leading section of No.1 Troop, had been wounded, how seriously nobody knew, save that he had received a bullet in his shoulder. Bill Fraser's troop had had a pleasant time strafing a road down which German vehicles were moving, and had sent many of these up in smoke and flames. Even squadron headquarters had taken part in this Hun-hunting, and the story was told of how Casey, one of the batmen, single-handed had captured a whole section of Germans. Apparently he had rushed about shouting *"'A' section on the left, 'B' section on the right, and 'C' section follow me"*, to such an extent that the Germans believed in the dazed and surprised state in which they were, that they were up against a whole company at least, and so surrendered willingly!

After Harry had given us this welcome news, he enquired after how we had fared. I told him about the shelling of earlier in the morning, and this he was inclined to pooh-pooh as indeed we also were by that time, for ever since the day had been completely free from sounds of battle, so that our confidence which had been momentarily shaken was fully restored once more.

Harry then left us to fetch our transport, and about an hour later we were driven into the town to re-join the rest of the squadron.

An enormous monastery right in the middle of the town, flanking one side of the main square, had been taken over as billets for the men. On the ground floor of this, with its bare stone passages and empty halls, the squadron was installed, and space and food were immediately procured for my section on their arrival.

Paddy came up to me, and after a few preliminary enquiries asked me if I had heard anything about a powerful counter-attack which according to rumour was developing. I told him about the shelling of the morning, but added that thereafter everything had been peaceful, and nothing had occurred to suggest the possibility of a counter-attack. Paddy told me that one or two Tiger tanks had been seen, and that No.3 Commando had claimed to have knocked out one of these, and so we were able to attribute the shelling of that morning to one of these tanks which had probably managed to penetrate to a point from where it could overlook the coastal stretch of flat country.

From then on rumours about the enemy counter-attack came pouring in, with ever increasing incoherence and urgency. By tea-time Paddy had received at least three messages from the brigadier commanding the leading infantry brigade, requesting that we should at once go out to strengthen the line against the oncoming enemy. Paddy was loth to permit this, partly because, like the rest of us, he found it difficult to believe that the situation was as serious as these messages made out, since we had been able to wander around the whole area only the day before without the slightest interference, but also because he considered the unit as his special charge.

To Paddy his men had been trained to such a pitch that they were not easily replaceable. They had to be of a high standard of efficiency, in view of the specialized tasks they might be called upon to do, and thus Paddy refused to allow some strange infantry brigadier, who had perhaps been flustered and worried by coming up against fairly strong enemy forces for the first time, to assume command over his valuable little unit and maybe cause it to suffer numerous and excessive casualties unnecessarily. In addition to these arguments, Paddy also considered that the men had done quite enough, and he refused to send them into action until he was himself sure that the need for them was fully necessary.

But by the time we had had our evening meal, there was nothing more we could do about it. The demands for our men in the line had by now become so frantic and irresistible, that it became imperative for three sections to be sent out that evening. Which sections were to be chosen? That was the question! It was generally accepted that our troop had had the lightest time during the initial landing operation, so it was decided to send out Tony's and Derrick's sections. But in view of the fact that my section had spent all the previous night out and had only just been brought back to the town, while all the rest of the squadron had been relieved the previous evening, we were spared, and instead, Sandy Wilson with his section from No.1 Troop were sent out under Tony.

A feverish fifteen minutes were spent in getting these sections ready and then they were off, cheerful as always but naturally rather sceptical as to the actual need for them. We watched them go with mixed feelings, wondering what lay ahead for them in the immediate future, and whether they would soon be allowed to return, unneeded.

I was tired after my two almost sleepless nights, and so went to bed early, where I slept like a log until dawn.

I awoke with the awful realization that something was wrong. What was the matter? What had I heard to cause such apprehensions in my mind. I sat up in bed to listen. Yes, there it was again. Clearly over the morning air the slow steady rattle of a Bren gun rang out, to be answered immediately by the roaring burst of a quick-firing machine gun which I recognized too well as being German. That was not much in itself, but the alarming feature of it was that both guns sounded as though they were less than half a mile away! And even while the horrible consequences of this fact were slowly sinking into my sleep-stupefied mind, my alarms were still further increased by the sound of a shell tearing the air overhead, landing nearby a second later with a deafening explosion.

The implications of these sounds were obvious. The enemy were within half a mile of the town, and evidently had command of the high ground on which we had been two days previously, and from which they would be able to observe every movement in the town. The rumoured counter-attack which yesterday had seemed to us no more than a few scattered alarmist reports, was now, beyond doubt an established fact, and everything pointed to our having to face a very sticky reception during the course of that day.

Early though it was, I found everybody up and about by the time I reached the mess. The atmosphere was strained and oppressive, for no one failed to grasp the seriousness of the situation in which we were, and to all of us, it was merely a matter of time before we were called out to take our place in the line, and help stem the German attack.

All that morning we hung around while rumours and reports came flooding in. Without a doubt it was a powerful counter-attack, and an all-out effort to recapture the town of Termoli which the Germans evidently valued very highly. They were attacking on at least a divisional scale, with tanks and artillery, and crack paratroop units as infantry. But the most serious aspect of it all, was that it looked extremely doubtful whether our troops would be able to hold them, for besides being outnumbered, these were for the most part inexperienced and green, and untrained in actual battle conditions. Previously the advance up Italy had met with little resistance, and had entailed no real fighting, beyond mopping-up and by-passing small rearguard elements which had been left to hold up our progress. But now, for the first time, our troops found themselves against a powerful enemy line, and for this they were obviously not prepared.

We had nothing to do all that morning, save wait in the mess, in an agony of suspense, listening to the frenzied whine of the shells, which were falling on the town in ever thickening profusion, and to the growing violence of the sounds of battle. We were put on half an hour's notice to move so that with the knowledge that we would certainly be called out to fight sometime during that day, the conditions of our waiting became almost intolerable through the strain that they entailed. Paddy was loth to send us out, but now that he knew the seriousness of the situation, he had no choice. Our sections who were already out had spent a comfortable night, we learned, but now they too were fighting hard to hold back the enemy.

The inactivity that was forced on us as we sat around in the mess that morning played on everyone's nerves. We found an old gramophone with some Italian records, and these Bill Fraser got hold of. To his delight he found among them 'Lili Marlene' sung by a female in Italian, and this he played through and through, the whole morning long, while outside the shells were falling nearer and nearer and the rest of us were expecting a direct hit on the house at any moment. But Bill did not seem to care. So long as he was able to listen to 'Lili Marlene', the war and the unpleasant threat hanging over us was forgotten by him. How we wished that we could have adopted that same detachment and unconcern which served to keep Bill so contented and oblivious of the furious battle developing around him.

We had a scraped-up lunch whilst still under this ominous atmosphere of uncertainty, knowing that any moment might see us called out to strengthen the line. Soon after lunch, about 2.30, the expected order came through. We were to prepare immediately, and every available man was to be rushed to help stem a renewed and powerful attack on a weak point of our line, on the eastern outskirts of the town. Transport was to take us to the required spot.

It only needed a matter of a few minutes for us to be completely ready. So that at 2.45pm the unit was assembled in the main square, and marched off to a side street flanking the public gardens, in which our transport was waiting.

Without a word the men began climbing into the trucks. To their delight my lads found that the driver of one of the lorries was McNinch who, because of a bad foot, had been left out of the battle and had come up as a driver. Naturally they all wanted to travel in the truck driven by their old friend, and since no definite allocation of trucks to sections had been made, I saw no reason to prevent them from climbing in behind McNinch. In fact I was on the point of mounting beside McNinch myself, when a small tornado materialized beside us in the form of Johnny Wiseman, who vehemently claimed that the truck in which we were was to be used by his section. Since he obviously appeared to know more about transport allocations than we did, we gave way and despite silent mutterings to the effect that 'surely one truck was as good as another' my section got down from McNinch's truck and slowly made their way over to the one in front, into which they clambered.

And at that moment the world seemed to fall to pieces around us, and from the resultant chaos and confusion there rose up a sight, the memory of which will never be stamped out from my mind.

For at just the moment when the squadron was packed into the half-dozen or so trucks, which were parked nose to tail in that narrow side-street, we were all transfixed by the frenzied shriek of a heavy shell, which suddenly distinguished itself from the normal noises of battle, deafening us with the rush of its passage and seemingly sweeping the whole world before it. Just as in one of those terrifying dreams when some danger is imminently threatening, and one finds oneself bound to the spot with chains, unable to make a move to escape it, so we stood or sat in our positions listening to the tearing roar of the approaching menace, and unable to transmit from our numbed minds the necessary commands to our limbs.

The human mind can stand so much and no more, so that when a horror too great for it suddenly materializes, the senses are unable to register exactly what happens, and the picture of the scene becomes mercifully blurred, vague and disjointed. When the first shell landed in the wall of a house immediately above the parked vehicles, blowing a gaping gap in the masonry and covering the whole area with dust and fragments, it became impossible for us to realize what was happening for five more shells followed the first in quick succession. All fell directly on the area in which we were, spreading death, destruction and confusion in that confined space.

The deafening roar and shock of that first bursting shell was such as to completely deprive us of feeling. As if in a trance we watched the wall of the house come down, slowly, infinitely slowly it seemed. And then amid the roar of further exploding shells the scene became covered with dust. Hardly a shout was raised from the mass of men piled onto the trucks – everything was too sudden for that. Only when the shuddering whine of the descending missiles had ceased, and when the clouds of dust had begun to settle were our minds able to register once more, and take note of what was happening around us. Figures

The truck in which McNinch and a section of I Troop were blown up.

of men vague and indistinct in the dust cloud, appeared, pale and shielding their eyes as they staggered out of the whirlwind. And then, as minds slowly recovered from the numbing shock, something like panic developed – there was a mad rush for cover, into alleys, doorways, corners. But what cover was there from those deadly shells which rained down from the sky, and were just as likely to blow one to pieces in whatever place one tried to hide oneself? The same feeling of helplessness gripped us all. The main thing was to get away – right away from this inferno, but where? From those heavy 105mm shells, no house was safe, no concealed or sheltered spot, for wherever you went they were liable to seek you out and destroy you.

As the dust subsided, and I realized almost unbelievably, that I was completely unhurt. I could hardly recognize the street, for great lumps of masonry and vehicles littered the roadway, and the scrambling mass of men rushing about in search of shelter added a further confusion to the scene. It took me some seconds to take in the awful extent of the damage we had suffered, for the rear half of McNinch's truck had virtually disappeared, merely a twisted and shattered hulk remaining.

Behind me I became aware of a commotion and there lay Bill Fraser, limp and motionless, his face an unnatural ashen grey. Over him Phil Gunn was bending, coolly making his examination. Poor Bill! The Fraser luck had not lasted indefinitely for, from the look of him lying there with his ashen complexion, I could not help feeling that he was seriously hurt.

Phil Gunn was very much in demand a second or two later, for as people came to their senses from the shock, a scene of gruesome disaster slowly dawned on their dazed eyes. Most of the casualties were dead, blown to pieces, and the wounded were a ghastly sight, such as to make hardened veterans turn pale and vomit feebly. But throughout, Phil Gunn worked methodically and calmly, refusing to be flustered by the ever-growing stream of serious casualties who were waiting on his treatment.

I found my section wild-eyed and shaking, scattered among the neighbouring yards and passages. By now the shelling had ceased, so that we were gradually able to overcome that intense and nauseating fear that we were at the mercy of the invisible enemy and that nowhere could we find shelter from him. It did not take long to get my section organized and together, for they were all stout-hearted lads and quickly rallied themselves, collected together in a neighbouring yard. The roll was called, and to my relief and amazement, I found that all were present.

Once I had seen to my section we looked around to see what else we could do to be of assistance. The street was now deserted; no one could quite pluck up the courage to go towards that blackened and twisted wreck that had once been a 3-ton truck. This reluctance was partly caused by the natural fear that that point was the central target of the threatening enemy shellfire, and who was to know what was still likely to come from that direction? Also our fears were partly due to the horror of what we knew we would see when we got there.

But soon a small figure stolidly trudged out towards the dreaded point, and from there started shouting orders to the pale faces peering round the doorways. It was Johnny Wiseman, whose section had been in the destroyed vehicle, anxious to see what could be done for the all too few remnants of his men. I took four volunteers and went forward to see what we could do, though loth indeed I was to do so.

As I came up to the truck I noticed in an abstract sort of way what appeared to be a carcase of meat lying in the middle of the road, exactly similar to those one sees hanging in butchers' shops. I remember vaguely thinking that there must have been a butcher's shop close by. But then an awful second later, that seemed to stretch into minutes so great was the revulsion I experienced, I saw that a few pieces of charred khaki cloth were sticking to the outside of the object I was examining. With my stomach writhing we went on to witness the most dreadful shambles any of us had ever seen. Piled around were the remains of what had been a minute or so before, twenty-five brave men in the prime of life, cheerful, strong, and good-hearted. And now...what was left! Here lay a man with half his head blown off, an arm lay there, and somewhere else an unrecognisable lump of flesh that had only a few seconds before belonged to a living organism pulsing with young life. In the back of the truck, over the sides and scattered over the road, lay the dead, piled high, a horrible and bloody carnage. A lump of flesh hung on the telegraph wires overhead. I could see no more!

Blindly I stumbled back my innards revolting at the sight which I had just witnessed. Never would I get over it – never, no matter what happened to me afterwards would I ever have to see such a sight again – such were the thoughts in my mind, as infinitely distressed I hurried away from the scene. For the rest of that day, the smell of death hung in the air around me, clinging to my clothes and to my hands. The smell of those poor scorched, fragmented bodies haunted my nostrils for days afterwards.

So overcome was I by the sight I had just seen, that I was unable to take much notice for the next five minutes of what was happening around us. Stretchers had been procured from somewhere and already those lucky enough to escape with wounds were being carried away to the dressing station. A young Italian girl who lived in the house which had been struck by the first shell, came running up and at the sight that met her eyes fell screaming to the ground, misery and frenzy on her distraught face. She had seen her father lying there, his belly ripped open. Two of the men led her away, still screaming, while we blocked our ears as best we could to keep those dreadful notes of distress from reaching our already overtaxed minds.

Many must have been the selfless deeds of devotion and bravery during those horror-stricken few minutes, which I was unable to record so numbed was I at the magnitude of the disaster. Gilmour, one of the men on the truck, came up to Johnny Wiseman, who was busy sorting out the wounded from the dead, and asked, holding his hand up to his head, *'Please sir, may I go to the hospital, I have lost an eye?'*

A young civilian girl, as calmly as though she were sitting in her own drawing-room on a peaceful winter evening, sat amid the rubble of what had once been a house, bandaging the less serious wounds and cleaning them, setting a fine example to the soldiers around.

And all the time Phil Gunn worked on, slowly bringing order to the confusion and chaos around him. Without a glance at the dead he concentrated on the living, arranging for their evacuation, as soon as he had examined them. Shaken as we were, we could not fail to admire his splendid coolness, as he worked patiently and without fluster to mend broken bodies and torn flesh.

In the midst of this confusion, young Ridler, the intelligence sergeant, came up with a message from Paddy, who had gone forward in advance of the squadron, and who was now anxiously waiting for their arrival and wondering what could have happened to delay us so.

'Major Mayne says that you must hurry, and come forward at once, without the slightest delay. It is very urgent,' he said to David Barnby, the senior officer present.

'Tell Major Mayne that we can't possibly come until we have sorted out this mess,' David replied.

'It's most imperative that you should, sir,' Ridler answered. *'I believe that the situation is very critical and that more men are vitally needed.'*

'Very well, we'll come as soon as possible. I'll send each section off as soon as they have reached some semblance of organization again,' said David, turning around in a harassed manner to see which of the troops huddled in the doorways seemed to be nearest to being in an organized state.

As I was standing nearby, and as I knew that my section were all together and ready to move off, my men were the first to go, so that in single file, we led a shaken, straggled procession up the main street of the town towards the eastern outskirts. Our nerves were tensed and our ears straining for any sound that might betray that the shelling was to be resumed. But apart from the continuous noises of battle, nothing further happened to renew our fears. It was with extreme reluctance that we came up to each crossroads, for we half expected to meet with some deadly reception as we crossed these danger areas. All around, we passed troops sitting in yards, or in doorways, singly or in pairs, shaken in appearance, and without order or formation.

Advancing in this way, we reached a railway bridge, and proceeded until we were met by a member of Paddy's forward party who led us off the road into the garden of a large villa, where we found Paddy calmly waiting.

'*Take your section over there, by that wall and get them into good positions,*' he said, indicating with a sweep of his hand the rough area into which we were to go.

It was an ideal defensive position. We were on the forward slope of a small hill, which rose up over the end of a wide and deep valley; this ran straight down to the road which we could see winding away below us. About 50 yards down the slope was a stone wall, and behind this a ditch.

I spread my men along the ditch, extremely thankful for its presence, and for the protection afforded by the wall in front, and at once we got busy scraping away at the mortar with our fighting knives, in order to make observation holes and firing slits in the hard masonry of the wall. I remembered sufficiently our experiences at Bagnara, to know that we would not stand much chance should the enemy succeed in coming close up to us, if we had to expose ourselves over the level surface of the wall each time we wanted to fire a shot.

Our field of fire was excellent. We could cover every inch of that valley down to the road, a winding stretch of which almost half a mile long we also had under observation. Beyond this road we could see the mouth of another valley, which ran off towards the high ground looming up about half a mile beyond. It was here that the enemy were, firmly established on the heights, and probing their way forward down that valley in an attempt to possess the road. The whole area where we were was under their observation, so that the slightest movement met with that terrifying whine of a 88mm shell.

On either side of the valley in front of us we could see our troops packed among the wooded crests complete with their transport. On the ridge to our left, a battery of 25-pounder guns was installed, while across the valley opposite them, we could see, here and there, a Bren carrier through the trees, or an infantry section post.

We spent the rest of the afternoon in that spot, in an agony of suspense, our normal reactions numbed by the horror of what we had experienced a short time ago, and our minds tormented by a myriad of alarms on the subject of the enemy attack which we knew was developing immediately to our front. Again and again movement seemed to be detected by one of the men. We strained our eyes through our glasses in the direction of that malignant valley-mouth across the road from which we expected, as each minute went by, the danger to materialize.

The shells fell in ever-increasing numbers, all around our position, the neighbouring crests and the railway bridge behind us. Every yard of the road was under the observation of these enemy guns. Under these conditions, movement along it was extremely dangerous and only attempted by very few vehicles. An ambulance streaked up that winding ribbon towards the town, and with relief we watched it disappear over the railway bridge and continue on its way unharmed. A Sherman tank clanked its way cumbrously down the hill towards open country and the bridge over the river, which was now under direct enemy observation. Anxiously we watched it continue its slow and painful journey, while the tearing, howling shells burst in death-dealing fury all around, and the noise of the battle dinned in our ears. Eventually it passed out of sight round a bend, still undamaged.

Piece by piece we began to formulate some vague picture of what was happening around us. That the situation was extremely critical we had no doubt, but we learned later that afternoon that the real danger lay in the fact that we were completely cut-off from any chances of help. Reinforcements could only arrive over the two bridges across the river, and these, although admittedly still in our hands, were as good as useless to us for the enemy could observe every movement around them from the high ridge which he held so strongly, and of course had the range to each bridge worked out so accurately, that it was suicide to work near these. The Royal Engineers had built a Bailey bridge over the river, before the counter-attack had developed, but this had been destroyed by a direct hit from a shell, and despite repeated and valiant attempts to rebuild it, these were doomed to failure almost before they were even started, so dominating were the enemy points of observation, and so accurate was their shellfire.

Tanks there were in plenty waiting to come to our aid, but they were all the other side of the river, completely unable to cross. An attempt had been made to wade the tanks straight through the shallow stream, but the bed was so soft and muddy that they had become bogged right down in the middle of the stream and no amount of exertion was able to move them again. Up to nightfall of that grim and fateful day, scarcely more than half a dozen tanks had succeeded in crossing the river.

The news that we were cut-off in this way rapidly spread among the troops who were across the river, so that their morale already dangerously low, was even further weakened. Many units, unaccustomed to battle conditions, had panicked, and abandoning their carriers, their bofors and anti-tank guns and their transport to the advancing enemy, had fled individually or in droves, back down the coast to safety.

Maybe these troops cannot be blamed unduly, for many of them were pitifully green, and only just sent out from England, and the suddenness and violence of the enemy attack must certainly have taken them by surprise. Not all the troops had fled; those who remained behind were in the majority, and these not only held out against all that the enemy could inflict upon them, but also against the insidious temptation that they too, like their comrades, could give up the exhausting struggle if they wished, and join the stream of pitiful, shamefaced refugees who were making their way to safety down the coast. For panic is an infectious thing: once it is allowed to take a hold, it spreads like wildfire, and through the medium of alarms, rumours and false reports, it can sweep a whole army in its path, changing it from a collection of co-ordinated fighting units to a mere rabble of frightened individuals anxious only for their own safety.

We learned later how the LCI which had brought us to Termoli had been waiting a few more miles back down the coast, ready to come up and take us off, should the situation so demand it. It was with amazement that their crews watched the stream of stragglers moving down the beach, many of whom hailed them, asking for a lift down the coast away from the fighting.

'Why, what is the matter?' the flotilla commander enquired, feeling extremely anxious for our safety from the disturbing sight that met his eyes.

'There has been a terrible counter-attack,' came the answer, *'it was impossible for us to hold it. The whole army is in retreat, if you don't move too you will find the Germans on you in no time. Already they have retaken the town, and there is no longer anything to stop them from advancing as far as they like!'*

The flotilla commander could hardly believe his ears. *'Why, what has happened to the commandos who first captured the town?'* he then asked.

'Oh, they are still back there somewhere in the outskirts: they are paid to do that sort of work,' came the callous answer.

It was no wonder that at this reply, the shrewd naval officer began to suspect the veracity of these reports and, refusing to take a single man on board, he held his flotilla ready to come to our immediate assistance, should he hear that that were necessary. Meanwhile, he made every effort to contact Paddy, over the wireless, and in this he was eventually successful. Paddy was surprised at the urgency of the terms of the messages he received from the flotilla, and it took him some time to persuade them that the situation was in hand, and that we would not be requiring their aid just yet.

Meanwhile we lay in our ditch, scanning the country to our front, and praying that the shells which were falling all around would somehow manage to miss us. Not much was said about the frightful slaughter we had all witnessed earlier that afternoon. It was just something we could not talk about. The fact that by rights my section should have been in that truck which was hit, made the whole affair all the more terrible.

The effects of this experience, the rumours and their fatigue, were visibly telling on the men. Silence took the place of their usual cheerful backchat, and as they painfully hacked away at the mortar in the wall with their blunt fighting knives, not a grumble made itself heard. To me, who knew these men so well, this latter fact was a significant pointer that things were not well.

As the afternoon lengthened, the shelling increased in violence; all of a sudden one of the men could take it no more – his nerve went, and throwing away his fighting knife, he lay groaning and sobbing in the ditch, as the shells howled overhead. Poor devil! He could not be blamed, for under the stress of war, that was something which could happen to anybody. The rest of the men were far from sympathetic, repeatedly urging him to 'shut up' or coming up to me requesting permission to move further away from him. Eventually they were forced to adopt the policy of ignoring him altogether.

The driver of a 3-tonner which was parked beside a haystack about 50 yards away came over to us, and stayed a while to have a chat. He was a stolid Yorkshireman of few words, unimaginative and yet infinitely sound. After spending about ten minutes with us, he got up to return to his truck.

'Well, it's been good to meet you. Good luck!' he shouted back at us over his shoulder as he disappeared behind a house.

'*Good luck!*' we replied in chorus.

A minute later, an extra loud whine of a descending shell warned us that one was going to land very close, so that we burrowed down into our ditch, blocking our ears and protecting our faces as best we could. An immense, shattering explosion momentarily stunned us, but when we eventually realized that we were still in one piece, we looked up to see a raging inferno in the place where the 3-ton truck had been. It had received a direct hit and was now burning so furiously that we could even feel the heat from it in our position. The flames quickly spread to the nearby haystack, and subsequently to the small farm cottage beside which the truck had been parked.

Soon a double danger began to materialize from the burning truck. For it had been loaded with ammunition, and as the flames reached this, shells, shrapnel and pieces of vehicle would be sent flying in all directions with the force of the repeated minor explosions which occurred in the burning vehicle. The din was terrific. The air was filled with the sound of the crackling flames spreading with venomous speed through the dry hay and the wooden roof of the cottage. Almost each second ammunition was exploding, sending out a stream of sparks and red hot metal in all directions, so that rescue and salvage operations became almost impossible. We wondered at the fate of the unfortunate driver with whom we had been chatting only a few minutes previously. In our ditch we were reasonably safe from the shrapnel falling all around, but the scene of destruction which we saw spreading before our eyes, accompanied by the nerve-racking roar of the flames and the exploding ammunition was a depressing experience.

And then as the twilight deepened, a new danger threatened, for the blazing vehicle and haystack lit up the whole area as bright as day, thereby providing an ideal landmark for any further shelling that the enemy might contemplate. The Germans were not slow to make full use of this direction-indicator, for as it drew darker, more and more shells began to whine over in our direction, to burst with their dull and stupefying roar all around the area in which we were.

Things were really beginning to get hot, and if what we were experiencing was regarded as being merely a prelude to worse horrors which would in all probability be following, we had good cause to feel ourselves to be in an extremely uncomfortable position.

Most of the men had succeeded in scratching some sort of loophole in the wall behind which they lay, so that by now this useful but monotonous activity could no longer keep their minds off the situation developing around them; they lay quietly behind their wall, strangely silent and subdued. Almost imperceptibly the darkness came upon us, veiling over, piece by piece, the area to our front, which from constant scrutiny we had come to know so well. And all the while the red glow of the burning truck gave an eerie illumination to the scene, sending fantastically flickering shadows darting among the shrubs and vines of the garden behind us, and here and there lighting-up momentarily some white face peering out from a patch of cover. Intermittent gun-flashes lit up the distant horizon.

At the moment when the twilight merged into the real darkness of night, a runner came up to me from Paddy, telling me to report to him straight away, bringing my section with me. I wondered what fresh horror lay ahead of us now.

We found Paddy at the entrance to the garden, standing there, immobile as a mountain, no trace of emotion discernible on his features. Clearly and concisely he gave me my orders.

'I want you to take your section back through the town again. It seems that the Germans are being held all right this side, but that on the other side they are putting in a dangerous attack along the axis of the railway line and troops are urgently needed *near the hospital to hold them. Tony, Derrick and Sandy are up there somewhere and from all accounts are having a pretty rough time. Take up a position behind the hospital and see what help you can give them.'*

We filed back through the battered and war-torn streets, our rubber-soled boots lending a ghostly silence to our progress. Only when we reached the town centre did we have the opportunity of seeing for ourselves the pitiful state into which some of our troops had allowed themselves, or more accurately had been permitted by their officers to get. Here lay two or three carriers, deserted and alone in the empty street, exactly where their drivers, panic-stricken by the rumours and the shell-fire, had left them. A couple of Bofors light anti-aircraft guns, deserted by their crews squatted in the square, their barrels pointed forlornly at the stars.

And all around us, in the shadows, in the alleys and in the doorways we felt rather than saw the presence of men – scared and shaken men, ready, like startled rabbits, to bolt for cover at the slightest sound. No one challenged us as we passed, no one came up to enquire whither we were bound.

At length, as we approached the western outskirts of the town, and left the monastery where our squadron had formerly been billeted as a vast black bulk to our rear, we gradually noticed that things were growing more organized. Groups of men were seen, clustered around anti-tank guns or around vehicles, and from these we were able to obtain directions to the hospital.

'*Be careful, if you are going that way,*' they warned us. '*The Germans are all round there, and can't be more than a couple of hundred yards ahead. They are creeping up the railway in small groups and infiltrating into the town.*'

So we continued on our way carefully, wondering how far forward we dared go, and where we would be able to take up a good position.

Just as we were passing the last houses of the town, a young lieutenant came up to us. He was scarcely more than a boy and yet he alone of all the people we had seen, seemed to be relatively unperturbed by the situation and unconfused by the various rumours that were flying around, and spreading their insidious, infectious disease.

'*Are you going to the hospital?*' his voice rang out clearly. '*Good. We need some more men there badly. We're holding them at present, but only just, so you will be useful. Watch out for small parties of Jerries creeping up the railway line. We've caught quite a few that way so far. Things should be all right by the morning. They're hoping to get sixty or so tanks across the river during the night. That's not certain but there seems a good chance of them being able to manage it.*'

How refreshing that encounter was to us. At least one man had his head screwed on the right way in this confounded town, we thought, as we continued on our way, decidedly cheered by a piece of optimism and common-sense, of the sort we had almost given up hope of finding in the unco-ordinated confusion of the battle.

We struck the railway line and followed this out of the town, suspicious of every shadow and startled at every sound, until we saw the square bulk of the hospital standing out, bleak and isolated on the far side of the track. Somewhere round here then we had to pick a position, but in the darkness this was far from easy, as it was impossible for us to tell where our nearest troops were, or if we would be in their way rather than a help to them. So despite the frequent warnings that there were no more of our troops in front of us, which we received from various odd soldiers whom we passed, accompanied by the information that we might expect to bump into the enemy any minute, we found it essential to go forward a bit to verify the doubtful reports. So leaving most of my section by a small railway hut, I took forward three men, with the object of having a look around. I was glad that I did, for we had hardly gone forward more than 20 yards, when we heard the vague murmur of voices, and saw one or two black figures on the skyline. There was no doubt that they were our troops so I approached and introduced myself.

We had stumbled across a section post, manned by all the odd batmen, cooks, drivers, clerks and mechanics etc. of an artillery battery, who had been rushed out to help ward off the threatening attack. In command of them was a captain, an old, administrative officer, who had probably never seen any fighting in this war at any rate.

But what a fine man he was. Being envious of the trench which they had got hold of, I rather hoped that this officer and his men would be just as keen to get out of the danger area as were most of the troops we had found wandering aimlessly about the town. But not a bit of it! For when I suggested that with our arrival, there was perhaps no need for an untrained collection of men such as his to be there anymore, so that we could use his trench and relieve him, he was not at all keen to jump at this opportunity.

For a long period he stood there in silence, pondering heavily. At length he appeared to make up his mind.

'I don't know how urgently we are needed here,' he said, 'but while things are as critical as we are led to believe they are I think I had rather stay. My OC said I could take the chaps out of it when the situation was restored, but none of us know what is happening yet, so I think I'll stay. We may prove useful.'

Little grunts of approval made themselves heard from my men behind me, and none of us failed to appreciate the qualities of this unknown officer, who with his motley crowd of men, should by rights have been one of the first to be withdrawn from the battle. What a strange battle, in which the trained fighting troops were running away and leaving the cooks, the clerks and the sick to remain behind and hold the line.

Also the information which the strange officer was able to give me, was trustworthy and rang true.

'*Good Lord, no! We're not the forward troops in this sector,*' he exclaimed in surprise in answer to my question. '*There are some commandos about 200 yards in front, and in front of them I believe there are some of your boys, so you see, now that you have arrived, we have quite a number of troops to hold the Germans off. But I think tonight is the critical time, and that they will make an all-out attack under cover of darkness. By dawn the situation should be completely restored. I did hear that a brigade of infantry are being landed by sea tonight and that they will be in action in the morning.*'

With at last something like a clear picture of the situation in my mind, I went back to my section and sited them around the small railway hut where I had first left them. Behind us in a deep gulley Alec's mortars had installed themselves, and behind him was Ted Lepine with the remnants of No.3 Troop, supplemented by certain elements of headquarters.

In fact by the time we were settled by the railway line, from our forward troops right back the three-quarters of a mile or so to the town was strongly picketed with defensive posts. Jerry would not find it easy to gain entry into the town by this route.

The shells were still falling in almost as great a profusion in this area as in the one we had just left, and so, partly for this reason, but partly also through the lessons we had learned at Bagnara, the first thing we did was to rake-up a couple of shovels with which to scrape out some sort of hollow that would serve to protect us against fire and shrapnel.

This task completed, we settled down to spend the night as best we could, with the continuous and varying sounds of battle vibrating in our ears. Somewhere to our left, a 'moaning Minnie' the new multiple mortar the Germans had only recently brought out, sent up salvos of bombs which swished through the air with an eerie sobbing effect before they exploded in a pandemonium of noise.

But gradually, as the night slowly counted off its long, dreary minutes, the hubbub became more and more intermittent, until silence was allowed to reign unchallenged, save by the passage of an occasional shell, fired as it were, just to show us that the Germans were still nearby and ready to carry on with their murderous intentions on the morrow.

Although at first we had been straining our eyes into the blackness of the night, to keep watch for those enemy patrols which might have penetrated as far as our position, as time went by and still nothing suspicious materialized, we were gradually able to relax sufficiently to permit all save the two sentries to stand down. We lay in silence on the springy turf, gazing up at the stars, and trying to find in the immeasurable extent and solitude of the universe visible above, some calming influence on the turmoil of our minds.

The message was passed forward to us from the rear that blankets were available and could be obtained from the monastery that had formerly been our billet. A couple of men were sent off and soon these returned with a load of blankets sufficient to give us at least some protection from the penetrating cold of the chill night air.

Suddenly a wild burst of firing from in front made us start to our feet, seizing our weapons and prepared in an instant for the attack which we had no doubt was now coming. For three or four minutes the rattle of a number of machine guns continued from the point where we knew our forward troops to be, vibrating in our ears and tearing to shreds the clear night air around us.

But after waiting tensely for several minutes we were greatly relieved to find that the firing died down completely, leaving in its place a silence seeming even heavier and more intense than before. From then until dawn our long vigil was disturbed by no more such diversions, and we were left alone with our thoughts, the silence of the night and the chill sea breeze as our only companions. It was learned later that the firing we had heard had indeed signalled the opening phases of what had appeared to be a determined attempt on the part of the Germans to thrust up the railway line towards the town. But the detachment of 2nd SAS who were in that sector of the line had managed to collect from the piles of stores and material thrown down at random by those of our troops who had retreated, a large number of Bren guns, to such an extent that these were issued out almost on the basis of one per man. At the first sign of enemy activity this formidable volume of fire-power was brought into such good effect that the Germans were persuaded to think twice about making an attack against what seemed to be such immensely strong resistance. Most of the Bren guns were blazing away in their direction, completely at random, without any definite target in view, but so effective was this hail of fire that the Germans could hardly know that it was coming from a mere bunch of about ten or twenty men!

As the chill mists of dawn slowly grew less opaque under the light and heat of the rising sun, two men with Bren guns who belonged to the crew of a Bofors gun sited nearby came up to our position to offer their assistance. This we gladly accepted, but they had remained with us for no more than an hour, when their sergeant fetched them away to man the gun. We persuaded them to leave their Brens however, for these and the additional fire-power they gave, were a great comfort to us and we knew that we would be able to put them to good use should the occasion so demand.

As the night receded, and our range of vision gradually extended we were overjoyed to be able to make out in the morning mist a truly cheering sight. For ahead of us were two large orchards and packed tightly beneath the trees were squadron upon squadron of our tanks, their guns facing the direction of the enemy. From the activity of their crews around them, we could not doubt that shortly they would be going into action, in an attempt to dislodge the enemy from the commanding high ground on which he had so firmly established himself.

In a moment the men had regained their customary high spirits. 'Look at them, they're everywhere,' they shouted jubilantly to each other. 'With that lot, we should soon be able to send Jerry packing.'

It was indeed a relief to know as an indisputable fact, that we had succeeded in getting so many of our tanks across the river that previous night. With these to help us, we should be able to hold our own against any attack which the enemy might contemplate.

Further good news reached us a short time later. A brigade of infantry had been landed in the town from the sea during that night, and it was rumoured that these troops would be counter-attacking soon after mid-day. They were an Irish brigade, full of the lust for fighting and the disregard for danger that were such characteristics of their race. These men, we knew, would not easily be forced to throw away their weapons and in a panic-stricken frenzy run from the battle area.

A shout from the nearby Bofors gun position made us swing round in their direction. They had spotted three enemy fighter-bombers swooping in at a low level from the sea onto the town. In a fraction of a second the gun was in action pumping up flaming shells towards the marauding planes, shaking our eardrums with its regular pulsation. But still the planes came in and dropped their small fragmentation bombs onto the harbour, before streaking off seawards again as fast as they could go. In silence we watched the bombs, small black cylinders against the clear, blue sky, leave the bellies of the planes and, turning over and over, start their groundward journey rapidly gathering speed until it was impossible to follow them with our eyes any longer.

That was the last we saw of the Bofors gun crew, for when we looked towards their position scarcely half an hour later, the gun stood alone and deserted, its barrel pointed in the direction in which the enemy planes had departed. The whole crew had, for some reason or other considered discretion to be the better part of valour, and had surreptitiously slunk away leaving their gun and ammunition behind them.

'Good riddance,' we thought. *'At least they have given us a present of their two Bren guns!'*

As it grew lighter the shells began falling fast and furious again, some landing close by us, and others in the town or in the green fields the far side of the track. Many we did not see land at all which must have come from our guns. It was quite impossible when heavy projectiles were ripping back and forth through the sky above our heads, to tell accurately whither each one was bound. Indeed the noises of the raging artillery duel became so intense that it was soon almost impossible to distinguish any one particular sound from the general din of that furious battle.

Through our overloaded ears the sounds of the battle – the whining, shrieking shells, the swooshing mortar bombs, the stupefying roar of bursting explosives – dinned in our minds, rendering coherent thought almost impossible. But from this hopeless confusion of sounds, one thing stood out clearly, namely that the intensity of our own artillery fire had considerably increased in comparison with that of the preceding day, and this fact told us that in addition to the tanks, supplies of much needed ammunition for our guns had been successfully brought across the river during the night. We had been told that on the previous day our guns had been practically out of ammunition on account of the enemy command over the one bridge across the river, over which supplies could be brought.

Meanwhile several of our Spitfires were leisurely and unconcernedly droning over the battlefield, ready to pounce on any further enemy aircraft which were rash enough to appear on the scene.

Suddenly the air seemed to shake at a new sound which rushed to assail our already overtaxed eardrums. In one continuous roar the Germans from their forward positions scarcely 600 yards up the railway from where we were, sent up stream after stream of green tracer at one of the Spitfires. It was an extraordinary sight, for the plane was at such a height that it seemed to be directly over our heads, and it was difficult to imagine that so close to us there were numbers of Germans gazing skywards at this solitary Spitfire, blazing away at it with every weapon they could muster. The plane, at which so much attention was directed, did not seem to be the least concerned. Slowly and gracefully it weaved around over the German lines, banking first on one wing and then on the other. And then suddenly, as if it could stand such nonsense no longer it left off its slow weaving, and streaked earthwards straight down the stream of bullets, its cannon blazing. In a long, low sweep, it regained height once more, and continued its casual and detached patrol in exactly the same area as before.

The sight of this stream of bullets blazing skywards from so short a distance ahead gave Alec, our mortar officer, whose section was just behind us, the idea of seeing whether he could not retaliate with a few well aimed mortar bombs. From then on throughout that day his two mortars were never silent, lobbing regular bombs over into the area which we knew to be covered so thickly by the enemy.

Shortly before mid-day the tanks massed in the orchards ahead, lined up, and slowly rumbled off into the open country beyond filling the air with the noise of their straining engines and churning tracks. We watched them in silence, until the last one had disappeared over the crest that formed the horizon to our front. And still, all the while, the shells rained down, throwing up more and more brown splotches on the smooth green of the open fields, and tearing more and more gaps in the already sorely battered buildings.

Our attention was then directed to a relatively small-scale individual battle which was being fought nearby. To our right and just the other side of the railway track, stood some large locomotive sheds, at one corner of which one of our Sherman tanks had taken up its position in support of Tony's section which we could now see about 200 yards ahead in the vicinity of a bridge over the line. This tank seemed to be directing its attention towards a cemetery which we could just see on the horizon 500 yards or so to our right front. We had noticed throughout that morning that any unnecessary movement on our part had met with some long-range sniping from somewhere, but only when we saw the tank sending streams of tracer machine-gun fire into the cemetery did we realize that this was in German hands and that it was from there that the occasional sniping was coming.

All that morning the tank poured burst after burst into the area of that cemetery and the large domed building that stood in the middle of it, without being able to dislodge from it the stubborn defenders. Soon its 75mm gun sent shell after shell with deadly accuracy at so short a range, into the building, tearing gaping holes in the masonry, so that we could hardly discern its outline anymore, so thick was the cloud of dust rising from the spot. At last, after the cloud had drifted away, we saw that the enormous dome which formed the roof of the building had vanished. Surely that would have driven out those persistent snipers or killed them where they lay! But no! Nothing the tank could do could dislodge them.

A cluster of smoke columns all around the cemetery announced that a battery of our artillery was now attempting to deal with this centre of resistance, but although the walls and buildings in the area were reduced by this concentrated fire to no more than a heap of rubble, the enemy sniping continued from the ruins, unaffected by the murderous destruction that had been poured into the area. Grudgingly we admitted to ourselves that the Germans in that cemetery were tough and brave fighters indeed, probably more fanatical in their stubbornness than any of us would have been in their place.

A gasp escaped us as a cloud of dust rose up around the spot where our tank had been. *'Hell! They've got it,'* someone shouted, but no, for as the smoke and dust rolled away there it still stood, and a second later the tinny sound of a burst from its Besa gun, showed that it was quite unaffected by the fact that a mortar bomb had landed only 5 yards behind it.

Bob Lilley, the troop staff sergeant had meanwhile joined us, bringing with him a box of cigarettes brought up by Franco who we heard had arrived in the town. These were quickly distributed for by that time none of us had a cigarette left. Not a grumble was raised at the fact that this cigarette ration consisted of no more than ten per man, and what is more that they were none other than 'V' cigarettes, a brand generally regarded as being completely unsmokable. Such was our desire for a cigarette at that time, that we were able to smoke even 'V's with relish!

Our troops were now able to move down the railway line in the comparative shelter of the cutting through which it ran, and we were dismayed to see quite a stream of men from our unit being carried or supported down to the hospital which lay just in front of us. Those poor chaps out in front must have been having a rough time, judging from the number of casualties we saw passing into the hospital. My mind was filled with worries about Tony, Sandy and Derrick who, with their sections, had now been out in the front line, bearing the full brunt of the enemy attack for nearly 48 hours. Even now we could see that despite the additional artillery and tank support, they were still not permitted to have a quiet time.

A sub-section of men suddenly appeared over the crest of the small hillock by the railway bridge behind the cover of which they hurriedly scrambled down, and took up improvised firing positions. Evidently, under the fury of the German attentions, their previous position had become too hot for them. A squad of green-bereted commandos was laboriously manhandling into a firing position one of the 6-pounder anti-tank guns that had been left deserted by its crew. Those three sections of our squadron who were out in front had been fighting continuously. No news had been received of them and it worried us to think of the condition in which they now probably were, after the gruelling time they had gone through.

Even as our minds were filled with such thoughts, Bob Lilley shouted that Tony was approaching down the railway track, and sure enough he was soon with us, greeting us like long lost friends whom he never expected to see again.

Poor Tony was very shaken. Through the mud and grime, his face looked drawn and haggard and a wildness in his eyes betrayed the ordeal which he had had to bear. Only with difficulty could he keep still for more than a few seconds, for his quick anxious movements and violent reactions to the slightest sound betrayed only too clearly that his nerves had been strained during the past two days, almost to breaking point.

He did not talk much, but lay with his eyes closed, thankful to reach for the first time since he had been sent out that evening two days ago, some place of at least comparative peace and safety.

Eagerly we questioned him, about our friends who were up in front of him, about the time he had had, and about the general situation of the battle. For a long time he did not answer, and then in a slow monotone he gave us some indication of his experiences since we had last seen him.

'I'm afraid I'm completely bomb-happy, Pete,' he started, *'those bastards have hardly left-off mortaring us since we went out. We lost Hodgkinson I'm afraid; a piece of shrapnel from a mortar bomb blew a hole in his back and although we did all we could for him, he died a few hours later. It was a miracle really that we did not have more casualties. I suppose you heard about poor old Sandy Wilson's section?'*

We had heard no news from up in front, so Tony went on to explain: *'Sandy was killed and practically his whole section was killed or wounded when their position was plastered by the Jerry mortars. His lads have been passing through us on the way to the hospital all morning. The mortaring has been the worst thing. The trouble was that we knew it was coming, for they were plastering every farm and every hilltop systematically, so that we could tell almost to the minute when it was time for our position to receive its dose. Of course the obvious thing would have been to get out to a place of safety from where we would be able to watch the show without danger, and then to return after it was all over, but you know, we felt we just could not trust the troops on our flanks. Honestly, they were so windy that the only thing that was keeping them in the line was the fact we did not go back. We felt that if we had gone back at all the rest would have gone back much further and for good, with no intention of coming forward again, and in that case we would have been even worse off. So you see, we had to stick it!*

'Can you believe it, but on one occasion when we did think it advisable to go back a few yards to a better position, the rumour immediately circulated that we had retreated! It's certainly no go having to fight under conditions like that!'

That was about all the coherent information we were able to get out of Tony, but it was apparent to all that his section had had an extremely rough time. I believe they were pinned down most of the previous afternoon and had been forced to take shelter from the murderous bomb splinters in a narrow culvert only a few yards away from the Germans. It must have been hell, and the stubborn hold which these sections kept on their positions throughout the battle, despite the battering they were receiving and despite the general low morale that was evident around them, is worthy of the highest admiration. If

Derrick Harrison's section HQ in action.

they had acted otherwise, the outcome of the whole Termoli battle might have been a very different story.

Tony then went off to find Alec, in the hope of arranging with him some effective sort of mortar fire into the area so thickly covered by the enemy. After a brief exchange of words, both of them went forward to see what they could do. But unfortunately Alec's wireless was out of order and there was no suitable covered site for his vulnerable mortars out in front, so he had to come back and fire them from the excellent position in which they were already mounted. A system of signals had been arranged with Tony, and Alec installed himself beside me, from where he was not only able to have a good view of Tony's position, but was also just within shouting distance of his mortars.

From then until well into the evening, both mortars were firing continuously, raking the area ahead with high explosive bombs, which penetrated into every corner and cranny in which the Germans might attempt to seek shelter. From his excellent observation post Tony directed the proceedings, in an attempt under these difficult conditions to concentrate the mortar fire in the areas in which it served the best purpose.

The system of signals evolved proved rather ineffective and soon these were supplemented by a despatch rider in the form of Corporal Moore, who drove madly up and down the railway cutting between us in a Jeep he had 'borrowed'. It was only after the battle was over that we discovered that this Jeep belonged not to a unit which had left the fighting to others, but to a young and officious Military Police lieutenant, who had somehow found himself in the battle area! He was all ready to kick-up an almighty fuss at the disappearance of his Jeep, and was even contemplating taking disciplinary action against Moore. Franco bore the brunt of this officer's ravings for quite a time, until he was forced with Tony's help to silence the abuse and complaints of the officer in question, with the explanation that the Jeep was taken as an emergency measure and an operational necessity, as indeed it was. This explanation was of course unanswerable at a time when the enemy shells were still falling around the town.

Meanwhile the news of the general battle situation was improving, so that the strain we had felt for so long was greatly lightened, and we were able to move around and discuss the events of the past few days among ourselves without so much of our former reticence. The tank attack which had been put in that morning had been successful and the threat to the town from the east and south had been removed with the Germans being thrown off the ridge of high ground from which they had been able to overlook both the town and its approaches over the river. All that now remained was to clear the enemy from the side of the town on which we ourselves were, and then our worries would be over.

We learned that with this aim in view the infantry were going to put in an attack at 3pm, and shortly before that time, elements of the Irish brigade which had been landed from the sea the night before, began to pass through us on their way forward. We were able to watch the initial stages of this attack, which seemed to progress smoothly and effectively, despite the continued sniping which still carried on from the area of the cemetery.

Those fanatically stubborn defenders refused to surrender and continued their sniping activities right until the cemetery was in the hands of our infantry, by which time the fire which they had caused to be brought down upon themselves, had left them lying dead amid the ruins of their stronghold. Not a man of that small party which had taken up its position in the cemetery the previous night, and which had carried on with its resistance in the face of overwhelming fire from our tanks, guns and mortars, was left alive by the time our troops reached the spot; but from all appearances not a man from among them had withdrawn to safety.

And all the time that this attack was going on, Alec's mortars continued to rain down high explosive bombs onto the area immediately ahead of our advancing infantry – he would never have been able to fire at this rate for more than half an hour on the stock of ammunition which the mortar section had brought with them, but fortunately fresh supplies were procured in large quantities, so that the mortars could continue firing without the possibility of any ammunition shortages materializing. It was a great day for the mortar crews. Never before had they been able to fire off such a vast quantity of bombs to such good effect. The mortar barrels became red hot, and by the constant firing their base-plates were driven so deep into the soft clay soil, that only about a foot of the barrel was eventually visible above ground level. The weapons had to be dug out and re-sited many times and by the time cease-fire was called both mortars were found to have cracked and buckled base-plates from the strain which had been imposed upon them. Each mortar fired nearly 300 bombs that afternoon, all of which must have fallen in a relatively small area. So the discomfort which the Germans must have experienced on this account, can well be imagined.

This was the first time I had seen Alec since we had landed – a period which seemed to stretch into many weeks but which in reality only amounted to a couple of days. During the occasional pauses in his directing the fire of the mortars, I was able to glean from him what had happened to his section after we had left them plodding so laboriously across the flat muddy coastal plain on the first night of our landing, in search of some suitable cover. Their mortars had not been in much demand during the original landing, and they had consequently been able to play around as infantry like the rest of the landing force. They captured a German NAAFI truck, or its equivalent, loaded with chocolate and cigarettes! A fact which aroused much comment from the examination of the stores, was that many of the cigarettes which had presumably been on their way down to the German front-line troops, were none other than Red Cross cigarettes of the type issued to prisoners of war. Whether the Germans made a habit of delivering these for their own consumption, or whether it was merely a temporary result of many Italian prisoner of war camps being closed down, we were never able to know, but it certainly gave us subject for thought.

The arrival of Corporal Moore in his Jeep, with a screeching of brakes, and in a flurry of dust, interrupted our conversation.

'*Captain Marsh wants as much mortar fire as you can possibly bring down,*' he said to Alec, '*in the area of the railway about a hundred yards longer range than the one you are now firing on. Also could you direct the fire of one of the mortars onto the beach. It's a wonderful target sir, wonderful – it really seems that the Jerries are pulling right out for the beach seems black with them. We are firing with all we have got, but they are almost out of range of our Brens. Oh if only we had a few more mortars or a Vickers machine-gun or two.'*

The end of the Termoli battle was in sight. The recent infantry attack had been successful, and now the Germans were retreating on this side of the town also – the last remaining direction from which they were threatening the town itself. Alec responded to Tony's call with all he had got, and for the next forty minutes his mortars were never silent. If the Germans had been reluctant to pull out of any area, that hail of terrifying bombs must have given them ample cause to think again.

The shells had meanwhile ceased to fall in the town or around our position, and the violent and continuous sounds of battle which had been going on all around us for the past two days were now carried away from us and the town of Termoli. The town was saved and in consequence, our presence in the line was no longer needed. For the first time since we had come out into the line, we were able to move about freely, stretch ourselves, and relax. The fighting was over and although we ourselves had not fired a single shot, the relief was immeasurable, to be able to feel that we were still alive, that the confusion and alarms and suspense were all no more than memories of the past, and that those howling, roaring shells were not landing around us anymore, and indeed need not be expected to do so again.

About 6pm we received the order from Paddy to pull back into the town. The fighting and shelling could be heard in a vague confusion of noise far off to our right. Stiffly we got up and filed back into the town. We must have looked a sorry sight, with our blackened and unshaven faces, our shambling gait – a sight which could well have been applied to retreating troops, withdrawing from the battle in face of overwhelming enemy pressure. So the elderly woman who with shouts and gestures met us at the edge of the town, exhorting us to turn round again and go back and fight the Germans, cannot really be blamed for her mistake. At least her intentions were good! Her senile cackle of delighted laughter, and the smiles creasing round her wrinkled old face as soon as she realized that not we but the hated *Tedesci* were *'finito'* was a cheering sight indeed.

We found the monastery untouched by the heavy shelling, and with no loss of time, the men were speedily installed in their old quarters. The cooks and headquarters staff had been busy preparing a welcome hot meal which was ready for the hungry and weary men as soon as they returned. Once we had seen to the welfare of our men, we trudged across the square to the house in which we had organized the officers' mess, only to find on arrival, a scene of indescribable confusion.

Although untouched by the shellfire, the building had been ransacked. Our kit had been completely turned out and anything of value had been removed from them. It was as though the enemy themselves had succeeded in taking possession of the building for a short while and had helped themselves to whatever they wanted from our kits, as lawful plunder of war.

But it was no enemy which had treated us so shamefully, but our own troops. The Irish brigade which had been landed in the town the preceding night had listened too strongly to the rumours that the town was likely to be retaken at any moment by the enemy, and that all the British troops who had previously been in it had fled in such confusion that they had left all their equipment behind. It was therefore only natural when these soldiers came upon our kits, strewn at random exactly as we had thrown them down, that they should have held the mistaken idea that the lawful owners of this equipment had fled from the scene, and were now miles down the beach to the east in the direction of safety.

And if it were likely that the Germans would shortly be in possession of the town what was the use of leaving these valuables to them?

In this way we stated the case for the action of these wretched Irish as favourably as possible, although we were naturally seething with indignation at this outrage. But it is doubtful whether the looting was activated by any such justifiable motives, and it is far more likely that greed and self-interest lay behind the whole affair. Although Paddy immediately lodged a complaint with the CO of the offending unit, none of the culprits had the decency to return a single article from the pile that had been taken.

Angrily we surveyed the scattered remnants of our kits, vainly searching for any little valuables or souvenirs which we hoped might have been overlooked and left to us. But everything was gone – cameras, binoculars, cigarettes and even money. I had a few 'V' cigarettes in a tin, which I would willingly have given away. But these were taken, and along with them the negatives of many of the photographs in this book, which by ill-fortune had been sharing the same tin. Needless to say, I never saw them again.

Whilst the cooks were busy preparing a meal for us, the padre came round to inform us that the funeral of all the casualties we had been able to collect would take place immediately. Whilst the fighting had been going on, his had been the unenviable task of sorting out and collecting, with the aid of a few headquarters men, the shattered and blasted fragments of what had once been human bodies. Many of that ill-fated truckload, were impossible to identify, but as best he could, the padre completed his gruesome and heart-breaking task, until he had all the pitiful fragments laid out in a neat row of separate graves, in the public gardens within a few yards of the actual scene of the tragedy.

Grave of McNinch and others, public gardens, Termoli, 5 October 1943.

It was dusk as we silently filed into the narrow street, with heads bared and softened tread. But the sight of that battered truck and of those crumpled, gaping walls conjured up for us again all the horrors which had been stamped so permanently on our minds by the events of that afternoon, only twenty-four hours previously. We could still smell that charred, musty and indescribably nauseating odour of the explosion, mixed with the heavy, clinging smell of death. Many of us felt sick and hopeless at the vivid memory which the scene brought so clearly to our minds.

It was soon over. In a quiet voice the padre read the service and dismissed us. Without a word we walked back to our billets, our spirits heavy, and troubled with the thoughts which filled our minds. The fears that had lain unspoken in the hearts of each man of my section had been confirmed. McNinch was dead: he had been blown to pieces in that truck along with seventeen others. I thought of him as I walked back to the mess – of his power over the men, his cheerfulness, and his amazing coolness in an emergency. There was a man who would be very hard to replace. I thought of his words at Bagnara, when he had said to me in a voice full of feeling, *'It's always the best that catch it. Charlie was the kindest hearted man in the section… and here am I, a drunken old reprobate.'*

And now he too was gone, taken by a vicious and unnecessary spin of Fortune's wheel, at a time when he should have been left out of battle. If he had been with the rest of the section he would undoubtedly have been alive at the moment. Again we wondered at the complex workings of Destiny – at the roundabout and complicated methods she would adopt to pick out one man and leave the rest. Again we were brought to realize how powerless man is to control his own life in opposition to her arbitrary whims and desires.

Eighteen men had died in that truck, many of whom, such as Sergeant O'Dowd and young Davidson, were hardened veterans of the desert and had been with the unit since it was first formed. Indeed it was most surprising that anyone had escaped from that shambles, and the fact that Fate had chosen to spare Sergeant Seekings, the sole survivor, was as incomprehensible as her decision to make McNinch die. This, I believe was not the first escape of this miraculous nature that Sergeant Seekings had experienced. He appeared to have a charmed life, a fact which served him in good stead throughout the whole course of the war.

As we sat at our meal in the mess the gloomy silence occasioned by the sad events of the past few days quickly relaxed and withdrew. It had become a custom with us not to let the deaths of our comrades affect our normal life, and we were determined to put out of our minds the memory of their loss. This did not mean that we had no regrets at the passing of such good men nor that we did not miss them, but in time of war when any day might see the death of a friend or a comrade it was useless to brood on these matters and allow our minds to be constantly filled with gloomy or morbid thoughts. Once a unit allowed itself to do this, its fighting efficiency would be irreparably impaired, and its morale permanently lowered. So our policy, in this case as with all the others, was to attend the funeral if there was one, and there pay due reverence and homage to the dead, and then immediately afterwards to cast the memory from our minds.

We may be accused of being callous in behaving in such a way, but I am convinced that our course of action was the right one. Those who had died would not have wished us to grieve on their account, in the same way as they themselves would not have grieved over the loss of their own friends. Thus although we were all cut-up at the losses the unit had suffered, and Paddy most of all, we chose to forget about it as soon as the funeral was over.

And so after our meal the vino was produced and glasses filled, and tired though we were, we could not resist sitting around yarning until well into the night.

I had not realized how bomb-happy most of us were. Occasionally a door would slam down below, or the faint rattle of a Bren gun burst would come drifting over from the front line, now a few miles from the town. At such sounds the conversation would abruptly cease – men would look at each other with startled eyes, as if expecting hell to be let loose at any moment, until they had ascertained the harmless nature of the interruption. And then, with sheepish looks they would carry on talking.

Naturally most of the conversation turned around the battle which had so recently been fought and won, and many interesting facts were learned. Apparently the Germans had laid great importance on the small town of Termoli, in view of its situation on the eastern end of the lateral main road running from Naples, and from a captured document we learned that they were determined to recapture it at all costs. With this aim in view the 9th Paratroop Division had been despatched from Naples and it was this unit which had given us so heavy a battering, before they were forced to withdraw.

Another interesting fact was that the church tower of the town was discovered to have been used as an artillery observation post and was beautifully fitted-out with flags, lamps, and radio. Almost certainly a German or Italian had been operating from there during the heavy shelling of the town. It had seemed uncanny to our troops how every movement of theirs seemed to have been watched and welcomed with a salvo of enemy shells. Indeed it is more than likely that the accurate fire which caused such havoc among our own unit as they climbed into their transport was not so much the result of a mere, unfortunate coincidence, but of deliberate direction by the enemy observer in the church tower behind us. The offender was never caught despite the rounding-up of numerous suspects.

Harry Poat, in his wanderings, had seen a lot of the battle and was able to relate many amazing stories. Among these was how a brigadier, probably the one in command of the leading brigade, had kept on turning up at points where there was no real fighting to speak of, during the most critical time of the battle, with the heartening battle cry of 'Don't waver!'

Tony told of a plan which was almost put into effect against the Germans on his sector of the front, which, had it come off, would undoubtedly have caused the Germans some surprise, and possibly heavy casualties. For in the neighbourhood of the hospital was found a railway wagon piled high with explosives, and it would have been no difficult task to harness this to a goods engine also found nearby, and send the whole lot snorting up the railway line in the direction of the Germans, after ensuring that the explosive was fused with some type of time mechanism which would fire it after a given period. There were probably many reasons why this plan proved to be impracticable, but we would have dearly loved to have seen it put into effect.

Johnny Wiseman and Alec Muirhead first experienced the initial signs of the enemy counter-attack under rather embarrassing conditions. After the squadron, with the exception of my section, had been withdrawn to the town upon being relieved by our main forces, these two decided to visit one of the LCIs which had brought us to Termoli, and which were now being used for evacuating the 300 odd prisoners which had been taken.

Unsuspecting that they might be overlooked by the enemy whom they thought at that time to be many miles away, they decided to have a brew-up of tea, and Johnny was just in the process of carrying a mess-tin full of boiling water precariously along the deck for this purpose, when he was rooted to the spot by the roar of an approaching shell, obviously coming in his direction. He could not take cover like everyone else on account of the boiling water and so perforce had to stand where he was and wait for the explosion. The shell landed scarcely 50 yards away, rocking the small craft and covering it with spray. The enemy had re-established themselves on the high ground overlooking the town and harbour and had started to shell our ships in earnest. Fortunately no harm was done and the craft were able to steam away at full speed to a safer spot, but the sight of Johnny standing there unable to move, with the dixie of boiling water in his hand, while everyone else hurled themselves flat on the deck must have provided much amusement. The story was quickly circulated and Johnny had to suffer much teasing to the effect that this must have been the first time he was known not to have taken cover!

Franco too had had adventures quite unbecoming to his dignity as a staff officer. As soon as he had heard that the unit had been relieved by the army he drove his convoy containing all the elements of our main camp into the town, and then took a truck down to Corps HQ to fetch the NAAFI ration, or similar stores, up to us. But by the time he arrived back, the enemy counter-attack had developed in full force and a long stretch of the road up to the town was under enemy observation and fire. Franco was ignorant of this situation and quite unperturbed by the fact that his 3-tonner was the first vehicle to cross the bridge which had at length been erected by the REs. It was a miracle how he succeeded in getting through, for even tanks had not dared to venture by that route in daylight. On arrival in the town he found a scene of indescribable chaos, and was forced to remain under these conditions until the battle was over. But although unaccustomed to such life in a frontline town, he managed to do some good work, in organizing the camp personnel and passing cigarettes up to our men in the line, as well as in procuring the much needed mortar bombs for Alec's section.

He was considerably worried by being challenged at the outskirts of the town by a strange soldier, who rudely pressing a bayonet to his paunch, harshly demanded the password. Now Franco had been told the password but in the excitement of the situation had unfortunately, for the moment, forgotten it, with the result that he had to undergo the indignity of having to stand there until he remembered, with the bayonet periodically jabbing harder and harder into his stomach, just to aid his memory. It was not a pleasant five minutes for him.

And then, even after he had contacted our unit, the story goes how the batmen took it upon themselves never to let him out of their sight, but to follow him like leeches wherever he might choose to go. The reason for this 'devotion' was very simply explained, for it was noticed that Franco was still carrying the little black bag, from which he was never known by the men to be parted, and Casey and the rest of them, thus made up their minds to be on the spot if, in the excitement of the moment, Franco should happen to put down his bag for a single second or if he should be laid low by some chance sniper's bullet. Their interest in the little black bag may have been partly caused by their certainty that it contained something of value, but the chief desire to get hold of it was that far back, even in the days at Azzib, the men had convinced themselves that Franco was robbing them of their PRI funds[1] and that the booty which rightly belonged to them, would be found in the little black bag in question.

Unfortunately for Casey and his companions, they were not given a single opportunity to carry out their evil designs, and to this day, Franco and his little black bag have not been parted.

The bag in question was nothing more than a harmless briefcase in which Franco merely carried certain regimental papers and administrative forms, and the suspicions of the men were of course completely unfounded.

Phil Gunn had some good news to give of Bill Fraser, about whom some of us had been worrying. He was not badly hurt and had only received a piece of shrapnel in the shoulder. He was in great form as he was being evacuated and could be expected back with the unit in a few weeks' time.

The Termoli battle was over, but only at a great cost to our gallant little squadron. For we had suffered nearly thirty per cent casualties. Of our nine operational sections, John Tonkin's had been captured to a man, Johnny Wiseman's had been blown to pieces on that ill-fated truck, and Sandy Wilson's had been almost wiped out by mortar fire. My section had been guided through the battle with complete safety and had undoubtedly had the easiest time, for we had not fired a shot throughout the operation and, except for McNinch who

---

1. President of the Regimental Institute's funds, non-public monies to be used for the benefit of corporals and lower ranks.

was not with us, had not suffered a single casualty. But it was an experience ever to be reckoned as one of the worst we went through, for although we ourselves did no fighting, in the narrow sense of the word, we shared in the horrors, the torments, and the suspense of those extremely critical few days. Without sleep and without peace of mind we had to undergo continuous shelling for nearly two days, while never knowing what the future had in store for us or whether the next few hours would see the enemy sweeping over our positions. And on top of it all we had seen our comrades blown to pieces before our eyes, even while some of our own troops were retreating, leaving depleted ranks to withstand the violence of the German assault.

It was certainly not a pleasant memory, or one which we were anxious to relive.

Chapter Eleven

Reorganisation and Recuperation

Nothing could have cheered us more than the speech which General Dempsey delivered to the unit the day after we were withdrawn from the line; it was a speech which for ever afterwards won him a place in our hearts for he made no bones about what he thought of us, and the words he spoke were calculated to stir up in us a pride in ourselves and in our achievements at just the time when we felt most in need of appreciation from someone in a high position.

And so, in one of the larger halls of the monastery, we all assembled to hear him. Previously our numbers would have been sufficient to fill the room completely, but now it was pitiful to see how small we were. The losses we had suffered were forcefully driven home to us as soon as we looked round the bare, unfurnished room and saw how inadequately we filled it.

In his shy, quiet voice the general addressed us briefly. He did not say much, but what he did say was sufficient to show his appreciation of our achievements. For it must have been one of the most flattering speeches ever delivered to a single unit by its commanding general, and in the simple, unassuming way in which he expressed himself, General Dempsey could not conceal the sincerity in his voice when he told us that, not only did he consider us the best fighting troops he had ever had under his command, but also the best disciplined.

General Dempsey then went on to talk about the past and of the principles which he had followed when planning an operation for us. As he spoke, it was obvious that here was a commander who placed the highest value on human lives, and who would never risk these needlessly. We learned that he would never consent to our undertaking a landing unless he himself felt confident that the leading elements of the main forces would be able to relieve us within twenty-four hours.

Such was the gist of what General Dempsey had to say to us. That he was sincere, none of us could doubt, and that he had nothing but the highest admiration for Paddy and his small unit was all too evident from the words which he addressed to us. His speech made us feel proud to have been working under so fine a commander and to have been so obviously appreciated by him. A little praise and a little recognition of past achievements can do wonders in encouraging a unit to continue to give of its best, and this General Dempsey was not slow to realize.

The general's talk set rumours flying and the next few days were filled with one conjecture after another as to our possible future destinations. Somehow or other a report that we were being sent home buzzed into existence and would not be stilled. After all, everyone knew that in the course of the next year the long awaited D-Day for the invasion of France would dawn, and what more natural than that we should be required in this campaign? So, although nothing definite was divulged, from that time on the growing certainty spread among us that soon we would be Blighty bound.

We were not nearly so impressed with the speech Monty gave us on the following day. The informal and unassuming way in which General Dempsey had addressed us, and with which he had been so successful in winning his way into our hearts, was entirely absent when Monty spoke. We had heard it all before from Monty, and it left us rather cold. The same old story of 'How I beat the Hun in the desert and how I am going to beat him again here' was trotted out to us, and thus it was no wonder that we all considered the parade a waste of time.

We remained a week at Termoli, while all the time expecting and hoping for an early move from the area, for most of us had come to hate the place on account of the unhappy associations tied up with it. It was a typical front-line town, battered and dead in every sense, and this exerted a stifling and oppressive effect on us all, so that we hardly felt inclined to talk in normal voices or to laugh and be cheerful.

We returned to the bridge over which all our supplies and reinforcements had to come, surrounded by shattered vehicles and the litter of battle. The green fields all around were torn by the tracks of the tanks and pitted with shell holes. In the river itself stood a Sherman, firmly embedded in the mud, with only its turret visible above the fast flowing water. Scarcely a hundred yards away was another, drunkenly leaning over at a perilous angle. One track had been torn off, and a huge twisted mass of metal, which had once been its turret, lay on the ground beside it. And all around, pitiful little white crosses marked the graves of those who had fallen, of friend and foe alike.

We went back down the road to have another look at the first position we had taken up, behind that wall at the head of the valley which ran down to the road. The burned out ammunition truck was scarcely more than a heap of ashes. Close by lay the twisted remnants of a 15cwt lorry. Evidently the area had been thoroughly blasted by the enemy guns, probably assisted by the beacon provided by the blazing truck. The villa immediately behind our position, and

Some of 'B' Section in Molfetta Harbour, Italy, October–November 1943

Ashurst, Telford, Stalker, Smith, Sergeant Lilley, Tideswell and Johnstone.

Officers' dormitory – John Tonkin and Rose.

in which Paddy had set up his headquarters, had received a direct hit from a heavy shell and now lay, a sordid heap of tangled ruins. It was just as well that we moved out from this area when we did, judging from the scene of desolation and destruction that surrounded it.

At last we received our long expected orders to move at short notice, as was usual on such occasions. One evening we were sitting calmly in the mess, and the next morning we were gone. Our LCIs, which had all along been anchored in the harbour, took us off and carried us southwards where we would be able to rest and recuperate.

It was an indescribable relief to be away from Termoli with its sounds of battle forever in our ears. At last we could completely relax without our hearts racing madly each time we heard a burst of machine-gun fire or a distant explosion.

We spent two uncomfortable days on the little LCIs, with hardly room to stretch our legs. The winter had set in and the weather was far from pleasant, with rough seas and torrents of rain so we were not even able to sleep on deck and thereby attain some relief from the crowded conditions. Some of us did indeed try this the first night, myself among them, but were soon driven below decks by the pelting rain.

We disembarked at Molfetta, a small port a long way down the coast. The former Fascist headquarters was requisitioned to form the officers' mess. This was an immense, flashily decorated house of lofty halls, gilded pillars and highly ornamented plasterwork, with enormous mirrors all around the walls. The largest room was made into a dormitory for all the officers except Paddy, and even though there were thirteen camp beds aligned along its walls, there still remained ample space for us to move about freely.

For over a month we lived at Molfetta. It was a pleasant enough little town, completely untouched by the war, still possessing its normal complement of civilians, and with its shops still carrying on a busy trade. The fashionable quarter was clean and spacious, with wide, tree-flanked streets of tall proud houses running out from the central square. But an unpleasantly large part of it was less attractive, for here was no more than a jumble of squalid buildings intersected by mean and narrow streets which sent up a medley of unpleasant odours to the skies and allowed the flies and the vermin to breed unhindered. Dirty and unkempt children thronged the narrow pavements, clutching with sticky hands at each soldier who passed, pestering him eternally with requests for '*Biscotti*' or a 'cigarette for Papa!'

Much attention was paid to sport, and as the town boasted a fine football ground and stadium, great pains were taken in training up a regimental team. When this was done, the local Italian team was challenged, and by posters and

No 2 sub-section, Italy, October–November 1943. Telford, Stalker, Ashurst, Davidson, Tideswell, Sergeant Storey.

advertisements the day of the great match was announced to the public.

It was perhaps the most extraordinary game of football ever played! The whole regiment turned out to shout its support while crowds of the townspeople thronged around the grandstand to watch the play. The traditional sportsmanship for which the Englishman is famed was not much in evidence during that match! Such was the contempt and hatred that our men felt towards the Italians that it was only with the greatest of difficulty that they were able to restrain themselves sufficiently to play a friendly game of football with them. But when they found their opponents to be twice as nimble as they, and by the skill and intricacy of their footwork able to run around them in circles, that was the last straw. Tempers were high and the game was dirty.

At half-time one of our men was sent off the field for very nearly assaulting one of the Italians in his fury. When towards the end of the second half, one of the Italian forwards so succeeded in incensing our goalkeeper that he left his goal and pursued him halfway across the field, eventually laying him low with a superb rugby tackle somewhere in the neighbourhood of the touchline! By methods such as these, we managed to hold our own with the nimble and tricky Italian players so that the game ended in a draw, but it was not a memory of which many of us could feel proud.

On the whole we had very little to do with the civilians, for it was such a short while previously that we had been fighting against these people that we had no inclination to fraternize with them or to trust them. But there was one woman who persistently went out of her way to make our acquaintance, a tall striking

Balcony of officers' mess, Molfetta, November 1943

Ted Lepine.

Peter Davis.

Derrick Harrison.

looking woman of about thirty-five, known by us as the 'Countess'. Her husband, the count, was a prisoner of war in Bombay, but for this she did not seem to bear us any malice, and made every effort to get to know us, and to organize for us dances and similar social functions which needed the support of the townspeople.

Her desire to be friendly may of course have been entirely genuine, but there was something suspicious about her. She was extremely keen to know personally every officer and although she asked no direct questions, it seemed that by a skilful manipulation of the conversation the information she was able to glean about the regiment in this way, must have been quite considerable. She expressed an open sympathy for the Germans and would tell how she had passed through the lines to fetch her son and had been protected throughout by a German officer against any possible evil designs on part of the soldiers towards her. Of course it may all have been quite true, but her manner was nevertheless sufficient to arouse in many of us a considerable distrust. I believe she was arrested on one occasion as a spy, or so she told us, but was released almost immediately as they could pin nothing on her.

One event occurred during our stay in Molfetta which served to make us more suspicious of the 'countess' than we would probably have been otherwise, even though she may have had nothing to do with what happened.

It was decided to hold a regimental dance one night, partly to provide some sort of amusement for the men, and partly as a first gesture of friendship towards the civilians. Great preparations were made – the date was fixed well in advance, the hall was taken over and decorated and a band engaged. Stocks of drink and refreshments were laid in. And so the forthcoming event was advertised throughout the town by means of posters announcing that all would be welcome and detailed preparations were made. In all these preparations the 'countess' was present, offering her assistance and acting as go-between between us and the civilians.

The great evening arrived and almost all the regiment turned up in that one hall in the expectations of a grand time. But although over 150 of our men were present at the dance, they were disconcerted to find that no women had chosen to put in an appearance, so that dancing had to be ruled out from the evening's programme. But we made the best of things, and the bar was well patronized so that none were anxious to leave while the drink continued to flow.

As we were in the midst of our festivities the whole building shook with the roar of a powerful explosion, and a second later the ceiling fell in upon us. It was an amazing sensation, to stand there, pressed up against the wall, watching the centre of the ceiling gradually cave-in. Slowly it bulged and parted; terribly slowly it seemed, until the electric wiring snapped under the strain and the hall was plunged into darkness. A second later, the whole mass fell upon us in a tangled heap of laths and plaster which raised up choking clouds of dust in the darkness and almost stifled us. Vaguely we wondered if we were buried alive or if the whole of the rest of the building was likely to follow at any moment. But gradually the confusion sorted itself out; matches and lighters were lit, and we were able to move around assessing the damage. Fortunately we had had sufficient warning of the fact that the ceiling was falling to crowd around the walls of the hall and we were thus able to escape the full brunt of the weight of the falling plaster, which for the most part landed in the centre. Beyond a few bruises, abrasions and minor cuts, no one was hurt, the hall was cleared within a few minutes and the crowd dispersed into the streets and thence to their billets.

At first we had thought that a bomb or grenade had been placed in the roof, with deliberate intent to wipe us out, but in fact it turned out that a single plane had flown over and dropped a single bomb, which had landed within 200 yards of the spot where we were.

We couldn't help wondering whether perhaps that bomb had been deliberately aimed at us. The fact that it was widely known throughout the town that the whole regiment would be in that hall that evening made it easy for the enemy to have been informed of this, and for him to have acted on the information.

The 'countess' had helped in the arrangements for the dance, and had actually been in the hall before the bomb had dropped, though she had left some time previously. Also it seemed that the civilians had been affected by some sort of propaganda warning them not to turn up, which may have accounted for their absence!

Of course it was only in our imagination that all these various circumstances were connected with the bombing incident, and there was not a shred of evidence with which we could substantiate the theory.

The landing of that bomb so close to the dance hall just about marked the end of our attempts at arranging such social functions in the future. Not indeed because we were afraid of the occurrence being repeated, but entirely through the effect of the incident on the minds of the civilians who, superstitious at the best of times, were thereafter prevailed upon by their priests to consider the bomb as a warning from above to the effect that dancing with the rude British soldiery was a sin which was not looked lightly upon in celestial spheres.

So no one would come to our dances in future. Knowing what some of the men could be like when they got going, perhaps it was wise of the Italian maidens to lend so obedient an ear to the warnings of their mothers and their priests. But in spite of the very real difficulties this caused, the sergeants' mess was undaunted, and made one more effort to organize a small private dance; but once again their exertions came up against a brick wall – not so much one of superstition and tradition this time, as of pure snobbery. Of the fifteen or so girls, who probably against their better judgement, had been persuaded to attend, two who had been asked privately by one of the sergeants, were considered by the rest as not being of quite the type with whom they liked to mix, and as a result soon after the dance commenced, the girls all ganged up in one corner of the hall whence they delivered an ultimatum to the effect that unless the two girls, to whose presence they so strongly objected, were asked to leave then they themselves would go.

We, in accordance with the true democratic principles of our nation would naturally agree to nothing of the sort, whereupon the dissenting majority of the women retired to the cloakroom where a council of war took place, for well on half an hour while the band continued to play and the two ostracized girls had a roaring time on the floor, dancing all the while, while the rest of us clustered round the bar.

We had not been at Molfetta for much more than a week, when one evening the door opened and in walked John Tonkin! A gasp of amazement followed by a bombardment of questions greeted his entrance, for we all expected that by now he should have been safely behind the wire in Germany. And yet here he was back with us!

The explanation was simple. A mere three days after his capture, even while he was being taken back from the front to the prison camp whither he was bound, he had eluded his guards and made good his escape, through both lines, and had found his way back to our unit.

Naturally he had many interesting and amusing stories to tell of his adventures since we had seen him last. The paratroops who had captured him had treated him extremely well and honourably, in a manner which rather put us to shame when we considered the way we had treated those prisoners who had fallen into our hands. Even his watch was not taken from him! Actually John said goodbye to this when a German sergeant came up and took it from him, but to his surprise, it was returned to him a few minutes later complete with a new strap! Evidently the sergeant had noticed that the strap was broken and had kindly offered to replace it!

The first night after his capture John was taken to the headquarters of the 9th Paratroop Division where he was made the personal guest of General Dietrich, who had been impressed by the fact that his paratroopers had captured an officer who was also a paratrooper, and was in consequence embarrassingly curious about our training and our role. John was given a first class dinner in the officers' mess at divisional HQ where he fed off the fat of the land and was filled with chicken and pork looted from the Italian peasants. The general was most friendly and patronizingly gracious, and throughout that meal, John found it difficult to remember that he was in fact a prisoner, and that these were his enemies with whom he was dining and drinking. Except for the language, the atmosphere in that mess seemed exactly the same as in our own – a free and easy, cheerful atmosphere, in which the future counted for nothing and the present for everything; an atmosphere which John had thought to be essentially English and which he was surprised to find in a German mess.

The general was full of talk about the Russian front, from which his division had apparently only recently been withdrawn, and he took pleasure in painting the horrors of the fighting there to his prisoner. After telling of the terrific fire-power which the Russians were able to mass, on such scale that if any movement on the part of the Germans was observed, they would bring down upon that spot the fire from forty mortars at a time, the general turned to John with a remark that struck him as being extremely quaint, when the circumstances of the conversation were considered:

'It was terrible,' the general said, with feeling, *'really terrible! I only hope that you will never have to experience anything like that!'* Indeed a peculiar remark to address to one's prisoner!

John managed to make his escape a couple of days later, while he was being taken back from the forward area by some German military police – the further he went from the lines, the worse treatment did he receive, and never again was he treated in the honourable and comradely fashion with which his original captors had received him. And so it was with no regrets as to the punishment he was letting his guards in for that he saw his opportunity one evening just as it was growing dark, of eluding them by jumping over the cab of the truck in which he was being taken, while their backs were turned, and then over a wall into a vine-covered valley. So well did he choose his moment that his escape was unnoticed for quite a time and he was able to get well away without hearing any signs of pursuit. He lay up for several days and then one night found his way through the lines to one of our forward posts. He had kept his eyes open during this time and was able to give our intelligence some valuable information about enemy troop locations and fortified positions.

Our stay at Molfetta was marked for us by only one other event, of sufficient significance to remain in our memories. This was the occasion of another of Paddy's outbursts, the worst I had ever witnessed, and the last time that he really went 'bad' through the influence of drink.

It all started by some of the officers entertaining in the mess one evening three or four nurses from the neighbouring hospital with whom they had become acquainted. It was so delightful to be able to talk to an English girl again after so long, that we all gathered in the ante-room to chat with them. Now women have never interested Paddy, and so he sat alone in a dark corner of the immense hallway, ominously brooding, a bottle of whiskey in his hand and a glass on the table which was emptied as quickly as filled. For the first time Paddy, who was essentially socially inclined, found himself alone, ignored and deserted by his officers. And what was worse, while the visitors were present, he was unable to exercise over his officers the power which he was accustomed to wield on normal occasions.

And so, all he could do was just sit there until someone noticed his mood, and the girls were hurried out before the trouble began.

And the trouble did indeed begin as soon as they had left. Pushing us all before him, like a flock of startled sheep, Paddy shepherded us into the ante-room and sat us around and made us fill our glasses and drink.

But it was soon evident that none of us were in a party mood. On previous occasions, parties had developed slowly and voluntarily on the part of several of the officers, so that Paddy had always had people to drink with him. But this was the first time he had tried to make us all drink, when none of us were willing to do so, and Paddy was not slow to realize that we were being singularly unco-operative. The idea infuriated him. After repeated vain efforts to make us sing, or drink faster, he started off on 'The tail of my coat' – a song, the implications of which we all recognized. At the expected point in the song down came his fist onto the table, with such mighty force that several glasses, standing on it bounced up into the air at the vibration and crashed to the floor.

With one sweep of his hand Paddy sent the rest of the glasses following, and then, towering above us he advanced into the middle of the room bellowing: '*So you won't drink with me! I know what you're thinking. There you sit smugly thinking to yourselves "He's drunk – a disgusting sight isn't it?"*' Whereupon he set about the room in search of further breakable objects.

Franco, the PMC could not stand by and see our precious glasses smashed in this wilful fashion and made a movement to restrain him. This was the last straw for Paddy that anyone should try and interfere with him. Seizing a whiskey bottle he was on the point of hurling it at Franco, when he fortunately noticed that it was still half full, and put it down, picking up an empty decanter instead. This missed Franco's head by a matter of inches and instead struck Tony in the chest. There followed a mad scramble for the door as Paddy advanced menacingly towards the first person he noticed in his way. Phil Gunn was picked up by the scruff of his neck, and hurled across the room. Tony followed, while somehow, the rest of us managed to make good our escape and barricade ourselves into the dormitory.

For several minutes we heard Paddy stumbling around outside and then, in a voice strangely controlled and calm after his recent outburst, he asked for a road map of southern Italy. Someone brought him one. Paddy thanked him politely and then saying he would have a look at Naples, he walked with extreme dignity from the room, down the stairs and out of the house. A moment later we heard his requisitioned civilian car start up below and drive away.

With relief we repaired to our beds, wondering how far he would get before he sobered up or met with a worse fate. He had expressed his intention of driving to Naples, despite the fact that this city was over 150 miles away, and had only just been captured from the enemy! In his present state he was just as likely to blunder into the enemy lines as reach Naples in safety.

It was indeed an eloquent expression of the sway he held over us, and of the respect we had for him, that although there were thirteen of us, none of us dared to stand up to him and attempt to restrain him. It was not a pleasant thought to take on those 17 stone of muscle and bone, when in the mood he was in; he was capable of committing murder.

The story ended happily. Paddy awoke the next morning from a very deep sleep to find an Italian civilian gazing down at his prostrate form in considerable awe. And the 'Itie' literally was gazing down at him, for although Paddy was still in his car, the car was on its side and the onlooker was peering through the door which now formed the roof. Paddy was completely unhurt and what is more surprising, no damage was done to the car!

Paddy was off whiskey for many months after that and it was obvious that he genuinely regretted the incident. Beyond seizing a razor with the firm intention of scarring his face to improve his appearance and add distinction to it, he never again gave expression to such homicidal tendencies!

One morning after we had been at Molfetta for several weeks, we were surprised to hear shouting and sounds of transport in the street below, and excitement became intense when we learned that a large convoy had just arrived, comprising all the camp staff, unit transport and heavy stores which we had left behind at Azzib so many months previously. After a long and varied journey, they had eventually found their way to us, and it must have been as pleasant for them to meet up with us again, as it was for us to be able to have all our personal kit in our possession once more, as well as to receive a huge batch of mail from home which had been kept hanging around the Middle East for so long.

With the arrival of this party from Azzib, the regiment was now virtually complete, and rumours about the prospect of our going home were infinitely strengthened by this fact.

Why, we asked ourselves, would they go to all the trouble of bringing this party over from Palestine to join us, if they were not considering sending us home? With all our personnel together once more, with our transport, stores and personal kit once again in our possession, we could now be sent home with the least prospect of being delayed by administrative difficulties.

Our month at Molfetta, flowed by quickly and without incident, while the rumour that we were shortly returning home persisted and grew stronger with each day that passed, though nothing further occurred to confirm it or give it support. And then, suddenly one day we received the long hoped for movement order. The regiment would move down to Taranto by train and report to the transit camp there. Surely that could mean only one thing, for Taranto was the port from which troops embarked for England!

And so we left Molfetta, full of excitement at the prospect of a speedy homecoming. Under such conditions, it was easy to put up with the discomforts of the transit camp at Taranto, with its mud, its complete lack of lighting and its air of gloom. For we were going home! Soon we would be rid of all this, so why worry at a little discomfort here and there?

Once installed in the dingy camp at last the rumours of the past month were confirmed. A ship would be sailing for England in two days' time, and we would be on her. For the rest of our stay at Taranto we eagerly watched the harbour from the road which ran along one side of it, until punctually on the day appointed, we saw a large two-funnelled liner steam in and moor by the quay. We were now certain that nothing could prevent us from going on the morrow as planned. After all, Paddy himself had gone off in advance by air, and was probably even now already back in England.

But a great disappointment was in store for us, for at the very last moment, the message was received that our posting was cancelled, and that we would remain where we were until we were sent further instructions.

The men took the news well, as they took everything that came their way, and the majority still allowed themselves optimistic hopes for an early homecoming.

But even so, we could hardly bear to look any more at that empty space in the harbour, at that bare quayside, from which that very day we were to have embarked on the ship which was even now steaming towards England.

Chapter Twelve

African Interlude

The rude manner in which our hopes of going home had been shattered, left us wandering round Taranto like ships without rudders. We had come here solely for the purpose of embarking for England and now that this prospect was indefinitely postponed, we seemed lost and out of place in this busy port, with even our immediate future a completely closed book to us.

For two days we explored this extraordinary town. It was extraordinary because the central part was built on a small island, and this was only connected to the mainland by a swing bridge which spanned a narrow channel separating the inner from the outer harbours. Every time a normal sized ship wanted to pass through this channel, the bridge had to be swung round to allow her to go through, and thus, for the period required for this operation the centre of the town was completely cut off from its outskirts. Usually it happened that the bridge was 'up' for an hour in the busiest part of the afternoon, so that streams of vehicles jammed up against each other on either side waiting to cross, while the pedestrians too massed at both ends of the gap. It seemed a most primitive arrangement for so large and thriving a port.

But meanwhile Harry, who in Paddy's absence was left in command of us, had been busy arranging for our disposal. We knew nothing about all this until early one morning we were marched out of the transit camp and down to the docks, where we embarked on a fleet of American LCIs.

These were too small a craft to take us to England, and ruling out that possibility, we were left completely in the dark as to our destination, until word was passed round that we were bound for North Africa, and that we would proceed to Philippeville and there remain as the guests of the 2nd SAS Regiment until our future was decided.

The voyage across the wintry Mediterranean was far from comfortable. Instead of the blue skies and smiling sea to which we had grown so accustomed during the summer months a bleak and cheerless view met our eyes. A sharp breeze tore at the surface of the steely water, whipping it into an angry motion which tossed our small craft hither and thither; rain, drizzle and fog exercised their customary depressing effect, and our spirits were therefore not high as we steamed away from Europe and back to Africa.

We could not help being amused at some of the methods the American navy had adopted, especially in connection with their navigation, and these at first caused us some concern! At the time when we were nearly level with Catania, on our journey southwards, Tony as was his custom, was on the bridge chatting to the skipper and the first mate, and asked when we could expect to reach Bizerta. The skipper replied that as they were now almost level with the toe of Italy it would be a good 48 hours steaming before we reached there!

Tony looked at him in amazement. *'But surely we are now just passing Sicily,'* he exclaimed, looking at the well-known, regular slopes of Etna, clearly visible above its surrounding foothills, *'that must be Mount Etna over there.'*

'Oh no', replied the American naval officer, confidently, *'that mountain is a mountain in Southern Italy!'*

Tony did not argue with him, although in his own mind he was positive that the skipper was mistaken, but by tactful enquiries he was able to establish the fact that neither of the officers on our particular craft had learned anything about navigation, that there was only one navigator in the whole flotilla, and that it was up to all the LCIs to keep well in sight of his ship!

We could not help wondering what would happen if the flotilla were to become separated in storm, fog or night, and what our ultimate destination was likely to be under those circumstances. However, fortunately no such thing occurred and we woke up one morning two days later to find ourselves in Bizerta harbour, as expected.

Extraordinary rumours were flying round Bizerta harbour that morning. Something was in the air and moreover, obviously something of the utmost importance, of that the American dockworkers were certain. In fact there was much talk to the effect that the Germans had made a peace overture, and that even now some Nazi general was on the way over to discuss terms. Otherwise why had the anti-aircraft defences of the harbour been warned not to fire at any unidentified planes that morning?

The Americans were certain that a large scale and important peace move was in progress, and so sure of this were they that many of them were staking high bets to that effect with our lads. We did not know what to believe, but we certainly had far more doubts than the Americans that the observed activity was due to the possibility of an armistice. But we were curious to know what lay behind all these rumours, since it was obvious that they could not have arisen from nothing. Only several days later did we learn that at that time the Teheran Conference was taking place, and that it was this which had given rise to all those vague and conflicting reports at Bizerta, and moreover which had caused the postponement of our posting home.

We were spared having to submit ourselves to the rigours of Bizerta transit camp. For Harry, on seeing the unnecessarily uncomfortable conditions which prevailed there, arranged an immediate train journey to Philippeville where we were to join the 2nd SAS Regiment.

Thus we spent the night spread out on the floor of a number of cattle trucks which bumped and jolted their way along the railway line to Philippeville, which, so we understood, lay along the coast about 300 miles to the west.

Two days and three nights were spent in that cattle truck before we eventually arrived at Philippeville early one morning. It was a far from comfortable journey, especially since the truck had previously been used for transporting coal, with the result that by the end of the journey, our clothes and bodies were black with grime and filth. The smoothness of our motion was further impaired, by the fact that the Arab brakeman inadvertently forgot to take off the brake for a considerable stretch of the journey, with the result that, after we had pointed out his error to him and this had been rectified, we found the wheel in question had become a trifle elliptical from the rough treatment it had had to undergo, and we thus spent the rest of the journey bumping up and down as though crossing a ploughed field on a bicycle!

Another amusing incident took place on one of the nights which we spent travelling in this way. All the officers had managed to get together in one truck, and had so spread themselves out, that it seemed that there was not an inch of floor space left unused. In the middle of the night, Johnny Wiseman woke up to find, that there was considerably less space than usual in which to move around. He could not account for the exceptionally tight squeeze, until he became aware of an inert sleeping figure occupying most of the small empty square around the doorway.

Now who on earth can that be? thought Johnny, by now wide awake, and sitting up to try and see which officer had moved from his customary sleeping position. But no, we were all accounted for, and there was still no clue as to the identity of the recumbent form by the doorway. By this time Johnny's curiosity had been thoroughly aroused, so that at length the vague and unpleasant suspicion formulating in his mind drove him out of his bed with the intention of giving the stranger a thorough shake and in this way finding out who he was. With a grunt, the sleeper awoke, stretched himself lazily, and then slowly looked up to see who had so roughly disturbed his slumbers. Johnny found himself gazing down at the unshaven face of an Arab, still completely at his ease, and unperturbed by his rude awakening! With a shriek of rage Johnny hurled himself at our nocturnal visitor, raising sufficient clamour to waken us all, and stir us into some semblance of action. The offender was dealt with in no gentle manner and cast off the train with a marked lack of respect.

The camp at Philippeville was one of the most charming I have ever seen. Beautifully kept paths ran through the bush-covered coastal sand dunes, on and around which the tents were pitched, in delightful irregularity. The undulating hillocks and undergrowth so divided up the camp that we were able to experience a pleasant sensation of solitude even when right in the middle of the camp area.

The night after our arrival a guest night was given in our honour in the officers' mess – after a first class meal, three pipers from a neighbouring unit were called in to play, marching round the tables as they piped, in the traditional manner. The colonel of the 2nd SAS, Bill Stirling – who incidentally was the brother of our former CO, David Stirling – delivered a speech of welcome. A very charming and sociable man, I thought him, but unpractical like his brother and without the compensating verve, dash and personality which had made David Stirling such an extraordinary character.

Dances were also organized in the camp, and for the first time since they left England many of the men were able to meet English girls in civilian clothes many of whom had come out to North Africa to work for NAAFI and had not at that time been issued with uniforms. The situation was considerably confused by there being many French girls also at these dances, and so the men soon found that they had to be very careful to whom they were talking, for it was at first difficult for them to know that the partner they had chosen might be able to speak English as well as they. In fact, one of the sergeants received quite a surprise when, in the casual manner which had been generally adopted in Egypt and Italy, he strolled over to ask a girl to dance. He felt sure that she was French, and was thus not too particular as to the words he used to request the pleasure of the next dance. His actual words were something like: *'Come on, worm, let's wriggle,'* but the wind was taken right out of his sails when he discovered that he was addressing an English NAAFI girl!

The longer we remained at Philippeville, the more confident we felt that very shortly we would be sent home after all. This optimism was, of course, entirely without foundation, and merely based on our conviction that Paddy, now in England, would be pulling all the strings in his power to get us over to join him. Everything was taken as a sign that soon we would be moving – a kit exchange, an issue of new battledress, signals from Paddy and Movement Control, and so when the movement order did eventually come no undue excitement was felt; no surprise or incredulity, for that was exactly what we had expected and had known would happen.

One morning, about a week before Christmas we found ourselves huddled once more in a filthy cattle truck, bound this time for Algiers. Indeed there had been no mention of our embarking there for home, but we were only too ready to put two and two together, knowing that Algiers was the port from which repatriation to England took place from North Africa.

After 48 hours in this crowded and uncomfortable train, which swallowed up the miles to Algiers so interminably slowly, we eventually arrived at our destination and were at once taken by transport to the transit camp in the Bois de Ferdinand, about 15 miles outside the town. As its name suggests, the camp was sited in a wood, not a nice, dry sheltering pinewood, but a tangle of undergrowth winding round the trunks of the scattered larger trees. It was pouring with rain as we arrived, and continued to do so for the remaining two days we were there. The water running in small rivers from the branches above, continually dripped on us as we passed below; the tents leaked and were so short of pegs that they seemed likely to be blown away by the wind at any moment; the ground became nothing more than a quagmire of red mud which sucked greedily at our boots and seriously impeded our movement. These were not the sort of surroundings any of us would voluntarily have chosen in which to celebrate Christmas, but we naturally could not have everything our way, and if this time we really were on our way home, then this fact alone was sufficient to offset the discomfort of our present conditions.

Even when the news that we were to embark for England was announced, many of us were sceptical. But we need not have worried. One such disappointment as we had experienced at Taranto was quite enough, and on this occasion nothing went wrong to interfere with the smooth operation of the embarkation programme.

We embarked on Christmas evening. Our Christmas dinner was eaten from our mess tins, as we stood under the dripping trees of the forest, with the rain soaking through our clothes and the mud weighing heavily on our boots. Nothing could have been more miserable and were we not on our way home we would certainly have been sadly depressed by these conditions. But we were kept sufficiently occupied to prevent ourselves from being overwhelmed with nostalgic memories of Christmases spent under happier circumstances, for no sooner was the Christmas dinner finished, than the roll was called and the squadron was bundled into trucks which bumped their way down to Algiers harbour.

And there she lay – the ship which was to take us home, looking incredibly beautiful in our eyes for this very reason!

We filed aboard her, as quickly as we could, so that we could be installed before the authorities changed their minds again and told us that we would not be going – for many of the men were firmly convinced that it was someone's job in Movement Control to raise our hopes and then to disappoint us again. But if this was the case he certainly slipped up badly on this occasion, for on the morning of 26 December, 1943 we slipped out of Algiers harbour on the start of our journey across the sea back to England.

Chapter Thirteen

Further Horizons

With our journey home our part in the African and Italian campaigns ended, and also, to a large degree the slice of unity, which can really only be found in a unit so small as was the SRS.

Our return to England was the closing of one door in our lives and the opening of another. Never again were we to see the shrub-covered stretches of Libyan or Egyptian desert, the green rocky mountains of Palestine, or the parched olive groves of Sicily or Italy. Henceforth we were to live and fight in a country more familiar to us – amid woods and orchards and grassy lanes, and the green, sweet-scented fields of North West Europe. That it was a change for the better, none of us could doubt, but it was with a strange feeling of regret that we grew to look back upon those sunny and carefree days spent on the shores of the Mediterranean.

For at the time the regiment left Italy its achievements had been recognized, and its worth proved. Maybe it did not do much fighting, in the sense of the ordeals the luckless infantryman has to go through day after day, without recognition and without glory, but what it did do was of the utmost importance in the large-scale operations which made up the Sicilian and Italian campaigns. We were never used unless we were needed, so that when we were called for, we always knew that there was much at stake in the way in which we acquitted ourselves.

Every man was happy and proud to be put to the use which had been chosen for him. The courage and stamina of this gallant little unit is not so much measurable by what it achieved, but rather by what it was willing to do. For it needs qualities which are not easily found, to wait patiently maybe for weeks at a time, for the operation which one knows is coming, and which is sure to be of a nature that calls for endurance, fearlessness, and discipline. The fears, trepidations and nervous strain which a gambler experiences, before he can know his fate, when having staked his all, he has to sit back and wait for the wheel to cease its motion, may be compared in many ways to the feeling and emotions that passed through the minds of each of our men during those monotonous, but tense periods between operations.

In any of the four operations we carried out, things could have ended very differently from the way they actually did, and that was the risk we took. The counter-attack we experienced at Termoli, could just as well have occurred on any of our other operations, or before we had been relieved by our main forces. Luck and the grace of God, saw to it that the gun battery at Murro di Porco was 'defended' by a bunch of cowardly Italians, with no stomach for fighting; that the Germans with their tanks and artillery did not choose to attack us at Augusta and that Bagnara was not more strongly defended. After the operation was all over, it was easy for us and others to say that it was all a walkover and that we did not do much, but that did not prevent our minds from being a torment of fears and uncertainties before we actually landed. And in addition, we also had to put up with the several operations for which we were made ready, and which (fortunately for us) were cancelled at the last moment.

In fact, the strain and suspense which gnawed at us during our periods of rest were infinitely worse than the actual fighting itself.

Apart from General Dempsey's personal opinion of us, it was clear that we were heard of and also appreciated in even higher spheres. Perhaps this is shown by the number of awards granted to the unit. These were too numerous among the men for me to attempt to list here, but in my section alone, Tunstall and McNinch were both awarded the MM, although unfortunately the latter was killed before his award came through. As regards the officers, Paddy and Tony received the DSO, Paddy receiving this award for the second time, for the achievements of the unit in Sicily, while Tony's stubborn stand at Termoli brought him his. In addition, Harry Poat, Phil Gunn and Johnny Wiseman each received the MC.

It seems reasonable to say that when we left Italy the regiment was at the height of its career and had reached a fighting efficiency, military knowledge and standard of discipline which it never quite attained again. Then it was small enough for everyone to be known to everyone else. With only 15 officers and 250 men under his command, Paddy was able to give every activity his personal supervision, and he was quick to remove any faults he discovered in the manner characteristic to him. It was Paddy's unit and under the orders of no one but him, so that he was encouraged to devote his entire attention to building up out of the men and officers under him, a perfectly co-ordinated body of men so thoroughly trained that they would react correctly to any situation in which they might find themselves.

Paddy's personal supervision was vital to the unit's success. For he was a born leader, with original, though none the less strong, ideas on discipline, a wonderful military instinct and an unrivalled personal strength and courage.

Officers and men alike worshipped him and would follow him anywhere, so great was their faith in his abilities, while he, in his turn, having the interests of the unit closest to his heart, continually devoted all his attentions to its welfare in every sphere of its activities. Under a leader such as Paddy, though many were the times that we cursed his wilful, unpredictable Irish ways, which gave him at the same time so forceful and yet so loveable a character, no unit could fail to be happy, proud of its abilities and ever willing to give of its best.

And it is largely for this reason that the spirit which ran through the regiment then – a spirit of unity, and singleness of purpose – did not show itself so strongly once we arrived back in England. For not only was the unit nearly trebled in size, with each of its troops an independent squadron, and almost on the same scale as the whole SRS had formerly been, so that the organization became too large and top-heavy for Paddy to be able to give it so thorough a personal attention as formerly. In addition, we were no longer independent and Paddy was no longer able to run his own show, completely without outside interference. For our enlarged unit, known as the First Special Air Service Regiment, became part of a brigade organization comprising in addition, the 2nd SAS, two French battalions and a Belgian independent company. A vast brigade headquarters was placed in control of us, with but little experience of the work which we were trained to do. Often it would infuriate us with its delays, inefficiencies and ignorance and tie Paddy's hands completely. Bureaucracy and routine were made to triumph over initiative and originality.

Thus Paddy delegated his command to his squadron commanders and only remained in control of those wider issues which directly involved the whole unit. He could do little else for the regiment was by now too large, and it was no longer possible for him to mould it as he himself most wished it, according to his own fiery and original character.

Our training in our camp at Ayrshire, which started as soon as we had returned from a month's leave, was of an entirely different nature to that which we had gone through at Azzib. For no more were we trained to work together as a whole, to raid, in our whole strength, stretches of enemy-held coastline. No more were battle-drill, co-ordination and precision the main features of our training.

We were to become again the saboteurs of the desert days, and in small parties, of one officer and five or six men, were to be parachuted behind the enemy lines in France and once there to move like hunted animals from one hiding place to another, keeping one step ahead of the enemy the whole time. We were trained so that we could sally forth by night or day with an intimate and complete knowledge of the area in which we were to operate, to blow up a bridge or a railway line here, to mortar a power station, factory or enemy camp

Peter Davis, England 1944.

3″ mortar training, Darvel, Scotland, January–June 1944.

Training jump, Prestwick, Scotland, January–June 1944.

there or, with our fast and heavily armed Jeeps, to lie in wait by the roadside at strategic points and from there to blast approaching enemy convoys with everything we had, until the battle became too hot for us and we had to slip away into the woods as silently and mysteriously as we had come.

The last winter of the war was spent idly for there was nothing for us to do while the line was more or less static. But with the coming of the final spring offensive our services were required again, and in armoured Jeeps bristling with machine guns, we took part in the final run through Germany. Here some of us met again our old friends, the 9th German Parachute Division, who apparently remembered us as well as we had remembered them, from conversations we had with prisoners taken, and which our men, taken prisoner, had with them. VE Day found half of us outside Bremen and the rest within 20 miles of Wilhelmshaven. We were at once withdrawn and sent to Norway to supervise the evacuation of the Germans who had surrendered there.

We returned to our camp at Chelmsford at the end of August 1945, and the regiment was disbanded in October. For those of the officers and men who were not lucky enough to be demobilized at an early date, the anti-climax and disappointments of those last few months of their army life must have been intense. To see disbanded the regiment with which they had served for periods varying from two to five years, and to see its members scattered, and then to have to join some other unit, separated from all the friends with whom they had lived and fought and travelled, was indeed a hard blow to bear.

And what of the officers whose names have so often been mentioned in these pages? How did Fate treat them after they left Italy? Casualties among our old hands were happily few in our subsequent operations, but a great loss was suffered in the deaths of Phil Gunn and Bob Merlot, both much loved figures in the regiment. It seems cruel that such fine men as these, who had gone through so much, should have to die in motor accidents far from the fighting zone. Their loss, and the manner of their going, was deeply felt by all who knew them.

Franco left us soon after we arrived in England to take up another staff appointment elsewhere, and Ronnie Lunt, the padre, transferred to 1st Airborne Division, but otherwise the rest of us remained together to the last, until we were finally separated by the unit being disbanded.

Paddy won a further two DSOs before the war ended, making a total of four in all. The first of these was given him for the work of his unit in France, but the second was earned by an act of extreme bravery which was so typical of this remarkable man. As one of his squadrons was racing through Germany in the last month of the war, the leading troop came up against unexpectedly strong opposition and was pinned down. The officer commanding it was killed and the

Fairford, June–August 1944

'C' Squadron Sergeants: Higham, Mitchell, Robertson, McDiarmed, Ridler, Lilley, Belsham, Storey, Badger, Shaw, Downes, Lowson.

A Section: Gaskin, Unknown, Reynolds, Crouch, Harrison, Squires, Howes, Mitchell, Farrel.

Fairford, England, June–August 1944

C Section: Jones, Unknown, Unknown, Mycock, Pagan, Kennedy, Clarke, Matt, Johnstone, Mitchell.

HQ Section: Storey, Glacken, Sanders, Stalker, Tunstall, P. Davis, Vautier.

situation was beginning to look extremely serious when Paddy came pelting up the road in his Jeep and drove it straight towards the enemy, regardless of their fire, with his guns blazing out their wicked streams of tracer. When he could go no further, he calmly reversed his Jeep and turned round, continuing to fire with his rear gun. Up and down that road he went, with such good success that he relieved the pressure on his forward troop and enabled them to press on once more.

Paddy was one of those extraordinary characters who only achieve recognition in time of war. While the war lasted, he was in his element, a real soldier of fortune. Never was he happier than when with his own trusted and tried unit under him, he was able to go out and match his wits against those of the enemy. But when the war ended he found himself suddenly at a loose end. Civilian life held no attraction for him, and yet a man of his qualities was no longer required in the army. So he joined an expedition to the South Pole, and would be there still, if his health had not let him down and compelled him to return home.

And now, this great soldier and born leader, has no men under his command, save perhaps a few clerks, for he spends his days clamped to a desk in a solicitor's office! It is a strong contrast and undoubtedly an unhappy one for him. With what regret he must look back on those wild, carefree days when he roamed the desert expanses of Libya, or drove through the grassy lanes of France, never short of sincere and trusted friends to drink and talk with, never finding time dragging monotonously or without interest.

In the last month of the war Sandy Davidson was killed when his Jeep blew up on a mine, while Lowson was badly wounded in the leg when a hidden enemy machine-gun post opened up on his Jeep, 5 miles within our own lines! But otherwise, except for a few changes, I was able to keep my old hands more or less together and the majority of them were still with me when the war ended.

The excitements, dangers and parties were as frequent during those latter years of the war as before, and yet, many were the times we looked back on those warm and stimulating days in the desert, in Egypt and in Palestine, when we were being built-up and trained out of nothing, when the war was not nearly won and we knew that we had a big job to do which it was imperative that we should do well.

How clearly we remembered the way Paddy used to drive us, chivvy us and guide us, towards his aim of making out of us a first-class fighting unit, working with speed, and precision.

And then when the time came for us to be tried out in Sicily and Italy, when we landed on that rocky coastline and waded through those gutless Italians as though they were not there. The pride we experienced, not so much in ourselves,

Fairford, England, June–August 1944

B Section: Livingstone, Stewart, Tideswell, Iredale, Unknown, Robertson, Unknown, Unknown, Unknown, Allan.

D Section: Lowson, Unknown, Smith, Ashurst, Goldie, Unknown, Kirby, Grierson, Bryce.

but in our being members of such an efficient fighting force under so trusted a leader, was one of the finest emotions that can ever stir the heart of a soldier.

The memories of those days are with us all. As we sit at our desks in our offices, or work at our trades, under conditions of routine and monotony, we at least have the consolation of being able to feel that once we were men – men working with a will towards a vital common objective, free to make our own decisions and use our initiative, and enjoying the height of physical fitness in an open-air life of activity and exertion.

Looking back on those days it is easy for us to realize that the friends we knew and lost, the McNinches and Tobins, need not be pitied. Honoured they certainly should be, but not pitied, for they died when they were happy, when they were really living in the full sense of the word and glorying in their existence. They were thankful for this chance to leave their workbenches and office stools, and instead to travel around foreign lands in sunny climes, where they could replace their sheltered, monotonous lives with an existence full of activity and variety, and join an ever increasing circle of comrades and friends. For the first time men had tasted 'life' and had possibly obtained more happiness and wider horizons in their 25 years than many old people who die peacefully in their beds.

Better to die happily having 'lived' a little, than never to have 'lived' at all.

Epilogue

Peter Davis returned to England in December 1943 and spent several months undergoing further training.

He embarked on two more operations, and was awarded the MC for the role he played in Operation Kipling (13 August–25 September 1944). Below is his original self-written report, requested by his superiors and reproduced with kind permission of The SAS Regimental Association:

'29 Aug. Whole of 'C' Sqn at FORET DE MERRYVAUX – Capt DAVIS', Lt BRYCE's and Sgt MITCHELL's patrols detailed to attack convoys moving Eastwards along the LA CHARITE-CLAMECY road. Moved off from camp 12.30 hrs. Owing to Sgt STOREY's jeep overturning, both occupants being injured, the move was much delayed and the party did not really start before 1600 hrs.

Intention was to take the three patrols to a point near the road to be attacked, and then to split up, but owing to the accident, and the fact that Lt BRYCE's jeep had to remain behind with the injured men, the original 9 jeeps were reduced to 7, and 19 men, and Capt DAVIS decided to make use of three jeeps as one force. Two 3″ mortars were also taken.

Arrived within 5 miles of road without mishap or contact with the enemy, and the remaining 5 miles to the chosen ambush position were made with the guidance of an FFI NCO, who caused much delay through leading the party the wrong way. 1800 hrs, arrived chosen ambush position, which proved unsuitable for jeeps, but excellent for mortars. Two jeeps with mortars were left here, remaining 5 jeeps proceeding to a small wood about 2 miles away, about 4 kms West of the village of NANNAY. Once again the guides lost their way, but eventually we arrived at wood 2230 hrs. Jeeps were concealed in the wood alongside the road, and an uneventful night was passed.

30 August. 0900 hrs 2 mortar jeeps re-joined main body. Still no movement along road, and it was decided to choose another road to attack. At 0930hrs, the jeeps were in the act of being manoeuvred onto the road in preparation for moving off, when the head of a German convoy appeared

Belgium, October–November 1944. Ron Grierson, Peter Davis, Derrick Harrison.

about 300 yds away. The leading vehicle, a civilian saloon car, together with an enemy section of infantry were immediately engaged by Tpr GRIERSON's and Tpr PAGAN's jeeps. After about a minute the enemy returned our fire with two light machine guns, rifle and machine pistols, but their fire was very inaccurate. Leaving these two jeeps to engage the enemy Capt DAVIS took a foot party of 6 men round the left flank, and Sgt MITCHELL did likewise on the right flank. The enemy leading section were in a ditch on the roadside and the left flanking foot party got to a point within 35 yds of them, when a lively S.A. and grenade battle ensued for about 5 minutes. PAGAN's jeep was then called up the road to spray the ditches, which he did, so effectively that the foot party was able to reach the enemy vehicle – beside it in the ditch we found three dead Germans, two seriously wounded, and one slightly injured. They were disarmed and one LMG, 3 rifles, 1 pistol, and grenades were taken. A Sgt Major (badly wounded) was in command of the section. Their unit was 338 STAMMKOMPANIE.

The prisoner who professed himself to be a Pole was not more than 18 years old, and extremely scared. He was only too willing to talk. In the car was found an Officer's map case which was taken and searched. Meanwhile the rest of the enemy column had retired, and beyond occasional sniping it was again quiet – the enemy appeared to be in considerable confusion as grenades and 2″ mortar bombs were seen bursting over half a mile away. It was learnt that the enemy column was about 250 men strong and from their operational order, which was captured in the map-case, it was also learnt that the force consisted of two infantry companies supported by M.G. Section, an A/T section and L.A.A. Section.

We then withdrew, leaving the dead and wounded, having disclosed to the wounded that we were English and the advance guard of a large force. We went back two miles down the road and took up an excellent position on a hill about 300 yds from the road,

Germany, April 1945. Jeeps refitting at Lowp.

behind a thick hedge. The mortars were sighted onto the road, 4 jeeps were sited covering the road and 1 jeep (Cpl JONES) was detailed to cover our flank and rear. A very good escape route was provided in the shape of a track leading into the FORET DA DONZY in which there was a maze of tracks. At about midday, LMG and rifle fire was heard in the direction from which we had come. Two civilians on bicycles later came up and told us that the Germans had just fired on them.

We remained in this position until 1915 hrs, when a very large convoy was sighted coming down the road below us, from the direction of LA CHARITE. Estimated 30 vehicles, including 5-ton lorries, civilian cars and scout cars. 3 lorries were towing light 20 mm cannon. The convoy stopped just beneath us, presumably to clear the village NANNAY. We engaged with 12 Vickers for 5 minutes – estimate 4,000 rounds fired.

Mortars did not have an officer and only fired three bombs. Enemy reaction was very strong and accurate – within 15 seconds of our opening fire they were replying. Three trucks dropped their side disclosing a 20 mm cannon which immediately went into action, together with heavy 2″ mortar and LMG fire.

Fire was exchanged fiercely for five minutes, during which time 2 large lorries and one civilian car belonging to the enemy were seen to be blazing fiercely; then, noticing that the enemy infantry were making good progress up the hill towards us, and suspecting the presence of enemy scout cars on our flanks, we withdrew to the pre-arranged RV in the centre of the FORET DA DONZY. Five out of the seven jeeps and 14 men met at the RV at approx 1945 hrs. The last jeep was followed by an enemy scout car, which seemed very disinclined to give battle and did not enter the wood. We waited one hour in the centre of the wood for the missing 5 men, but for fear of being surrounded, withdrew towards DONZY under cover of dusk at 2045 hrs. Meanwhile the enemy continued to give battle hotly for 1½ hrs after we had disengaged….

At about 2130 hrs, 3 ambulances arrived to pick up casualties, and made several runs to LA CHARITE. Several sources report that between 30 and 40 of the enemy were killed, and twice that number wounded. The enemy took everything away with them, so an accurate estimate of damage done is impossible. Civilians report that the convoy was composed of 37 vehicles and about 600 men, and the convoy moved back towards LA CHARITE with 15 vehicles in tow. 2 Germans were wounded by their own officers in an attempt to make them fight. The FFI in LA CHARITE reported that the Germans realised that the attack was made by British troops, and there was considerable apprehension in the town that these attacks were the prelude to larger ones. Barricades were created, and similar precautions were taken in LA CHARITE….

12 Sep. A report came through that 18,000 Germans West of the LOIRE were thinking of surrendering. Capt DAVIS assumed the rank of Colonel, with a view to making it easier for the Germans to surrender. (He later resigned this office in favour of Capt BARNBY). Left camp 1800 hrs with 12 jeeps.

13 Sep. Composed a letter in NEVERS to the German commander, to the effect that we had been detailed by General PATTON to take charge of his surrender and to disarm his men. We then crossed the LOIRE and

Norway, Bergen, July–August 1945

Germans waiting to be searched.

German columns marching to docks.

at MORNAY we heard that there was a German column just up the road. Capt DAVIS went forward in a jeep, under a very large white flag, to parley with the German commander, a Lt Colonel. From him, he learned that the 18,000 Germans, under Gen ELSTER, had already surrendered to the Americans, and were to proceed to ORLEANS with all their transport and arms, and under no circumstances were they to give up their arms before their arrival there. We then decided to find General ELSTER and find out from him (a) whether there were any Germans in the area who had not received the order to surrender, and (b) whether there were any Germans, including SS troops, who had refused to surrender. We followed in the tracks of the General as far as Bourges, but were unable to locate him. At BOURGES, Col BOURGOIN, C.O. 4th French Para Bn, requested us to help him to picket the entrances to the town, to prevent any of the surrendering German columns from entering and causing alarm and despondency among the civil population. Jeeps were picketed as instructed, but no enemy seen.

14 Sep. The force returned to camp by patrols. Convoys of Germans, who had surrendered, fully armed, were seen at many points. We arrived back in camp and remained there until moving to BRUSSELS.

On account of civilian reports that small parties of Germans with and without arms, and in uniform or civilian clothes, were moving by night in an attempt to escape to Germany, one patrol was sent out each night to form a road-block, and establish the identity of all.'

Captain Davis took part in Operation Howard (6–29 April 1945). Hitler committed suicide on 30 April 1945. Germany was surrendering to the Western Allies and, in these last days of the war, Captain Davis was wounded whilst rounding up surrendering Germans. He later said that he noticed a certain look on a German officer's face, and realized that this officer was not going to surrender. Fortunately he ducked to his right, the bullet went through his left shoulder, but killed a young German girl who was running across the road behind him.

Captain Davis was in Norway, overseeing the disarmament of 300,000 Germans, when the war ended.

Appendix

England, June–August 1944

'C' Squadron Officers. Standing: Tony Marsh, Roy Close, Stewart Richardson, 'Titus' Oates, Tom Bryce, Derrick Harrison, John Reynolds, M. Mycock. Sitting: Peter Davis, Tim Iredale, Colin Rosborough.

Tony Marsh.

Fairford, England, June–August 1944

Derrick Harrison and Tony Marsh.

Derrick Harrison preparing for 'Kipling' operational jump.

Derrick Harrison preparing for 'Kipling' operational jump.

France, August–September 1944

Peter Davis cleaning magazines for Vickers guns, Forêt de Merryvoux.

Sergeant McDiarmid, Forêt de Merryvoux.

St Amand Camp. From L to R: Harry Poat, Paddy Mayne and Fraser McCluskey.

Belgium, October–November 1944

Brussels – Brigadier's inspection. Peter Davis's troop on parade.

Heath near Meppen Squires and Peter Davis's Jeep.

Defensive laager in forest near Neuvrees, April 1945.

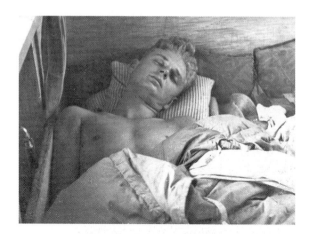

Edwin Mycock, Bergen,
Norway, August 1945.

Peter Forbes.

Sergeant McDiarmid and Tom
Bryce.

Tony Marsh, Bergen, Norway, August 1945.

Edwin Mycock.

Paddy Mayne aquaplaning on Bergen Fjord.

Tony Marsh.

Fraser McCluskey.

Peter Davis.

Bergen, Norway, May–August 1945

Peter Davis, Tarleston and Ted Badger.

Pat Reilly, Peter Davis, Edwin Mycock.

Letter from Harry Poat congratulating
Peter Davis on being awarded the
Military Cross.

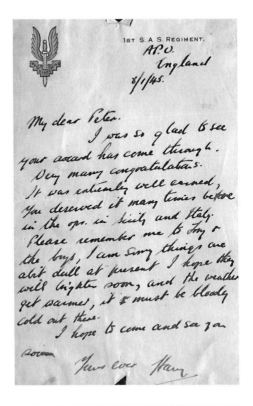

THE MILITARY CROSS

Captain (temporary) Peter Julian Geoffrey DAVIS (184425).

Army Air Corps.

Captain DAVIS was the leader of a troop of "C"
Squadron, 1st Special Air Service Regiment, Army Air
Corps, who were operating behind the enemy's lines in
the Auxerre area, harrassing the enemy's lines of
communication and causing confusion among the retreating
enemy troops.

On the 4th September, 1944, at about 1700 hours,
Captain DAVIS placed his troop in position to ambush
enemy convoys retreating along a main road near the
twon of NANNAY.

After a short while a very large enemy convoy came
along, vastly superior in numbers of men and much more
heavily armed than Captain DAVIS' troop.   In spite
of that, Captain DAVIS carried on with his plan and
opened fire at the given moment.

So calmly did he carry the plan through and so
well had he sited his position that despite heavy enemy
counter-fire, no less than Fifteen German trucks were
destroyed and very heavy casualties suffered by the enemy.
During the fighting, Captain DAVIS inspired his men with
his coolness and calculated determination.   Not until
he was absolutely satisfied that no further damage could
be inflicted, did he order his troop to withdraw and then,
although by that time heavy machine gun and mortar fire
was being directed at his position, he personally remained

behind and covered the withdrawal with ......

Citation for Military Cross.

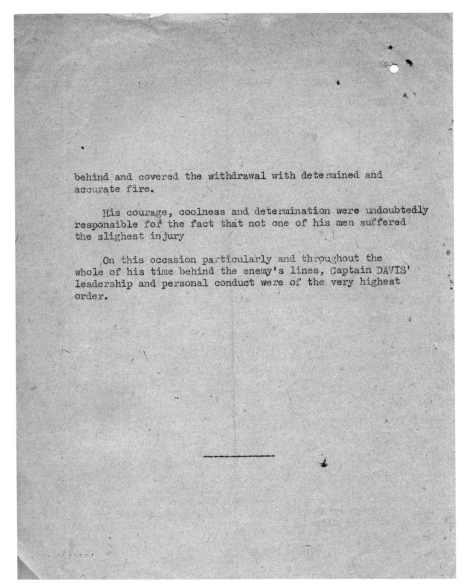

behind and covered the withdrawal with determined and
accurate fire.

His courage, coolness and determination were undoubtedly
responsible for the fact that not one of his men suffered
the slighest injury

On this occasion particularly and throughout the
whole of his time behind the enemy's lines, Captain DAVIS'
leadership and personal conduct were of the very highest
order.

Citation for Military Cross.

Tel. No.—   SIOane 3477 Ext. 209.

> Any further communication
> on this subject should be
> addressed to :—
> The Under-Secretary of State,
> The War Office
> (as opposite)
> and the following number
> quoted.

THE WAR OFFICE,
(M.S.3),

LONDON, S.W.1.

4 February, 1947.

Your Reference........BM/2674/9(MS3V).

Sir,

    I am directed to refer to your
letter dated 28th January, 1947 and
in reply to attach for your information
a copy of the citation relating to an
award of the Military Cross conferred
on your son, Captain P.J.G. Davis
(184425), A.A.C.

      I am, Sir,
        Your obedient Servant,

D.S. Cowans Fairweather
Major

for   Lieutenant-General,
       Military Secretary.

Geoffrey Davis Esq.,
Hindfell,
Whatlington,
Battle,
Sussex.

Pumb. 36994   1541

SUPPLEMENT
TO
The London Gazette
Of TUESDAY, the 20th of MARCH, 1945
Published by Authority

Registered as a newspaper

THURSDAY, 22 MARCH, 1945

CENTRAL CHANCERY OF THE ORDERS OF KNIGHTHOOD.

St. James's Palace, S.W.1.
22nd March, 1945.

The KING has been graciously pleased to give orders for the following promotion in, and appointments to, the Most Excellent Order of the British Empire, in recognition of gallant and distinguished services in the field:—

To be an Additional Commander of the Military Division of the said Most Excellent Order:—

Brigadier (acting) Michael Arthur Green, O.B.E., M.C. (21150), late The Northamptonshire Regiment (seconded Royal Air Force Regiment).

To be Additional Officers of the Military Division of the said Most Excellent Order:—

Lieutenant-Colonel William Edgar Bush, D.S.O., M.C. (11109), The Green Howards (Alexandra, Princess of Wales's Own Yorkshire Regiment).
Lieutenant-Colonel Henry Alastair Campbell (8424), The Argyll and Sutherland Highlanders (Princess Louise's) (seconded Royal Air Force Regiment).
Colonel (temporary) George Hew Fanshawe (13054), The Queen's Bays, Royal Armoured Corps.
Lieutenant-Colonel (temporary) Henry Walter Featherstone, M.D. (51644), Royal Army Medical Corps.
Major (temporary) Frederick Charles Lowenbach (301614), General List.
Major (temporary) Henry Hopkinson Augustus Thackthwaite (125296), Royal Army Service Corps.

To be Additional Members of the Military Division of the said Most Excellent Order:—

Major (temporary) Fergus Chalmers Wright (236640), General List.
Captain (temporary) Alexander Francis Lionel Colson (226289), Corps of Royal Engineers.
The Reverend Peter Gordon (87276), Chaplain to the Forces Fourth Class Royal Army Chaplains' Department.
Captain Owen Stanmore Hetherington, M.B. Ch.B. (22000), New Zealand Military Forces.
Lieutenant Donald Lowe (242250), Corps of Royal Engineers.
Captain (temporary) Alfred William Tindall Lucas (95192), Corps of Royal Engineers.
Jemadar Muthulingam (14571), Queen Victoria's Own Madras Sappers and Miners, Indian Army.
Captain (acting) Frederick Ernest Porter (117769), Royal Horse Artillery.
Captain (temporary) Hermann André Schoofs (241731), General List.
Major (temporary) Bowman Scott (151430), Royal Corps of Signals (seconded Royal Air Force Regiment).

Major (temporary) Filmer George Evan Walford (100418), Royal Tank Regiment, Royal Armoured Corps (seconded Royal Air Force Regiment).
Captain (temporary) Arthur Francis Stevenson Wright (201265), Corps of Royal Engineers.

CENTRAL CHANCERY OF THE ORDERS OF KNIGHTHOOD.

St. James's Palace, S.W.1.
22nd March, 1945

The KING has been graciously pleased to approve the award of the British Empire Medal (Military Division), in recognition of gallant and distinguished services in the field, to:—

No. TML.79383 Company Sergeant-Major Robert Okaki, African Pioneer Corps

CENTRAL CHANCERY OF THE ORDERS OF KNIGHTHOOD.

St. James's Palace, S.W.1.
22nd March, 1945.

The KING has been graciously pleased to approve the award of the British Empire Medal (Military Division), in recognition of gallant and distinguished services, to:—

No. 1769806 Gunner Herbert Leonard King, Royal Regiment of Artillery.

War Office, 22nd March, 1945.

The KING has been graciously pleased to approve the following awards in recognition of gallant and distinguished services in North West Europe:—

The Distinguished Service Order.

Brigadier (temporary) Gerald Grimwood Mears, C.B.E., M.C. (21160), late Royal Regiment of Artillery (Shrewsbury).
Lieutenant-Colonel (temporary) Arthur George Proudlock (38421), Royal Regiment of Artillery (Primnay).
Lieutenant-Colonel Richard Edward Black (34653), Corps of Royal Engineers (Harrietsham).
Major (temporary) Hugh Rose (66450), The Royal Scots (The Royal Regiment) (Guilane).
Lieutenant-Colonel (temporary) Archibald Ian Buchanan-Dunlop (39416), The Royal Scots Fusiliers (Crieff).
Lieutenant-Colonel Walter Anderson Venour (32188), The Manchester Regiment (Spilsby).
Major Maurice Robert Lonsdale (38726), The North Staffordshire Regiment (The Prince of Wales's) (Seaford).

1542   SUPPLEMENT to the LONDON GAZETTE, 22 MARCH, 1945

Lieutenant-Colonel (temporary) Brian Forster Morton Franks, M.C. (89085), Army Air Corps (London, S.W.10).

Bar to the Military Cross.

Major (temporary) Stephen Reginald Martin Jenkins, M.C. (64559), 4th/7th Royal Dragoon Guards, Royal Armoured Corps (Lymington).

Captain (temporary) Edward George Wright, M.C. (149391), The Hampshire Regiment (Bournemouth).

The Military Cross.

Major (temporary) Richard William Stratton (170578), Royal Armoured Corps (West Malling).

Lieutenant John Percival Griggs (304711), Royal Armoured Corps (Thornton Heath).

Lieutenant Martyn Holt Leppard (245250), Reconnaissance Corps, Royal Armoured Corps (Broxbourne).

Lieutenant John Edgar Rogerson (289321), Reconnaissance Corps, Royal Armoured Corps (Ashton-under-Lyne).

Lieutenant Ernest Anthony Royle (245258), Reconnaissance Corps, Royal Armoured Corps (Cheadle-Hulme).

Captain (temporary) Kenmure Hector Alexander Gordon (160033), Fife and Forfar Yeomanry, Royal Armoured Corps (Henley-on-Thames).

Captain (temporary) Michael Anthony Sutton (189008), 2nd County of London Yeomanry (Westminster Dragoons), Royal Armoured Corps (Aldershot).

Major (temporary) Duncan Robert Riach Pocock (109422), Lothians and Border Yeomanry, Royal Armoured Corps (Scarborough).

Captain (temporary) John Anthony Gauntley (269301), The Nottinghamshire Yeomanry, Royal Armoured Corps (West Bridgeford).

Major (temporary) Denis Greenway Goode (75570), Royal Regiment of Artillery (Chipping Campden).

Major (temporary) John Ewart Marnham (85851), Royal Regiment of Artillery (Holyport).

Major (temporary) Walter Jack Scott (124317), Royal Regiment of Artillery (Keynsham).

Major (temporary) Ernest Alfred Tonge (145721), Royal Regiment of Artillery (Bournemouth).

Major (acting) Edward Lionel Knyvet Augustus Carr (166677), Royal Regiment of Artillery (Boscombe).

Major (acting) David James Ramsay (95294), Royal Regiment of Artillery (Woburn Sands) (since killed in action).

Captain (temporary) Robert Graham Cosgrove (145590), Royal Regiment of Artillery (Kings Worthy).

Captain (temporary) Roy Stuart Marshall, M.M. (224271), Royal Regiment of Artillery (Whitley Bay).

Lieutenant John Simon Hunter-Gray (271536), Royal Regiment of Artillery (Oxford).

Lieutenant Clifford Lavender Keeler (272845), Royal Regiment of Artillery (Harborne).

Major (temporary) Andrew Aitken Gray (154298), Corps of Royal Engineers (Leicester).

Captain (temporary) John Paul Bennett (137195), Corps of Royal Engineers (Cullompton).

Lieutenant Kenneth Highton (256831), Corps of Royal Engineers (Sheffield).

Lieutenant Basil George Holliday (228021), Corps of Royal Engineers (Purley).

Lieutenant Douglas Frank Jackman (201243), Corps of Royal Engineers (London, W.7).

Lieutenant John Hamilton Lockyer (201713), Corps of Royal Engineers.

Lieutenant Douglas Dalgarno Murray (219720), Corps of Royal Engineers (Aberdeen).

Lieutenant George Frederick Rocke (233956), Grenadier Guards (Warlingham).

Major (temporary) John Pelham Mann (124557), Scots Guards (Salisbury).

Captain (temporary) Michael Wood (291419), Infantry (Simla).

Captain (acting) Joseph Telford Cameron (124702), The Royal Scots (The Royal Regiment) (Edinburgh 7).

Lieutenant Terence Desmond Rennie (288245), The King's Regiment (Liverpool) (Wirral).

Major (temporary) Harry Cranbrook Allen (124567), The Bedfordshire and Hertfordshire Regiment (Bournemouth).

Captain (Acting) Lewis James Thomas (265852), The Royal Welch Fusiliers (Llandudno).

Lieutenant George Chapman Carmichael (277749), The King's Own Scottish Borderers (Edinburgh).

Major (temporary) Stanley Storm (138822), The Cameronians (Scottish Rifles) (Stonehaven).

Lieutenant Ralph Morgan (302126), The Worcestershire Regiment (Cropthorne).

Major (acting) Geoffrey Lionel Holland (126165), The Duke of Cornwall's Light Infantry (Richmond, Surrey).

Captain (temporary) Geoffrey Derek Hodgson (78904), The Royal Sussex Regiment (attd. The Dorsetshire Regiment) (Hassocks).

Major (acting) Harold Rodney Adair Dartnall (278359), The Hampshire Regiment (Winchester).

Lieutenant Sydney Walter Jary (296804), The Hampshire Regiment (Ilford).

Major (temporary) George Reginald Hartwell (93937), The Dorsetshire Regiment (Bournemouth).

Lieutenant Alfred Horace Wright (329968), The South Lancashire Regiment (The Prince of Wales's Volunteers) (Wallasey).

Lieutenant Peter Albert Hands (299581), The Oxfordshire and Buckinghamshire Light Infantry (High Wycombe).

Major (temporary) Basil Avery Tarrant (284581), The Royal Berkshire Regiment (Princess Charlotte of Wales's) (Reading).

Major (temporary) Ernest Raymond Butler Field (113042), The Wiltshire Regiment (Duke of Edinburgh's) (Parkstone).

Lieutenant John Falconer McFarlane (162670), The Highland Light Infantry (City of Glasgow Regiment) (Gourock).

Major (acting) William Redpath Bruce (240700), The Argyll and Sutherland Highlanders (Princess Louise's) (Glasgow, C.3).

Captain (temporary) Peter Julian Geoffrey Davis (184425), Army Air Corps (Warnham).

Captain (temporary) Derrick Inskip Harrison (145763), Army Air Corps (Wembley).

Captain (temporary) Cecil Leylaid Riding (180311), Army Air Corps (Lockerbie).

Captain (temporary) Willis Michael Sadler, M.M. (282465), Army Air Corps (Sheepscombe).

The Reverend Mark Green, B.A. (257733), Chaplain to the Forces, Fourth Class, Royal Army Chaplains' Department (London, S.W.7).

The Reverend James Oswald Welsh, B.D. (123182), Chaplain to the Forces, Fourth Class, Royal Army Chaplains' Department (Dalkeith).

Lieutenant Lawrence Arthur Wagstaff (262261), Royal Army Service Corps (Formby).

Lieutenant Derrick Edmund Will Wigg (232183), Royal Army Service Corps (Gorleston).

Major (Temporary) Eric George Wilbraham (94979), Royal Army Medical Corps (West Norwood).

Captain John Oldroyd Forfar, M.B. (227049), Royal Army Medical Corps (Broughton Ferry).

Captain Allan George Seymour Hill, M.B. (135094), Royal Army Medical Corps (Edinburgh 11).

The Distinguished Conduct Medal.

No. 3715768 Trooper Richard Piper, Royal Armoured Corps (Cleator Moor).

No. 404454 Troop Sergeant-Major Percy Guest Parkin, 4th/7th Royal Dragoon Guards, Royal Armoured Corps (Breaston).

No. 3132466 Lance-Sergeant William Allan, The Royal Scots Fusiliers (Crieff).

No. 14424561 Lance-Corporal Arthur John Beck, The King's Own Scottish Borderers (Croydon).

No. 3853876 Sergeant (Acting) Patrick McVeigh, The Loyal Regiment (North Lancashire) (Kilmarnock).

No. 14216814 Private Michael John McGee, Army Air Corps (Aughnacloy, Co. Tyrone) (since died of wounds).

The Military Medal.

No. 968769 Gunner Ernest George Stanton, Royal Horse Artillery (Sheffield).

No. 7952743 Corporal David Muir Ross, Royal Armoured Corps (Paisley).

No. 6296146 Trooper David Thomas Simpson, Royal Armoured Corps (Borstal).

No. 7899634 Sergeant James Alton Driffield, 4th/7th Royal Dragoon Guards, Royal Armoured Corps (Relperby).

No. 552556 Sergeant Frederick Herbert Harris, 4th/7th Royal Dragoon Guards, Royal Armoured Corps (Gloucester).

No. 4534374 Sergeant William John Waters, 4th/7th Royal Dragoon Guards, Royal Armoured Corps (Bradford).

No. 813601 Trooper Andrew Ward Fisher, 15th/19th The King's Royal Hussars, Royal Armoured Corps (Hebden Bridge).

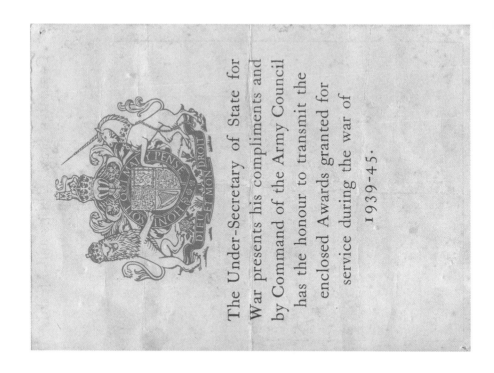

BUCKINGHAM PALACE.

I greatly regret that I am
unable to give you personally the
award which you have so well earned.

I now send it to you with
my congratulations and my best
wishes for your future happiness.

George R.I.

Captain P.J.G. Davis, M.C.,
      Army Air Corps.

1939–45 Star, Africa Star, Italy Star, France and Germany Star, Defence Medal, War Medal 1939–45.

1939–45 Star, Africa Star, Italy Star, France and Germany Star, Defence Medal, War Medal 1939–45, Military Cross.

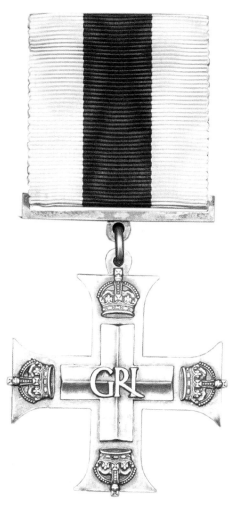

Military Cross.

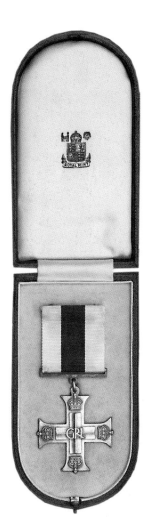

Index